Restructuring
Retirement Risks

Restructuring Retirement Risks

Edited by

David Blitzstein, Olivia S. Mitchell, and Stephen P. Utkus

OXFORD
UNIVERSITY PRESS

OXFORD
UNIVERSITY PRESS

Great Clarendon Street, Oxford OX2 6DP

Oxford University Press is a department of the University of Oxford.
It furthers the University's objective of excellence in research, scholarship,
and education by publishing worldwide in

Oxford New York

Auckland Cape Town Dar es Salaam Hong Kong Karachi
Kuala Lumpur Madrid Melbourne Mexico City Nairobi
New Delhi Shanghai Taipei Toronto

With offices in

Argentina Austria Brazil Chile Czech Republic France Greece
Guatemala Hungary Italy Japan Poland Portugal Singapore
South Korea Switzerland Thailand Turkey Ukraine Vietnam

Oxford is a registered trade mark of Oxford University Press
in the UK and in certain other countries

Published in the United States
by Oxford University Press Inc., New York

© Pension Research Council, The Wharton School,
University of Pennsylvania, 2006

The moral rights of the authors have been asserted

Database right Oxford University Press (maker)

First published 2006

British Library Cataloguing in Publication Data
Data available

Library of Congress Cataloging in Publication Data
Data available

Typeset by SPI Publisher Services, Pondicherry, India
Printed in Great Britain
on acid-free paper by
Biddles Ltd., King's Lynn, Norfolk

ISBN 0–19–920465–9   978–0–19–920465–6

1 3 5 7 9 10 8 6 4 2

Preface

Retirement security is the central policy concern of our time. Masses of aging Baby Boomers stand on the verge of retirement in developed nations around the globe. Pension systems everywhere confront crushing challenges, and governments often appear confused about which direction they should move. Contributors to this volume clarify the discussion by addressing the question: 'What are the new risks and rewards in pensions, and what paths can stakeholders chose to solve these problems?' The chapters herein set their sights on employees' needs and expectations, employers' intentions and realizations, and policymakers' efforts to resolve the many challenges. Despite the fact that retirement systems face deep stresses exacerbated by volatile capital markets, poor corporate earnings streams, weak macroeconomic performance, and international turmoil, nevertheless contributors to this volume show courage and creativity in plotting the course ahead over uneven terrain.

This book owes much to its contributors and particularly to our two collegial co-editors for this latest book in the Pension Research Council Series, David Blitzstein and Stephen Utkus. Support for the research was generously provided by the Wharton School, the Pension Research Council, and the Boettner Center for Pensions and Retirement Research at the University of Pennsylvania. The manuscript was expertly prepared by Virginia Jurika and Michael Stevko. On behalf of the Pension Research Council and the Boettner Center at the Wharton School, we thank our collaborators and supporters for ensuring that retirement security stays at the core of our work.

Olivia S. Mitchell
Pension Research Council
Boettner Center for Pensions and Retirement Research
The Wharton School

The Pension Research Council

The Pension Research Council of the Wharton School at the University of Pennsylvania is an organization committed to generating debate on key policy issues affecting pensions and other employee benefits. The Council sponsors interdisciplinary research on the entire range of private and social retirement security and related benefit plans in the USA and around the world. It seeks to broaden understanding of these complex arrangements through basic research into their economic, social, legal, actuarial, and financial foundations. Members of the Advisory Board of the Council, appointed by the Dean of the Wharton School, are leaders in the employee benefits field, and they recognize the essential role of social security and other public sector income maintenance programs while sharing a desire to strengthen private sector approaches to economic security. More information about the Pension Research Council is available on the Internet at http://pensionresearchcouncil.org or send email to prc@wharton.upenn.edu.

Contents

Part I.   Perspectives on Pension Risks and Rewards

Part II.   Pooling Pension Risks and Rewards

Part III. New Strategies for Managing Retirement Risk

List of Figures

List of Tables

Notes on Contributors

Peter Albrecht is the Chair for Business Administration, Risk Theory, Portfolio Management and Insurance, and Managing Director of the Institute for Insurance Science, both at the University of Mannheim. His research interests are risk management and insurance, investment management, old age provision, and actuarial mathematics. Previously he was a professor of Operations Research at the University of Heidelberg. He received his doctoral degree and habilitation in Business Administration from the University of Mannheim.

David Blitzstein is the Director of the United Food and Commercial Workers International Union (UFCW) Negotiated Benefits Department where he advises local unions in collective bargaining on pension and health insurance issues and consults with the Union's 150 jointly trusted health and welfare and pension plans nationwide. Mr Blitzstein also serves as trustee of the UFCW Industry Pension Fund, and the UFCW National Health and Welfare Fund. Mr Blitzstein represents the UFCW as a member of the working committee of the National Coordinating Committee for Multiemployer Plans. In addition, he serves on the Pension Research Council Advisory Board at the Wharton School; he is a member of the Employee Benefits Research Institute and the National Academy of Social Insurance. He received the BS degree from the University of Pennsylvania and he received the MS in Labor Studies from the University of Massachusetts in Amherst.

Henning Bohn is a Professor of Economics at the University of California at Santa Barbara. Previously he served on the Finance faculty at the Wharton School of the University of Pennsylvania. He has published widely on government debt and fiscal policy, and his research focuses on macroeconomics, public economics, and international finance. He received his Ph.D. from Stanford.

Phyllis C. Borzi is Research Professor, Department of Health Policy, School of Public Health and Health Service, The George Washington University Medical Center and Of Counsel, O'Donoghue & O'Donoghue LLP, Washington, DC. Her research interests focus on employer-sponsored benefits; discrimination based on age or disability; access to health insurance; managed care; health and retirement policy issues; and legal issues relating to employer-sponsored benefits. She was part of the Pension and

Employee Benefit Council, Subcommittee on Labor–Management Relations, Committee on Education and Labor, U.S. House of Representatives; and Majority Legislative Associate, Task Force on Pension and Welfare Plans, Committee on Education and Labor, U.S. House of Representatives. She received the BA degree from Ladycliff College, the MA from Syracuse University, and the J.D. from Catholic University.

Joachim Coche is Senior Economist, Risk Management Division, at the European Central Bank, in Frankfurt, Germany. His research interests focus on asset allocation, issues arising in risk management, and fixed income markets, particularly foreign reserves management. Previously he served as Senior Analyst, Portfolio Research, at the DZ Bank Frankfurt, Germany. He received his Masters and Doctorate in economics from the University of Osnabrueck, Germany.

Julia Lynn Coronado is a Senior Research Analyst at Watson Wyatt Worldwide. Her interests include pensions, retirement saving, social security, and pension finance. Before joining Watson Wyatt Worldwide, Julia was an economist at the Federal Reserve Board of Governors. She received her BA from the University of Illinois Urbana-Champaign and the Ph.D. from the University of Texas at Austin.

Douglas Fore is a Principal Research Fellow at the TIAA-CREF Institute. His research interests include the determinants of pension plan type. Dr Fore earned the Ph.D. in Economics from the University of Colorado.

Brian J. Fuller is a Principal and actuary in Mercer's Richmond health care and group benefits practice, where he is involved in complex financial modeling projects on the design, pricing, and valuation of life, health, and disability income programs. Previously he worked for a regional insurance company analyzing life and health experience, and setting underwriting pricing guidelines, as a systems consultant for pension and welfare valuation and data collection software needs, and an actuarial assistant for a regional consulting firm. Brian received the BA in mathematics from the University of Virginia. He is an Associate of the Society of Actuaries, an enrolled actuary, and a member of the American Academy of Actuaries.

P. Brett Hammond is head of the Investment Analytics Group at the Teachers Insurance Annuity Association-College Retirement Equities Fund (TIAA-CREF). His current work focuses on inflation-indexed bonds, domestic and foreign asset allocation in taxable and tax-deferred settings, Social Security reform, defined contribution pensions, and executive compensation. Previously he was Director of Academy Studies at the National Academy of Public Administration, where he was responsible for a wide range of projects including studies on the changing relationships between Congress and the executive, American governance, public trust and confidence in radioactive waste management, and federal Medicaid management. He also served on the faculty of the University of California (Berkeley and Los Angeles) and has consulted with the Office of Technology Assessment and Multinational Strategies, Inc. He received the BS in economics and politics from the University of California, Santa Cruz, and the Ph.D. from the Massachusetts Institute of Technology.

Sarah A. Holden is a Senior Economist in the Research Department of the Retirement, Tax and International Division at the Investment Company Institute. Her research interests include 401(k) plan participant behavior, defined contribution retirement plans, individual retirement accounts (IRAs), and the role of mutual funds in the retirement market. Previously she served as an Economist in the Research and Statistics Division (Flow of Funds Section) of the Federal Reserve Board. She received the BA in math and economics from Smith College and the Ph.D. in economics from the University of Michigan, Ann Arbor.

J. Nellie Liang is the Assistant Director of the Division of Research and Statistics of the Federal Reserve Board's overseas Capital Markets and Flow of Funds sector. Her research interests include retirement savings plans, payout policy, and corporate finance. She received her Ph.D. from the University of Maryland.

Raimond Maurer is the Chair and Full Professor for Investment, Portfolio Management and Pension Finance, Finance Department, Goethe University Frankfurt. His research interests focus on issues in institutional investors, asset management, real estate, and pension finance. Previously he was on the faculty at the University of Mannheim's National Research Center. He is also a member of the German Society of Insurance and Financial Mathematics, scientific director of the German and program coordinator of the German A.F.I.R. Group (Actuarial Approach for Financial Risk). He received the doctorate and Habilitation in Business Administration from Mannheim University.

Neal McCall is an economist in the Office of Financial Institutions Policy, U.S. Treasury. His research interest is pension regulation. Previously he served as an economist at the U.S. Department of Housing and Urban Development. He received the Ph.D. degree in economics from the University of North Carolina.

David McCarthy is a faculty member at Imperial College, London. His research focuses on pensions, finance, and actuarial studies. Previously he was a postdoctoral fellow at the University of Oxford. He received the Ph.D. in Insurance and Risk Management from the Wharton School and he is a Fellow of the Faculty of Actuaries, Edinburgh, UK.

Olivia S. Mitchell is the International Foundation of Employee Benefit Plans Professor of Insurance and Risk Management, the Executive Director of the Pension Research Council, and the Director of the Boettner Center on Pensions and Retirement Research at the Wharton School. Concurrently Dr Mitchell is a Research Associate at the National Bureau of Economic Research and a Co-Investigator for the AHEAD/Health and Retirement Studies at the University of Michigan. Dr Mitchell's main areas of research and teaching are private and public insurance, risk management, public finance and labor markets, and compensation and pensions, with a US and an international focus. She received the BA in economics from Harvard University and the MA and Ph.D. degrees in economics from the University of Wisconsin, Madison.

Anthony Neuberger is Professor of Finance at Warwick Business School, University of Warwick, England. His research interests are pensions, investment management, risk management, and financial markets. He received the BA in mathematics and philosophy from Cambridge University, the MBA from London Business School, and his Ph.D. in financial economics from London University.

Anna Rappaport is an independent consultant, advocate, writer and speaker, recently retired from Mercer Human Resource Consulting; her main focus is to advocate for women's retirement security. She has been a Fellow of the Society of Actuaries for over forty years and served as President of the Society of Actuaries. She currently chairs the Society of Actuaries Committee on Post-Retirement Risk and serves as a member of the Boards of the Actuarial Foundation, the National Academy of Social Insurance, the Women's Institute for a Secure Retirement (WISER), the Profit Sharing Council of America, and the Pension Research Council. She earned the MBA from the University of Chicago.

Ralph Rogalla is a research assistant at the Goethe University Frankfurt, Finance Department. His research interests are pension plan transitions, asset-liability-management for pension plans, strategic asset allocation, and real estate finance. He is currently working on his doctoral degree in finance at the Goethe University Frankfurt, Finance Department.

Stephen P. Utkus is the Director of the Vanguard Center for Retirement Research, where he conducts and sponsors research on retirement savings and retirement benefits. His current research examines attitudes and expectations regarding retirement, financial markets, and employer-sponsored retirement plans; the psychological and behavioral aspects of participant decision-making; trading and investment behavior among retirement plan participants; fiduciary issues arising from retirement programs; and global trends in public and private pension plans. Mr Utkus serves on the Pension Research Council Advisory Board and he is also a Visiting Scholar at the Wharton School. He received the BS in Computer Science from MIT and the MBA in Finance from The Wharton School.

Salvador Valdés-Prieto is a Professor of Economics at the Catholic University of Chile. His research interests are pension economics, financial regulation, industrial organization, and political economy. He has worked as a consultant to the World Bank; as an adviser to governments of Chile, Mexico, Peru, Bolivia, and China; and consulted with various companies on antitrust and regulatory issues. He received the Civil Engineering degree from the Catholic University of Chile, and the Ph.D. degree in Economics from the Massachusetts Institute of Technology.

Jack VanDerhei is a faculty member at Temple University's Fox School of Business and Management in the Department of Risk, Insurance, and Healthcare Management. His research focuses on employee benefits and insurance, particularly financial aspects of private defined benefit and defined contribution retirement plans. Previously, he was on the faculty of The Wharton School of the University of Pennsylvania. He has consulted with the Pension Benefit Guaranty Corporation, the U.S. Department of Labor, the International Foundation of Employee Benefit Plans, and the International Society of Certified Employee Benefit Specialists program. He received the BBA and MBA from the University of Wisconsin, Madison, and the MA and Ph.D. from The Wharton School of the University of Pennsylvania.

George Wagoner is a Principal and Chief Healthcare Actuary at Mercer Human Resource Consulting. His research interests include human resources strategic planning, consumer-directed healthcare, managed care, retiree healthcare, pharmacy, long-term care, dental and vision care, disability programs, and life coverages. Previously he worked as Chief Actuary for a major non-profit health insurer and for the group division of a regional insurance company. He is a Fellow of the Society of Actuaries, a member of the American Academy of Actuaries, and a former member of the board of directors and vice-president in charge of health care activities for the Conference of Consulting Actuaries. Currently he is a member of the board of directors of The Health Project, which presents the C. Everett Koop National Health Awards honoring cost-effective health promotion and disease prevention programs. He received the BS degree in mathematics from Davidson College.

Mark J. Warshawsky is Assistant Secretary for Economic Policy of the U.S. Treasury. His research interests focus on public and private pensions, annuity markets, and public policy. Previously he was Deputy Assistant Secretary for Microeconomic Analysis, U.S. Treasury; and he also served as Director of Research for TIAA-CREF. He received the Ph.D. degree in Economics from Harvard University.

John D. Worth is Director at the Office of Microeconomic Analysis of the U.S. Treasury. His research interests focus on pension regulation and financial market regulation. Previously he served as economist at the U.S. Treasury and at Welch Consulting, in Santa Barbara, California. He received the Ph.D. degree in economics from the University of Southern California.

Tongxuan (Stella) Yang is a researcher at the Radian Guaranty, Inc. Her research has focused on pension plan investments, pension funding, and employee choices regarding pension plans. Previously she worked at the Industrial and Commercial Bank of China. She received the BE degree from the Shanghai Jiao Tong University, the MA from Peking University, and the MA and Ph.D. in Insurance and Risk Management from the Wharton School of the University of Pennsylvania.

Frank Yeager is an actuarial analyst in Mercer's Healthcare and Group Benefits practice, where his responsibilities include pricing, reserving, and working with health plan design issues and contribution strategies. He earned the BA in mathematics and a Masters in Operations Research and Industrial Engineering from Cornell University. He is currently pursuing Fellowship in the Society of Actuaries.

List of Abbreviations

ABO	Accumulated Benefit Obligation
AIME	Average Indexed Monthly Earnings
ASB	Accounting Standards Board
BIG	Below Investment Grade
CFFI	Center on Federal Financial Institutions
CMS	Centers for Medicare and Medicaid Services
COBRA	Consolidated Omnibus Budget Reconciliation Act
CPI	Consumer Price Index
CRRA	Constant-Relative-Risk-Aversion
CWB	Covered Wage Bill
DB	Defined Benefit
DC	Defined Contribution
DRC	Deficit Reduction Contribution
EBRI	Employee Benefit Research Institute
ECB	European Central Bank
EDF	Expected Default Frequency
EGTRRA	Economic Growth and Tax Relief Reconciliation Act of 2001
EIU	Economist Intelligence Unit
ERISA	Employee Retirement Income Security Act
ESOP	Employee Stock Ownership Plan
FASB	Financial Accounting Standards Board
FRS	Financial Reporting Standard
GASB	Governmental Accounting Standards Board
GDP	Gross Domestic Product
HAS	Health Savings Account
HCEs	Highly Compensated Employees
HDHP	High Deductible Health Plan
HI	Hospital Insurance
HIPAA	Health Insurance Portability and Accountability Act
HMO	Health Maintenance Organization
HRA	Health Reimbursement Arrangement
HRS	Health and Retirement Study
IASB	International Accounting Standards Board
ICI	Investment Company Institute
IFL	Implicit Fiscal Liability
IRA	Individual Retirement Account

IRC	Internal Revenue Code
IRS	Internal Revenue Service
LTC	Long-Term Care
MA	Medicare Advantage
MA-PDPs	Medicare Advantage Prescription Drug Plans
MFR	Minimum Funding Requirement
MINT	Modeling Income in the Near Term
NASI	National Academy of Social Insurance
NDT	Nondiscrimination Testing
NHCEs	Nonhighly Compensated Employees
OG	Overlapping-Generations
OPEB	Other Nonpension Postemployment Benefits
PAYGO	Pay-As-You-Go
PBGC	Pension Benefit Guaranty Corporation
PBO	Projected Benefit Obligation
PDPs	Prescription Drug Plans
PFFS	Private Fee-for-Service
PIA	Primary Insurance Amount
POS	Point-of-Service
PPF	Pension Protection Fund
PPO	Preferred Provider Organization
PSCA	Profit Sharing Council of America
PUC	Projected Unit Credit
S&L	Saving and Loan
S&P	Standard and Poor
SEC	US Securities and Exchange Commission
SMI	Supplemental Medical Insurance plan
USBLS	US Department of Labor, Bureau of Labor Statistics
USGAO	US Government Accountability Office

Part I

Perspectives on Pension Risks and Rewards

Chapter 1

Understanding the Uncertainties of Retirement

David Blitzstein, Olivia S. Mitchell, and Stephen P. Utkus

An aging-population tsunami is sweeping the world, and capital markets have buffeted pension plans while retiree health care costs rise without letup. This coincidence of shocks marks a crucial moment for global retirement security, since public and private retirement systems everywhere have fared poorly just as the massive Baby Boom generation moves into retirement. Clearly urgent efforts are needed to enhance risk management for public and private pension systems around the world. This book explores three aspects of the evolution of risk and reward sharing in retirement, to offer guidance to pension fiduciaries, plan participants, and policymakers. First, we focus on new perspectives for assessing retirement risks and rewards. Second, we evaluate efforts to insure retirement plans. Last, we provide several new strategies for managing retirement system risk. This chapter briefly previews the remarkable findings by contributors to this rich and interesting volume.

Perspectives on Retirement Risks and Rewards

Many long-held beliefs about the pension system have been undermined in the last few years. Traditionally, pension stakeholders believed that firms which offered a defined benefit (DB) plan would bear the bulk of the pension plan risk. But recent corporate bankruptcies involving massively underfunded DB plans have clearly demonstrated that workers and retirees are also exposed to capital market risk in such pensions. And even though DB plans are seriously underfunded in many developed nations, many have not yet come to grips with this new reality. Instead, sponsors and participants often elect to simply wait for rising markets to bail out the system—a leap of faith that we contend represents poor policy and wishful thinking on stakeholders' part.

Indeed, there are several sources of uncertainty in the retirement mix. In his chapter, Henning Bohn explores the role of technological change and productivity, future fertility and longevity patterns, and health shocks. Bohn argues that productivity represents the greatest source of long-term uncertainty. If productivity increased 1 percent annually over a generation, today's children would earn 35 percent more than today's workers, and their children in turn would be 80 percent wealthier. If productivity grew at 3 percent, today's youths would earn 140 percent more than their parents and their children would earn 500 times more. Nevertheless, the retirement security debate tends to focus mainly on asset valuation rather than productivity risk which is often overlooked. Using an overlapping-generations (OG) model, Bohn shows that some groups—namely active workers—are more exposed to even more productivity risk than others—namely retirees. He also demonstrates that demographic risks must be taken into account since large cohorts, such as the baby boomers, have a disadvantage compared to smaller cohorts in demanding wages; further, its flood of retirement saving tends to depress asset returns. Another demographic risk is uncertain longevity: the good fortune of living longer is bad news financially. As a result, increasing retirement age along with longevity improvements make sense and annuitized pensions help share longevity risk.

Taking the perspective of participants, Phyllis Borzi notes that only a decade ago, some 40 percent of US families had at least one member enrolled in a DB plan, but the figure has now dropped to 20 percent. Defined contribution (DC) plan coverage rose from one-third to over one-half over the same period, but she worries that the average 401(k) balance is not large, amounting to only about $77,000 in 2003. This highlights 'accumulation risk' or the possibility that workers will not build up enough saving or underestimate the amount of money they will need in retirement. Another obstacle to accumulating retirement saving arises from 'breaks in coverage', due to unemployment or disability, reducing contributions, and employer matching. Furthermore, she points out that employees often lack the knowledge to invest wisely: in a corporate DB plan, the costs of hiring professional investment advice are spread across the entire group, but if workers invest on their own, they often invest too conservatively and tend to hold too much undiversified employer stock.

Due to the relatively recent arrival of DC pensions on the scene, today's retirees have not had an entire career to invest in this sort of plan. To assess their likely future role, Sarah Holden and Jack VanDerhei describe their model that estimates projected future saving patterns in the 401(k) context. Their model tracks amounts contributed, asset allocation, and whether loans are taken; they also consider whether participants change jobs and whether they roll their accruals into individual retirement accounts (IRA). The research indicates that workers who remain in a 401(k) plan for their entire careers will replace about half of their pre-retirement salary in the lowest income quartile if they reach age 65 between the years 2030–9; replacement rates of two-thirds would be anticipated for the highest income quartile. Combined with social security, retired low-paid workers could receive over 100 percent of their preretirement income, while higher earning retirees would expect over 80 percent. But they also show that replacement rates would be much lower, around 25 percent, if workers experience long breaks in service unless they have the self-control to contribute to an IRA.

Discussions of retirement income risk should also acknowledge the huge problem of retiree medical care, addressed in the chapter by Brian Fuller, Anna Rappaport, George Wagoner, and Frank Yeager. In the USA, larger employers traditionally offered early retirees continuation of medical coverage until age 65, and most also offered supplemental coverage once the retiree attained age 65 and was eligible for government-provided Medicare. (Most small- and mid-sized firms offer no supplemental coverage.) Yet there retiree health insurance provision has dropped steadily: a decade ago, almost half of all large employers offered retirees health care insurance if they were below the Medicare age, and some 40 percent offered coverage to the Medicare eligible. These figures are now down to 26 and 20 percent, respectively, and continue to fall. This is the result of concern over rising retiree medical costs that have risen at double digit rates for a decade; health insurance premiums for pre-Medicare retirees are now 25 percent higher than active workers. It is also worth noting that 5 percent of claimants account for more than half of the medical care costs, leading to the problem of adverse selection in the health insurance risk pool. If employers try to recoup costs by increasing the employee share of premiums or other costs, healthier participants will tend to drop out, leaving only the sickest, most expensive beneficiaries—a phenomenon sometimes called the 'health plan death spiral'. More generally, aging workforces and continued double-digit increases in health care costs are leading employers to boost retiree health premiums, drop coverage, or move to a defined-dollar approach where retirees must bear the brunt of future premium increases.

Pooling Pension Risks and Rewards

The recent wave of DB pension fund terminations has prompted many to review the role of pension insurance, offered by the US government for the last thirty years and recently adopted in the UK. In their chapter, Julia Coronado and Nellie Liang investigate whether this pension insurance has influenced financial practices in firms offering DB pensions. The authors note that the insurance premiums charged were not properly risk based, thus distorting funding and possibly asset allocation decisions. In fact, they conclude that the inefficient premium structure creates moral hazard and exacerbates underfunding, mainly through inadequate contributions. They find little evidence that pension funds offered by firms close to bankruptcy got into trouble by holding riskier assets in their portfolios.

The flaws in the US DB guarantee program have produced a $450 billion shortfall in the insurer's reserves, in part because the rules are overly complicated and offer few incentives for sponsors to prudently fund their plans. Authors Neal McCall, Mark Warshawsky, and John D. Worth outline several key principles that they contend should guide reform proposals, placing great emphasis on the view that DB plans should be seen as financial intermediaries providing workers with a promise of deferred compensation. They also propose that DB plan sponsors and participants are economic actors who respond to incentives in a predictable way. Finally, they note that no DB plan will live forever, so provisions should be made for termination. These principles imply that an insurer cannot provide an open-ended guarantee without exposing itself to extraordinary risk. Their reform proposals stem from the observation that pension assets and liabilities must be measured in a transparent and timely manner. Whereas under current law, plan sponsors may compute an 'almost infinite number' of liability calculations, they argue for a single liability measure. They also argue against discounting expected future benefit payments using a single discount rate, and they favor a seven-year amortization period for annual increases in funding shortfalls. Finally, they additionally propose restrictions on the extension of new benefit promises by sponsors that fall below minimum funding levels. Their proposals address the incentives for plan sponsors in financial trouble to promise generous pension benefits rather than raise wages, putting more participants and the government insurer at risk. Under their proposal, bankrupt companies would not be allowed to raise benefits if they were 20 percentage points below their required funding level. Investment-grade sponsors would be unable to increase benefits if they were below 40 percentage points of their targeted funding level.

Plan sponsors hoping for reform of the US guarantee system should take to heart aspects of the newly created Pension Protection Fund (PPF) in the UK, as described by Anthony Neuberger and David McCarthy. This chapter projects a set of likely scenarios for the recently established PPF and concludes that the UK insurer will likely have many years of low claims, interspersed with troubled periods of high demand. As a result, the UK fund would require huge reserves, which the authors conclude will be politically difficult to maintain. Since the PPF will face lumpy and irregular claims, relatively small in normal times but huge after a market downturn, the authors argue that the UK reserve fund design is economically nonviable. These same lessons apply not just to the UK design but to any reserve fund attempting to guarantee private DB pension claims.

New Strategies for Managing Retirement Risk

Traditional DB plans are moving quickly to extinction, driven by systemic risk, economic and accounting issues, and administrative problems. Brett Hammond and Douglas Fore assert that the biggest problem is that traditional plans did not keep up with dramatic changes in the labor market. Consequently, these plans are now concentrated in troubled industries such as steel and airlines. Additionally, accounting rules permitted sponsors to smooth asset values and underfund their plans. To counteract these trends and enhance DB benefit systems, the authors favor the recently adopted European accounting standards that require market-based accounting and curb smoothing of asset values. They also propose a new framework for DB plans that would emphasize portability. Once common actuarial standards and plan designs are adopted, workers could purchase service credits and carry them along when they change jobs.

In view of the growing popularity of company-sponsored DC plans around the world, it is worth knowing how they are designed and what they accomplish. In the USA, plan sponsors have a great deal of leeway regarding employee contributions, employer matches, investment menus, the availability of loans, and various other plan features. The chapter by Olivia Mitchell, Stephen Utkus, and Stella Yang demonstrates that a wide range of US 401(k) plan design features are a function of the average wages of a workforce—better-paid employees are more likely to have more generous matching contributions, as well as 'better' noncash features such as greater access to loans. Drawing on data for more than 500 401(k) plans covering more than 740,000 participants, the authors show that corporate match rates *offered* range from 0 to 18 percent; the median match offered was 3 percent of pay. They also note that *actual* employer match rates fell below 2 percent of pay, since not all employees opted to contribute the full amount. For lower-paid employees, employer matching elicits a positive impact on contributions up to 3 percent of salary, but there is little response above that level. Because of the impact of average workforce earnings on plan design, the analysis shows that a low-paid clerical worker employed at a high-wage firm would be likely to have a richer plan with a more generous match and other appealing attributes; the same worker employed at a low-wage firm would have far less rich opportunities to save.

A different approach to pensions in Europe, described by Peter Albrecht, Joachim Coche, Raimond Maurer, and Ralph Rogalla, explores a hybrid plan which combines elements of both DB and DC plans. Their chapter traces how a traditional DC pension can be adapted to include, for instance, minimum and maximum benefits, and minimum as well as maximum return guarantees in the individual investment accounts. The authors also show that capping investment returns is the best way to share investment risk and returns more equally between plan sponsors and participants. Further, the analysis explores optimal asset allocation-given benefit and return features. For instance, if the plan caps investment returns, the optimal investment strategy would rely on a high exposure to bonds and low exposure to equities. Additional costs of these guarantees will vary according to their structure, with estimates ranging from 0 to 250 percent of contributions depending on the plan design.

Turning to public pensions, the chapter by Salvador Valdés-Prieto asks how to mitigate political risk in unfunded social security systems which arise when demographic and economic shocks require action but politicians cannot take urgently needed action. He proposes developing contracts and rules that remove discretion from politicians by securitizing the revenue stream dedicated to social security. This would be facilitated by having the system issue Covered Wage Bill bonds, representing the future revenue from payroll taxes dedicated to social security. Participants could trade these assets with their prices set similarly to mutual fund net asset values. This scheme would offer a means to restructure pay-as-you-go social security systems while internalizing transition costs, as the payoff to the new bonds would depend on system financing and economic performance.

Conclusions

While private and public retirement systems face deep stresses, made worse by volatile capital markets, uncooperative interest rates, poor corporate earnings streams, anemic macroeconomic underperformance, and international turmoil, progress is possible. Those charged with protecting the pension institution understand that there is a deep-seated need for restructuring of these valued and long-standing retirement institutions, to restore the promise of future retirement security. This volume informs the debate by bringing to the fore lessons from research and practice on these topics so critically important for the future of retirement security.

Three lessons can be drawn from the current DB pension crisis. First, DB plan funding is extraordinarily sensitive to investment returns and volatile swings in asset prices, much more so than previously believed. Second, mature DB plans have become highly leveraged, with assets rarely well-matched to liabilities. Third, while DB pensions should be long-term investors, in practice they confront lethal short-term market risks that have undermined their survival. Experience shows that pension-funding ratios can drop 30 percent in a single year. These problems arise from several sources, including outmoded pension actuarial and accounting practices which assume incorrectly that assets always earn an equity risk premium. This has produced confusion over smoothing assets and liability value, allowing corporations to convey plan assumptions to generate profit and create incentives to undertake an asset–liability mismatch.

Going forward, the 'pension deal' between employers and participants must be seen as a contractual relationship requiring transparent and accurate information so that both sides know what risks they are sharing (see Frijns 2003). If stakeholders are required to finance shortfalls, they must also be included in the sharing of surplus. The contract should also include clearly stated, targeted, pension formulas that describe the risk-bearing agreement between various stakeholders in the pension plan. Both the reform of traditional DB pensions, as well as the continued growth of hybrid and DC pension designs, will be central to this transformation of risk-sharing among the affected parties. Indeed, retirement security is the central policy issue of our time: it can no longer be shunted off to the side.

Reference

Frijns, Jean (2003). 'Redesigning DB Pension Plans: The Case for Risk-Sharing Cooperatives', *The Ambachtsheer Letter* #209. Toronto: K.P.A. Advisory Services, Ltd.

Chapter 2

Who Bears What Risk? An Intergenerational Perspective

Henning Bohn

Governments in most developed countries promise pension and medical benefits to their elderly citizens. As the number of retirees is growing rapidly, the burden of retiree benefits has become painfully obvious. Uncertainty about the future complicates the planning for retiree benefits. If the future is brighter than expected, who will reap the gains? If it is worse, who will cover the added cost?

This chapter examines the impact of uncertainty on different cohorts at an aggregate or macroeconomic level. Macroeconomic analysis helps evaluate different risks and the policies affecting them in context, and it also enforces a consistent recognition that society as a whole faces an uncertain future and must bear the resulting financial risks. These risks include a tremendous uncertainty about the future path of technical progress, medical innovations, and trends in fertility and longevity—risks so huge that common stock market risks are small in comparison. Tax, pension, and health care policies have a major impact on who bears these risks.

Risk-sharing is instructive as a general perspective on public policy because it avoids divisive battles about redistribution. Everyone is better off if risks are shared. Risk should be seen as a symmetric chance of outcomes better or worse than expected. Furthermore, economic risks are often compensated by gains in expectation, creating interesting risk-return trade-offs. The key challenge for economic policy is therefore not to minimize risks, but to allocate risks to those best able to bear them. If risk-taking is rewarded in the market, a related challenge is to maintain incentives for risk-taking and to focus policy interventions into areas where markets fail. Once actual outcomes are observed, however, public policy is inevitably a battle between known winners and known losers, leaving little scope for disinterested economic analysis. Risk-sharing is not only a natural perspective looking forward—a search for mutually beneficial insurance arrangements—but equally instructive looking back: to what extent can existing social institutions be explained as solving risk-sharing problems?

Intergenerational risk-sharing is fertile ground for finding market failures because future generations are naturally excluded from insurance markets. Welfare improvements are possible because a government's power of taxation gives it a unique ability to make commitments on behalf of future generations. Fiscal institutions such as social security and Medicare formalize such commitments. The government's power to oblige future generations also creates potential for abuse. Risks might be shifted haphazardly onto future generations by governments catering to current voters. The merits of government intervention are therefore an open question—a question inviting economic analysis.

In this chapter, we first identify the key issues and mechanisms of risk-sharing and illustrate them with policy examples. Next we examine three major risk factors: (*a*) macroeconomic risks, particularly uncertain productivity growth and uncertain asset values; (*b*) demographic risks, due to uncertain fertility and longevity; and (*c*) medical expense risks, due to uncertain health care needs and cost. For each risk factor, allocations of risk under current and proposed policies are compared to efficient risk-sharing and to a laissez-faire allocation.

Aggregate and Generational Risks

The future rarely unfolds as expected. Over the typical life cycle, individuals face uncertainty about earnings and job prospects, their health and family status, the return on their savings, and ultimately about the time and manner of their deaths. Some of these risks imply financial burdens that add up across cohorts and over time—driven by macroeconomic disturbances—while other risks wash out.

On a macroeconomic level, uncertainty about earnings and the returns on saving have common roots, namely uncertainty about technological progress that determines factor productivity and asset values, as well as uncertainty about demographic developments that determine the supply of labor relative to capital. In turn, demographic uncertainty can be attributed to more fundamental shifts in fertility, longevity, and health (e.g. disability). Health and mortality can perhaps be traced to even more fundamental factors such as innovations in medical technology.

Tracing risks to their fundamental sources is most easily done at an aggregate level to avoid the confounding effects of idiosyncratic noise. Tracing risks is important for economic and policy analysis because common sources of risk create positive correlations that make risk-sharing difficult. Because individuals are exposed to different sources of risk as they age, it is instructive to aggregate risks by cohort (birth year) or by generation (a collection of cohorts). Risks that remain significant for an entire generation are essentially macroeconomic. Such risks are more difficult to manage than idiosyncratic risks because they may not cancel out. Risk-sharing is nonetheless promising because different generations are often exposed unequally to the various sources of aggregate risk.

Managing Aggregate Risks

Three main mechanisms exist for managing aggregate risks: markets, families, and governmental fiscal policy. Financial markets and insurance markets have serious limitations with regard to aggregate risks. In practice, markets work well for sharing many short-term risks between cohorts with largely overlapping lifetimes. However, they cannot provide insurance when there is a very large age difference between cohorts, one large enough so that the older cohort's life risks are largely known, when the younger cohort arrives. In aggregate, the insurance industry is 'owned' by the same generation of savers for which the industry provides insurance. Similarly, corporate pension promises are made by firms that are collectively owned by cohorts as they approach retirement. Consequently, neither insurance policies nor private pensions can provide significant protection against aggregate risks.

The most promising venue for private risk-sharing is probably intergenerational risk-sharing, at least, if risks are defined at the national level. Intergenerational risk-sharing has been puzzlingly ineffective in practice, however. Saving has historically flowed mostly into domestic investment. Investment portfolios are strongly biased toward domestic securities. The analysis later will therefore take mostly a closed-economy perspective, as appropriate in a world with strong home bias.

A second mechanism is intrafamily exchange and altruism, as expressed through bequests and *inter vivo* gifts. In theory, altruism can fully solve all risk-sharing problems, especially if combined with an intracohort sharing of idiosyncratic risk. As shown by Barro (1974), the Ricardian neutrality proposition has dynastic families behaving like a single infinitely lived economic agent, making generational issues moot.[1] Empirically, however, risk-sharing within families is highly imperfect, as documented by Altonji et al. (1996). Parental altruism toward children is undoubtedly an important explanation for education expenditures, but overall the life-cycle model is a good first approximation for individual behavior. Risk-shifting through bequests may nonetheless occur 'accidentally', if mortality is uncertain and assets are not annuitized.

The third risk-sharing mechanism is fiscal policy, via social insurance programs, general taxes and transfers, and through public debt. The most important international risk-sharing programs in the USA are social security old-age benefits and retiree medical insurance (known as Medicare and Medicaid). Public debt also plays an equivalent role for intergenerational redistribution, as it tends to be refinanced repeatedly and passed on to future generation just like pay-as-you-go (PAYGO) pensions. In this setting, taxes are a general purpose risk-sharing device: they socialize the tax share of whatever tax base they are imposed on. Particularly important in the generational context are consumption taxes and capital income taxes; the latter broadly construed to include taxes on saving, including individual interest, dividend, and capital gains income, corporate income, and on real property.

Economists have shown that fiscal risk-sharing is sometimes constrained by tax distortions, as the excess tax burden grows more than proportionally as labor income tax rates rise. Because risk-sharing leaves taxes rates unchanged on average, distortionary taxes per se are not an issue. Also not at issue are capital income taxes: if stochastic capital income is to be taxed for risk-sharing purposes, saving distortions can be avoided by compensating up-front incentives. A convex excess burden does imply a welfare loss, if risk-sharing calls for variations in labor income tax rates. This is conceptually an enforcement problem inherent in all insurance. After an insured event occurs, one or the other party must be forced to pay up. For intergenerational risk-sharing, convexity means that payments are more costly to collect from future generations than they are to disburse. The welfare impact is roughly proportional to the labor supply elasticity and could be minimized by collecting risk-sharing related taxes at times in the life cycles where labor supply elasticities are small. The distortion issue is noted later where relevant.

Three Policy Examples

Examples are instructive to illustrate the role of policy and to convey two key points. First, none of the risk-sharing mechanisms can eliminate the underlying risks. Therefore, one should be skeptical of policies offering safety to some group, without disclosing who is supposed to provide the guarantees. Second, details matter. Risk-bearing is often determined by subtle features of economic institutions that are often ill-defined or poorly understood.

Who Ensures That Social Security Is Safe?   Social security—by which we mean old-age benefit programs—are known to experience recurrent financial problems, which are mainly attributable to the contradictory way in which such programs account for risk. Benefits tend to be set—in the defined benefit (DB) world at least—according to a fixed formula. In the USA, payroll tax rates are also supposed to be constant, but even if budgets initially balance, the risk profiles of benefits and taxes are inconsistent. Consequently, benefits and taxes are bound to drift out of balance if the economy does not grow exactly as expected, or if demographic trends fail to exactly match expectations. Honest planning should acknowledge that either tax rates or benefits must vary in response to economic and demographic disturbances.

In the reform milieu, two paradigmatic structures can be envisioned: a DB model, which will inevitably entail variable taxes to pay the set benefits or a Defined Contribution (DC) model, which entails variable benefits. DB and DC are instructive points of reference (used later) because more complicated transfer systems are conveniently characterized by how they compare to DB and DC.

For the US social security system, which is a DB model, having a Trust Fund has complicated an assessment of the system's risk-sharing structure. Having the Trust Fund does help smooth temporary fluctuations in revenues and benefits, but it cannot solve the deeper problem of uncertainty. In 1983, Alan Greenspan's Commission to reform social security raised taxes and reduced benefit growth rates, apparently believing that building up a surplus in the Trust Fund would fix the system's uncertainties. Nevertheless, even if true in expectation, the fix was bound to fail in practice. Since 1983, the Trust Fund and the resulting chaos in federal accounting (Trust Fund accounting conflicts with national Unified Budgeting) have obscured the fact that policymakers have not addressed the key questions of whether social security should be seen as a DB or a DC system, or something in between.

If social security is viewed as a DB model, then it is reasonable to think of it as creating 'safe' claims; in other words, it entails an unconditional obligation on future generations to finance promised benefits. To honor this obligation, tax rates will have to rise whenever payrolls grow less than expected, and vice versa. By contrast, if it were seen as a DC model, social security benefits would be contingent claims worth as much (or as little) as the payroll tax revenue dedicated to them. Either way, future benefits payable and taxes collected are influenced by a multitude of economic and demographic disturbances.

The DB versus DC question is crucial for those who expect to live off social security in old age, but there is little agreement over which is the right interpretation. US political rhetoric for many years supported the DB view, but more recently the government has adopted more of a DC perspective, as seen in social security statements warning of benefit cuts when the Trust Fund is exhausted. If widely accepted, this new view would have a major impact on risk-sharing in the USA, as it would expose retirees to additional risk of future economic and demographic changes. If increases in payroll taxes are deemed to be politically infeasible, this supports the DC interpretation. We examine both interpretations in later subsections.

What Are the Risk-Sharing Implications of Social Security Reform? The policy debate over whether to hold equity investments in social security illustrates some of the risk-sharing implications of seemingly minor differences in program design (Bohn 1999). For instance, consider two alternative proposals: permitting workers to convert part of their social security taxes to a DC-type individual account, as suggested by the 2001 Presidential Commission, versus the Clinton administration's plan, which proposed to invest part of the Trust Fund in the stock market while maintaining a DB promise. The individual accounts approach reduces risk-sharing, scaling down the traditional system proportionally. Under the Clinton plan, by contrast, equities in the Trust Fund are effectively owned by future tax payers, so equity risk is shifted across generations.

Now consider two modifications that might be thought of as relatively modest. First, suppose the individual accounts were combined with a minimum-return guarantee. Financial economists know that a return guarantee is economically equivalent to a put option on the stock market, which in turn is equivalent to a transfer of fractional ownership to future generations which back the guarantee (Smetters 2001). In this sense, an individual account plan with a guarantee has remarkably similar risk-sharing implications to the Clinton plan. Furthermore, the put option argument applies even without explicit guarantees, if those who earn low returns in their individual accounts would be eligible for welfare benefits.

As a second example, consider the Clinton approach to equity investments in the Trust Fund, but now with a DC view of social security where gains and losses in the Trust Fund would accrue to retirees. Clearly, the risk-sharing implications are equivalent to nonguaranteed individual accounts: no intergenerational risk-shifting. Trust Fund investments rule out individual debt-equity choices, of course. Even this microeconomic difference vanishes if individual accounts are restricted to a single index fund.

In summary, the risk-sharing implications of equity investment proposals depend on the specifics. Individual account plans imply very little effective ownership if accompanied by guarantees or by means-tested supplemental supports. Conversely, having the Trust Fund diversify its investments has very different risk consequences, depending on whether the system is seen as a DB versus a DC plan.

Who Bears the Financial Risks of Medicare?   In the USA, retiree medical benefit promises have traditionally been presented as a categorical commitment, just like social security. Retiree Hospital Insurance (HI, known as Medicare Part A) is financed by the same payroll-tax mechanism as are old-age benefits. Medicare is of interest because of two important complications: substantial uncertainty about medical expenses and the cost-sharing structure embedded in the Supplemental Medical Insurance plan (SMI, known as Medicare Part B and Part D). If Medicare benefits are seen to be a promise to 'cover all medical needs', then it follows that the system can be interpreted as a DB plan with less predictable costs than the old-age social security system. In this view, benefits are contingent on the uncertain cost of existing treatments and contingent on medical discoveries that may vastly increase beneficiaries' perceived needs. Both create what I will call *medical-expense risk*. Cost projections under this DB interpretation are enormous and highly sensitive to alternative assumptions. Clearly, this interpretation exposes future generations to substantial risks, to be examined in more detail later.

Cost-sharing in SMI complicates the assessment, as SMI has always required retiree contributions, and there is a history of cost-shifting between HI and SMI. To the extent that rising health costs could be shifted to SMI, retirees will retain some of the aggregate medical-expense risk. On the other hand, most SMI coverage is financed from general tax revenues, and many retirees have limited income. As long as medical care in retirement is viewed as entitlement, medical-expense risk is thus largely carried by future generations.

This allocation of risk would be reversed completely if aggregate expenditures were capped. For example, Kotlikoff and Burns (2004) propose that Medicare be converted into a voucher program subsidizing individual insurance purchases. They argue, somewhat misleadingly, that vouchers provide full insurance and are sensitive to preexisting conditions. But a key assumption in their approach is that vouchers increase in value no faster than the growth rate of wages; if aggregate medical expenses rose faster, the vouchers would cover a declining share of each retiree's medical expenses. A capped voucher system therefore places aggregate medical-expense risk onto the retiree generation.

These examples illustrate how program rules determine the allocation of risk within and across generations. The lesson is clear—there is no free lunch. With proper accounting, governments cannot make macroeconomic risks vanish; instead, the risk is simply reallocated. The observation leads to the next question: how *should* society allocate aggregate risks?

A Benchmark: Equal Risk-Sharing

A natural benchmark for risk-sharing is the proportionate pooling of risk. Everyone bears the impact of any conceivable good or bad economic outcome in proportion to his normal consumption opportunities. Risk-pooling is the unique efficient allocation if everyone has the same relative risk aversion. If risks were allocated differently, individuals with above-average risk exposure would be willing to pay a higher price for risk-reduction than individuals with below-average exposure. Unequal risk exposures are therefore indicators of economic inefficiency.

Risk-pooling provides a clear guideline for policy and a roadmap for economic analysis. To improve welfare, policy should shift risks from cohorts more exposed to a given source of risk to those initially less exposed. To find policy improvements, one must assess who bears how much of each risk in the market, how the risks would be allocated with efficient sharing, and then compare the market allocation with the efficient allocation.

Two clarifications and two caveats are in order. First, efficient policy regarding risk-bearing and risk-sharing should focus on consumption (or more precisely, the marginal utility thereof) and not income. Because labor supply and savings opportunities differ across cohorts, consumption pooling usually entails unequal exposures to income risk. Second, risks can be shared with future generations by variations in capital accumulation. Most economic disturbances therefore trigger consumption responses in current and future periods. Efficiency requires that retiree consumption and working-age consumption respond equally in every period, usually with declining amplitude over time.

The first caveat is to emphasize that aggregate risks have a market price. In finance terms, aggregate risks are systematic risks. On financial markets, securities with systematic risk trade at a discount to safe assets, or equivalently, they promise an expected return above the safe interest rate. The same principle applies to aggregate risks that are reallocated through fiscal policy and may be nontradable. To make everyone better off, a policy must offer compensation to those required to bear more risk—a risk premium. The acid test for a welfare-improving policy is that those relieved of risks are better off *after* paying the risk premium. Unfortunately, economic theory has trouble explaining empirically observed risk premiums, notably the equity premium. While risk pooling provides a straightforward benchmark for how risk should be allocated, the magnitude of the compensation is sometimes difficult to determine.

The second caveat is that risk exposures must be adjusted if individuals differ in their intrinsic risk aversion. Less risk-averse individuals demand a lower price for bearing risk and should bear more risk in an efficient allocation. The literature on habit formation suggests that older people, the retiree cohort, may be more risk-averse than younger, working-age individuals. Later I will return to this caveat.

In any case, efficient risk-sharing has implications that are robust to differential risk aversion. Most importantly, for economic efficiency, everyone would have to be exposed to aggregate risk in the same direction. If a disturbance hit only working-age cohorts, or only retirees, or both generations in opposite directions, risk-sharing is always inefficient. Moreover, if one cohort is more risk-averse than another, it should be proportionately less exposed to all types of risk, yielding testable restrictions in a world with many sources of risk.

A Tractable Analytic Framework

The risk-pooling principle has most power if applied across multiple risks. Because examining and aggregating the joint effects of all the various risks on different cohorts is not an easy task, it is instructive to take a stylized perspective on work and asset accumulation over the life cycle to see how the principle can be evaluated. The classic Diamond (1965) two-period overlapping-generations (OG) model provides a convenient framework.

In the Diamond model, all cohorts in the workforce are grouped together into a single working-age generation, and all retirees are treated as a single retiree generation. Children are attached to their parents' households. Changes in longevity can be modeled as changes in the relative length of working-age and retirement. While this description of the life cycle is clearly simplified, it helps highlight key elements of intergenerational risk-sharing without getting lost in the minutiae of how individuals lead their lives. Incomes during the working-age period are mainly wage incomes; wages after taxes are divided between consumption and saving. Saving is invested in financial markets, and it ends up financing either domestic capital accumulation, government bonds, or investments abroad. Income for the retiree generation is from capital and other assets. Retirees use asset income, asset sales, and transfers from the government to finance retirement consumption, medical care, and (perhaps) bequests.[2]

What can this framework tell us about who bears what risks? The following sections will examine each of the major risks.

Aggregate Risks (I): Macroeconomic Risks

Uncertain Productivity Growth. Productivity growth is quantitatively the most important source of long-run economic uncertainty. With 1 percent annual productivity growth for a generation, for example, our children will earn 35 percent higher incomes (compounding 1 percent for 30 years), and our grandchildren 80 percent more. With 3 percent annual productivity growth, our children would instead earn 140 percent more and our grandchildren almost 500 percent more. Without productivity growth, per capita incomes would stagnate. The 0–3 percent range falls well within the range growth rates experienced around the world.

Who bears the risk of such growth uncertainty? Because labor and capital shares in national income are essentially constant, growth uncertainty has an equal impact on wages earned by working-age households and on capital incomes earned by retirees. But equal income effects do not imply equal consumption effects; there are three main issues to consider. First, the retiree generation owns not only the earnings but also the principal value of accumulated real and financial assets. Because asset values are less sensitive to growth than earnings (see later), existing assets reduce retiree generation's exposure to productivity risk, leaving workers relatively more exposed. Second, government transfers and taxes augment retiree incomes at the expense of working cohorts' incomes. Because net transfers tend to be less sensitive to growth than wages and capital incomes, fiscal policy further reduces retiree exposure to productivity risk while increasing working cohorts' exposure. Third, the working-age generation may respond to unexpectedly high or low productivity by altering its saving rate and work hours. The study of labor supply and savings responses is unfortunately complicated because several income and substitution effects interact. In Bohn (2004), I show that savings and labor supply responses tend to further magnify the impact of productivity shock on working-age consumption.

Key distinctions must be made between income and productivity shocks and between temporary and permanent shocks. Negative *income* shocks can be absorbed by working more; however, negative *productivity* shocks reduce not only income but also the hourly wage, which makes a productivity slump an inefficient time to work more. Having variable labor supply therefore does not enable working cohorts to bear more productivity risk. The permanence of shocks matters because the young can absorb temporary shocks by consumption-smoothing over the life cycle. A change in productivity *growth* is, however, a permanent disturbance to the economy's productivity level, which rules out consumption smoothing.[3] The permanence of shocks also matters because high future productivity raises interest rates, which has income and substitution effects. Assuming a low elasticity of substitution (consistent with empirical estimates), high-productivity growth reduces the savings rate and therefore magnifies the impact of productivity shocks on working-age consumption.

Overall, the OG approach yields an unambiguous conclusion: *working-age individuals are more exposed to productivity risk than retirees.* This result may seem to conflict with the notion that capital incomes are more risky than wage incomes. There is no conflict, however, if one properly distinguishes productivity risk from asset valuation risk—to be examined next.

Uncertain Asset Values.   Returns to capital are subject to a second source of risk, namely the uncertainty about the price at which seasoned capital can be sold to the next generation. This topic includes the much-discussed stock market and housing market risks. Because asset valuation risk falls primarily on the retiree generation, retiree incomes can be more volatile than working-age incomes.

The main social mechanisms for sharing such valuation risk include capital income taxation and bequests. Capital income taxes yield return-contingent government receipts that reduce the need for taxes on future generations. This gives future generations an exposure to the current return on capital. Income taxes unfortunately reduce saving incentives. One policy response in the USA has been to provide savings incentives up-front and fully tax the returns, as exemplified in 401(k) and 403(b) plans and traditional IRAs. Another policy response has been to tax capital gains and dividends at reduced rate, or to exempt capital income entirely (e.g. Roth IRAs). The distinction is important because risks are shared in proportion to the marginal tax rate. A tax system with taxed returns and up-front incentives provides much more risk-sharing than tax-exempt savings.[4] The other important mechanism is bequests. For risk-sharing purposes, bequests are equivalent to a self-imposed capital income tax that benefits future generations.

Evidence on Productivity and Valuation Risks. Empirical evidence is consistent with wage income being relatively more exposed to productivity risk than capital income. I have computed 30-year-ahead 'generational' covariance matrices from annual 1875–2002 US gross domestic product (GDP) data and S&P500 prices and dividends (Bohn 2004). Here I find a generational standard deviation for GDP of $\sigma_Y = 35$ percent, a 64 percent standard deviation for equity returns, and a 41 percent correlation between the 30-year-ahead forecast errors.[5] If one interprets the data in terms of a Cobb–Douglas aggregate production function, the standard deviations of wages and productivity equal the standard deviation of GDP. If capital is financed with equity and debt (about 26 percent debt) and debt is essentially safe, the standard deviation of capital (R^k) can be determined to be $\sigma_{R^k} = (1 - 0.26) \times 0.64 = 47$ percent. One may also decompose the return on capital into a GDP factor, plus an orthogonal asset valuation factor (V), $R^k = \pi \times Y + V$. The above estimates imply a factor loading of $\hat{\pi} = \mathrm{cov}(Y, R^k)/\mathrm{var}(Y) = 0.58$ and $\sigma_V = \sqrt{\sigma_{R^k}^2 - \hat{\pi}^2 \sigma_Y^2} = 43$ percent.

Even my long data-set covers only a small number of nonoverlapping generational periods. The generational variances and covariances are therefore best viewed as point estimates subject to substantial specification uncertainty.[6] It is nonetheless reassuring that the estimates match economic theory quite well. Notably:

(1) The factor loading below one indicates that capital returns are less exposed to productivity risk than output and wages—about 58 percent as much.

(2) The inequality $\sigma_{R^k} > \sigma_Y$ confirms the conventional wisdom that returns on capital investment are more volatile than wages.

Note that these estimates are also consistent with productivity uncertainty as the dominant source of consumption risk at long horizons, especially looking several generations ahead. This is because future generations bear valuation risk for a limited number of years, between work and retirement, whereas their exposure to productivity risk grows with the forecast horizon.

The differences in riskiness between retiree and working-age incomes are promising for intergenerational risk-sharing. They suggest that working-age cohorts benefit from shifting productivity risk to retirees, while retirees benefit from shifting asset pricing risks to subsequent generations.

Linking Income to Consumption: A Quantitative Analysis. Quantitative insights about the efficiency of risk-sharing can be obtained by combining the data with a calibrated version of the OG model. Table 2-1, which builds

TABLE 2-1 Productivity and Asset Pricing Risks

	Scenarios (Responses to unexpected changes in percent)					
	Laissez-faire	Laissez-faire with bequests	Efficient solution	Calibrated policy	More taxes and wage-indexing	All safe transfers
	(1)	(2)	(3)	(4)	(5)	(6)
Panel 1A: Higher productivity (35 %)						
Consumption in retirement	26	26	34	25	28	17
Consumption in working age	36	35	34	37	35	41
Disp. Income in working age	35	34	30	35	33	39
Capital investment	32	31	23	31	29	37
Panel 1B: Higher asset values (40 %)						
Consumption in retirement	40	40	13	27	21	27
Consumption in working age	0	4	13	7	10	7
Disp. Income in working age	0	4	16	8	11	8
Capital investment	0	5	22	10	14	10

Source: Author's calculations.

Notes: Columns refer to different policy scenarios, as follows.
Col. 1: Basic overlapping generations economy without government and no bequests.
Col. 2: Like Col. 1 with accidental bequests.
Col. 3: Responses with efficient risk-sharing. (Key characteristic: Equal consumption responses.)
Col. 4: Economy calibrated to US data and fiscal institutions: partially wage-indexed social security, defined-benefits public health, safe public debt, capital income taxes with 15 percent marginal rate.
Col. 5: All transfers wage-indexed, public debt wage- or GDP-indexed, capital income tax with 30 percent marginal rate, otherwise like Col. 4.
Col. 6: All transfers inflation-indexed, otherwise like Col. 4.

on Bohn (2001, 2004), shows how differential income risks translate into unequal consumption exposures.[7] Each column presents the risk-sharing implications of a different policy scenario. Entries in Panel A show percentage responses in both generations' consumption, in working-age income, and in capital investment to an unexpected 35 percent increase in productivity growth. The 35 percent change can be interpreted as generational standard deviation or as 1 percent per year compounded for

30 years. Panel B shows responses to an unexpected 40 percent increase in asset values, also about a standard deviation.

The responses are symmetric and scalable. Negative disturbances would have the reverse effects; smaller or greater shocks would have proportionally smaller or greater impact. The percentage values can therefore be interpreted as exposures to risk. They can be used contemporaneously to assess the efficiency of risk-sharing between current retirees and current workers, or prospectively to examine risk-sharing between future retirees (current workers) and future workers (current children and unborn).

Column 1 shows the allocation of risk in a laissez-faire economy without bequests. Higher productivity raises working-age consumption, incomes, and capital investment by about as much as productivity (35 percent), but retirement consumption by substantially less (26 percent). Unexpectedly high asset values affect only retirees. Column 2 adds bequests to the laissez-faire economy, specifically that 20 percent of retiree resources are bequeathed to working-age cohorts.[8] Retirees remain exposed to the same risks as before, but working-age cohorts bear a little valuation risk. The more diversified income slightly reduces working-age exposure to productivity risk. Column 3 shows the allocation one would obtain with perfectly pooled risk. Retiree and working-age consumption would respond equally to both shocks. Because savings respond more to productivity shocks than working-age consumption, disposable income in working age should be less sensitive to productivity shocks than retiree income. The efficient allocation of valuation risk cuts retirees exposure by more than two-thirds, and it shares valuation risk with future generations through substantial variations in investment. Column 4 adds a stylized representation of US fiscal institutions to the market economy with bequests. The retiree generation receives partially wage-indexed, annuitized social security benefits: 5 percent of GDP on average, 50 percent wage-indexed to proxy indexation to age 60. They receive medical benefits that are unresponsive to productivity risk: 3.5 percent of GDP. They pay income and consumption taxes: 3.5 percent of GDP with 15 percent marginal rate; and they hold safe government bonds: 2.5 percent of generational GDP. The relative magnitudes of transfers and taxes match Auerbach et al. (1999) generational accounts for age 65, rounded for simplicity.

If one compares the calibrated policy (Column 4) with laissez-faire (Column 2) and with the efficient allocation (Column 3), one finds that *fiscal policy magnifies the generational gap between working-age and retiree exposure to productivity risk.* This is largely because public debt, medical benefits, and social security (the nonwage-indexed part) provide safe claims to retirees. While safe transfers reduces retiree exposure to risk, they force the government to collect fixed revenues from the next generation's stochastic wage income. This increases the relative risk exposure of working-age cohorts. Policy also shifts valuation risk from retirees to workers, largely because of the capital income tax, but not as much as risk-pooling would require.

Columns 5 and 6 illustrate the impact of alternative policies. Column 5 assumes fully wage-indexed transfers: a 30 percent (doubled) tax on capital income, holding savings incentives and the generational account constant through compensating transfers. Column 6 assumes that all retiree transfers are fixed in real terms. The allocation with wage-indexing and higher-marginal tax rates is evidently closer to risk pooling than current policy, whereas fixed benefits yield a more uneven allocation of productivity risk.

Overall, Table 2-1 demonstrates how fiscal policy influences risk–sharing and how it could improve the allocation of risk. Note that a better sharing of productivity risk would make labor income taxes less variable and therefore reduce the excess burden of taxation. Hence tax distortions cannot explain the imperfect sharing of productivity risk. They may help explain why valuation risk is not fully shared.

In general, the public policy debate is quite incoherent regarding how much risk retirees should be expected to take. Two popular positions which embody this conflict are those who would (a) encourage equity investments in pensions and (b) provide guaranteed benefit promises. Both positions are inconsistent with risk pooling. To justify (a), one would have to consider retirees to be highly risk-tolerant, but in this case retirees should bear much more productivity risk, contradicting (b). To justify (b), one would have to view retirees as intrinsically more risk-averse than younger individuals. This might justify fiscal institutions that provide safe income to retirees, but it would argue strongly against pushing retirees into equity investments. If retirees are about as risk-averse as younger cohorts, welfare improvements can be found in the direction of more wage- or GDP-indexing, either within social security or via GDP-indexed public debt.[9] Not all indexing is beneficial, however. For example, if productivity shocks are negatively correlated with inflation, as evidence suggests, inflation-indexed government debt yields less risk-sharing than traditional nominal debt.[10]

Aggregate Risks (II): Demographics

Uncertain Fertility. It is clear that fertility changes can have major effects on the economy and on intergenerational transfers: the baby-boom and baby-bust phenomena are prime examples. Unfortunately, the public pension debate has mischaracterized the phenomenon by focusing on the fiscal burden that falls more heavily on smaller cohorts than on larger ones.

Macroeconomic theory suggests that being born into a small cohort is actually good news. When a small cohort enters the labor force, workers are scarce and retirement saving from the preceding larger cohorts provides a high capital–labor ratio. When small cohorts move toward retirement, subsequent larger cohorts provide the labor that allows retirement savings to earn a high return. In a world without PAYGO transfers, risk-sharing would therefore call for net transfers from small cohorts to larger ones. In a world with PAYGO transfers, higher-payroll taxes on smaller cohorts can be interpreted as risk-sharing—not as a fiscal problem, but as solution to a demographic risk sharing problem.

Table 2-2 provides a quantitative assessment of who bears the risk of variable cohort sizes. Panel A displays responses to an unexpected 15 percent decline in the labor force (about the decline between the baby boom and baby bust: 79 million births in 1945–64 versus 69 million births 1965–84).[11] Columns 1–6 display the allocation of risk for the same scenarios as in Table 2-1, with the clarification that transfers are of the DB variety in Columns 4 and 5 but DC in Column 6. The laissez-faire allocations

TABLE 2-2 Demographic Risks: Fertility and Longevity

	Scenarios (Responses to unexpected changes in percent)					
	Laissez-faire	*Laissez-faire with bequests*	*Efficient solution*	*Calibrated policy*	*More taxes and wage-indexing*	*All safe transfers*
	(1)	*(2)*	*(3)*	*(4)*	*(5)*	*(6)*
Panel 2A: Baby-bust decline in the workforce (−15 %)						
Consumption in retirement	−7.9	**−7.9**	**0.1**	−4.2	−2.1	−7.6
Consumption in working age	4.0	**4.4**	**0.1**	**2.2**	1.2	3.9
Disp. income in working-age	4.5	4.8	0.1	2.5	1.4	4.4
Capital Investment	5.5	5.6	0.2	3.2	1.7	5.6
Panel 2B: Increased longevity (+15 %)						
Consumption in retirement	−15.0	**−15.0**	−6.7	**−11.6**	−8.6	−15.0
Consumption in working age	−5.9	**−5.1**	−6.7	**−6.3**	−6.5	−6.0
Disp. income in working age	0.0	**0.0**	−4.6	−1.9	−3.5	0.0
Capital investment	12.4	12.6	**0.0**	7.7	3.0	13.0

Source: Author's calculations.

Notes: Same scenarios are as in Table 2-1. Panel A considers a 15 decline in cohort size, roughly matching the US baby-boom to baby-bust transition. Panel B assumes a 15 percent increase in the retirement period (about two years). Transfers are annuitized defined benefits in Cols. 4 and 5, and defined contributions in Col. 6.

illustrate the benefits of being in a small cohort (Columns 1 and 2). The consumption of the retired 'baby boom' generation declines, whereas the income and consumption of the working-age 'baby bust' generation rise. Efficient risk-sharing calls for a slight increase in both generations' consumption (Column 3), as permitted by a slight increase in per capita income. The policy (Column 4) calibrated to resemble the US yields consumption responses in the same opposing directions as laissez-faire. The smaller absolute values indicate better risk-sharing. The policy alternative with more DB transfers (Column 5) provides more risk-pooling than the calibrated policy, whereas the DC system (Column 6) provides virtually no risk-sharing. In summary, a DB transfer help share demographic risk.

Empirical evidence on the effects of demographic risk is unfortunately scarce. Evidence exists on the labor market, where the wage effects of a variable cohort size are well documented (e.g. Welch 1979). Capital market effects are difficult to document, perhaps because the start of retirement savings is more variable cross-sectionally than a cohort's entry into the labor force. Capital market effects are also obscured by high asset price volatility and perhaps by international capital flows. Population aging is a worldwide phenomenon, however, so the scope for international diversification is limited. Despite the scarcity of evidence, economic theory is probably a better guide to the future than naive trend extrapolations that assume a disconnect between demographic change and factor prices.

Uncertain Longevity. Around the world, mortality has long been on a declining trend. The main intergenerational impact is on life expectancy in retirement, or longevity, for short. Increased longevity is obviously good news for the retirees. But unless all retirement income is annuitized, increased longevity has a negative impact on living standards. It requires a reduced rate of per-period consumption.

Efficient risk-sharing calls for a sharing of longevity risk with subsequent generations. On a microeconomic level, annuities are the obvious risk-sharing tool, but they are subject to adverse selection and often unavailable. Most assets are held in nonannuitized form, which leads to substantial intergenerational transfers through accidental bequests. On an aggregate level, longevity risk is virtually impossible to insure in the market. Insurance providers are owned collectively by the generation that seeks insurance. Insurance between nearby, but distinct cohorts would have to be signed far in advance, before too much about actual longevity is known. Therefore, the government has a unique role as a provider of longevity insurance backed by future generations, providing a rationale for annuitized public pensions.

The degree of inefficiency without public pensions depends heavily on retiree attitudes toward bequests. To the extent assets are bequeathed intentionally—say, to a close relative or to a favorite charity—there is no inefficiency.

To the extent that bequests occur because annuities are unavailable, public pensions improve retiree welfare. I interpret the popularity of public pensions as indication that most retirees like annuities (i.e. do not have altruistic bequest motives strong enough to make the risk-sharing problem moot).

Not all annuitized public pensions share aggregate longevity risk. The key design issue is if per-period pensions and related medical benefits are fixed regardless of longevity (i.e. of the DB variety), or if payroll taxes and other contributions are held constant (i.e. the DC model). In the former case, increased longevity requires higher taxes. In the latter case, increased aggregate longevity must lead to reduced per-period benefit payments. Table 2-2B provides a quantitative perspective on how fiscal policy allocates longevity risk. It shows responses to a permanent 15 percent increase in longevity during retirement (equivalent to about two years). Under laissez-faire, per-period retiree consumption declines one-for-one with longevity (see Columns 1 and 2). Because working-age cohorts also expect a longer retirement, they increase savings and reduce consumption, but only fractionally. Efficient risk-sharing simply calls for sharing current resources (Column 3). Savings remain unchanged because the longevity increase is permanent and leaves no scope for risk-sharing over time. The calibrated allocation (Column 4) shares longevity risk better than laissez-faire due to annuitized social security and health benefits, but not completely. An expanded transfer system (Column 5) comes closer to risk-pooling, documenting the risk-sharing role of an annuitized DB model, whereas the DC system (Column 6) is as inefficient as laissez-faire.

The retirement age is an open question in this context. One may of course allow early retirement at an actuarially reduced pension. The deeper question is how the normal retirement age should relate to longevity. Medical improvements that extend a generation's ability to work may be viewed as a positive demographic shock. Risk-sharing would then suggest that individuals capable of working longer should indeed work longer and share the gains with other cohorts. The gains may be small, however, because if retirement ages are individually optimal, working longer increases lifetime income by about as much as it reduces utility from leisure, leaving no first-order gains for sharing. A related issue is the baseline for insurance. Only unexpected changes are insurable. If one started with naïve static expectations, any increase in longevity would trigger payments from those living short lives to those who have the financial misfortune of living longer. Insurance against good news—living longer—is counterintuitive from a distributional perspective. If insurance is conditioned on a positive trend path for longevity, in contrast, only deviations from this path are insurable and would trigger increased or reduced intergenerational transfers.

Conditioning on the trend is perhaps the best argument for linking retirement age to longevity. It seems unfair to let generations who die early pay for the predictably higher expenses of longer-living generations.

But to avoid slipping from a DB to a DC world, the normal retirement age needs to be fixed well before a cohort approaches retirement. An exemplary implementation is the increase in retirement age from 65 to 67 in the USA, which was announced decades in advance.

Finally, we note that tax distortions may impose limits on sharing demographic risks. Fertility and longevity risk are shared by imposing higher working-age taxes on unexpectedly small cohorts and on cohorts that follow unusually long-lived ones. It is an open question to what extent tax distortions explain why demographic risk-sharing is incomplete in practice. Distortions do provide another rationale for link normal retirement age to the longevity trend.

Aggregate Risks (III): Health Care

The growth in medical expenses has reached a stage where health care deserves treatment as a macroeconomic risk factor. The social security debate has been remarkably silent about health issues, even though Medicare and Medicaid are growing much more rapidly and—looking forward—will impose the greater fiscal burden. It is tempting to avoid discussing the issue, because health care raises delicate questions about preferences over life, death, and human suffering. I will nonetheless attempt a welfare-theoretic analysis as policymakers simply cannot afford to ignore the issue.

Two very different perspectives are currently influential in the health care debate. One view is that every person is entitled to health and survival, regardless of wealth or income. Under this view, public spending on health care will grow at an exogenous rate, driven by an ethical obligation to pay for all health care that is technically feasible. The economic implications of this are troubling, with fiscal projections totaling \$38 trillion in present value for Medicare (Gokhale and Smetters 2003). Cost uncertainty creates a huge need for insurance. The opposing view is that people buy health care like other commodities; consequently, the demand for health services responds elastically to changing relative prices and to rising income. Growth in medical spending is thus endogenous, driven in part by technological innovations that reduce quality-adjusted prices, in part by rising incomes, and in part by inefficient insurance arrangements that provide false price signals. Insuring expenditures would then be misguided. The insurable events are instead the discoveries of new treatments and the resulting changes in relative prices. The need for insurance depends on health consumers' price elasticity. If innovations reduce the price of curing a health problem, expenditures fall if demand is inelastic; stay constant if demand has unit elasticity, or rise if demand is elastic. In practice, new treatments tend to increase overall medical spending, suggesting that demand is more than unit-elastic. Setting aside the well-known static inefficiencies of third-party insurance (a topic best left to microeconomics), the key macro implication is that rapid growth in medical spending may well be an efficient response to medical innovations and price-elastic demand.

These contrasting views have some common macroeconomic and intergenerational implications. Medical expenses are bound to increase as share of GDP, either unavoidably (view 1) or because it is optimal (view 2). The generational implications follow from the correlation between age and medical needs: risk-sharing, of whatever type appropriate, will go in the direction of working-age cohorts providing insurance to retirees.

The source of rising medical expenses is important for the distributional baseline. Even if one takes an entitlement view of what society should cover, one must acknowledge that growth in medical expenses is largely driven by new treatments. Intergenerational insurance against health care cost is thus analogous to longevity insurance. Just like longevity insurance, insurance against medical expenses insures against the financial implications of good news—the discovery of new treatments. Just like longevity insurance, such insurance is awkward from a distributional perspective. Why should we be responsible for the medical expenses of future generations who we expect to be more healthy, wealthy, and longer living than we are? The fiscal balance rule of generational accounting appears questionable in this context because it obliges current generations to share the cost of treatments not yet invented (Gokhale and Smetters' $38 trillion estimate includes some amount of this).

Intergenerational risk-sharing is again about the impact of changes relative to a given baseline, and it is applicable regardless of baseline. For analytic purposes, I divide health care into two conceptually distinct types, roughly corresponding to the two views. Type 1 consists of life-saving or life-lengthening treatments prerequisite for normal life (life-saving care, for short). Type 2 consists of items that make people feel better, here called discretionary care, for short. In the OG model, one may think of life-saving care as affecting the probability of reaching a certain age, but not utility from consumption conditional on survival, whereas Type 2 health care enters into each period's utility function. Risk-sharing with Type 1 medical expenses is centrally about the value of life—an issue where normative answers are outside the scope of economics. If, however, one takes a certain level of life-saving care as given, and if such care enters separably into individual preferences, efficient risk-sharing calls for the unexpected cost to be shared. The usual principles of risk-sharing apply to the generations' nonmedical consumption.

Efficient risk-sharing with Type 2 medical expenses is a straightforward exercise in welfare analysis. Health care prices enter the price index for consumption. Assuming discretionary care has a higher weight in retiree consumption, an unexpected decline in quality-adjusted medical prices implies a decline in the price index of retiree consumption relative to the price index of working-age consumption. If the elasticity of substitution between health care and other consumption is above one, as presumed in the discretionary view, then efficient risk-sharing calls for retirees to share with working-age cohorts the welfare gains from lower medical prices. Real consumption would increase for all cohorts, but consumption spending would decline for retirees while rising for working-age cohorts.

Table 2-3 provides a quantitative illustration. The setting is the Diamond model described above, now with a distinction between medical and nonmedical consumption. Retirees are assumed to have twice as much health care needs as working-age cohorts.[12] Columns 1 and 2 contrast two extreme scenarios, 'Full Coverage' of retiree medical expenses (the DB approach) versus 'Capped Benefits' (the DC approach). Efficient risk-sharing is shown in Column 3. Consumption spending refers to total consumption, including private- and government-provided health care, with nonmedical consumption as *numeraire*. For reference, public spending in the USA covers about 65 percent of retiree health care. As Medicare drug coverage is rolled out, this percentage is likely to increase.

Panel A explores the implication of a permanent 30 percent increase in medical needs, meaning an increase in expenses that is unavoidable and separable in preferences from other consumption.[13] The Full Coverage scenario imposes the cost entirely on the next generation of taxpayers, leaving nonmedical retiree consumption unchanged. The Capped Benefits scenario holds overall retiree spending unchanged, forcing them to fund the incremental medical expenses from reduced nonmedical spending. Working-age households also face increased medical expenses, but their response is mainly driven by their expectations about retirement. In the Full Coverage scenario, savings and investment decline as workers pay higher taxes to fund retiree medical expenses without having to worry about increased own expenses in retirement. In the Capped Benefits scenario, working-age savings and investment increase in expectation of higher medical expenses in retirement.

The standard for efficient risk-sharing with separable preferences is an equal response of nonmedical spending. In the setting of Table 2-3A, this implies covering 27 percent of costs (Column 3), forcing retiree and worker nonmedical consumption to decline. Efficiency also implies a zero savings response because expenses increase equally in current and future periods. The 27 percent value is sensitive to the example parameters. The zero investment response is robust—a hallmark of an efficient response to a permanent shock.

Table 2-3B presents a setting where individuals have preferences with constant elasticity of substitution over real medical and nonmedical consumption. Prices are assumed to decline by 30 percent, the elasticity equals 2, so medical expenses also increase by 30 percent. But now the increased

TABLE 2-3 Uncertain Medical Spending: Needs-driven or Innovation-driven?

Scenarios (Responses to unexpected changes in percent)

	Full coverage for retirees (1)	Capped benefits for retirees (2)	Efficient risk sharing (3)
Panel 3A: Inelastic increase in medical needs			
Consumption spending in retirement	6.6	**0.0**	1.8
Consumption spending in working age	−1.6	−1.4	−1.4
Nonmedical Cons. in retirement	**0.0**	−8.5	**−6.2**
Nonmedical Cons. in working age	−6.4	−6.1	**−6.2**
Disposable income in working age	−3.6	**0.0**	−1.0
Capital investment	−8.0	2.9	**0.0**
Medical cost coverage	100	0	**27**
Panel 3B: Elastic response to medical innovations			
Consumption spending in retirement	6.6	**0.0**	−0.7
Consumption spending in working age	**0.0**	0.5	0.6
Nonmedical Cons. in retirement	**0.0**	−6.6	−7.4
Nonmedical Cons. in working age	−3.9	−3.4	−3.4
Disposable income in working age	−3.6	**0.0**	0.4
Capital investment	−11.5	−1.2	**0.0**
Medical cost coverage	100	0	**−11**

Source: Author's calculations.

Notes: Panel A assumes medical expenses are inelastic/needs-driven and increase 30 percent. Panel B assumes a 30 percent decline in quality-adjusted health care prices and an elastic response of medical consumption. Responses are computed for the calibrated model with stylized US policy, as detailed in the text. Col. 1: Retiree medical expenses are fully government funded on the margin. Col. 2: Retiree medical benefits are held constant. Col. 3: Efficient risk-sharing.

spending reflects a relative price chance favorable to retirees. Full Coverage (Column 1) raises retiree consumption, reduces working-age consumption and capital investment as savers expect full health coverage in retirement. Capped Benefits (Column 2) leaves retiree spending unchanged and triggers an individually optimal shift from nonmedical to health care consumption. Workers also shift away from nonmedical to health care consumption, and they reduce savings slightly because lower-cost health care yields greater benefits in retirement than during working age.

Efficient risk-sharing (Column 3) now calls for retirees to share the positive effect of lower health care prices with working-age cohorts by accepting reduced transfers. Retirement spending declines, nonmedical consumption declines even more, whereas working-age income and consumption spending rise. The numerical values are again example specific, but the efficiency of a benefit reduction and the zero investment response are robust. These results apply to any permanent price decline provided permanent retirees consume relatively more health care than younger cohorts.

International Risks: Wars and Foreign Assets

Wars. The risk of war is a major risk omitted in the analysis earlier. This is because burden-sharing is the standard paradigm of war financing, so risk-sharing does not provide much new insight. War expenses and war-related damages are negative shocks to the national resource constraint. A draft could be interpreted as a negative but temporary shock to working-age productivity. In an overlapping generations setting, efficiency would call for risk-pooling across generations. The results of a formal analysis would presumably resemble Barro's (1979) tax smoothing model.

However, the OG model gives different answers than that provided by the representative agent literature solving Ramsey tax problems. In representative agent models, the risk of war is best shared instantaneously through state-contingent claims (Lucas and Stokey 1983). In the OG model, efficient risk-sharing includes future generations. Their contributions to war finance cannot be collected instantaneously and requires taxation over time. State-contingent debt therefore does not avoid the need for a dynamic fiscal response to wars and other temporary shocks.

Foreign Assets. Foreign assets are the focus of international risk-sharing, as highlighted by Shiller (1993, 1999). He views international and intergenerational risk-sharing as alternative insurance mechanisms, and in his book (1993) he explains in some detail how international financial markets would help share income risks. In the same spirit, one could imagine macromarkets for country-specific fertility risks, longevity risks, and health care risks.

Unfortunately, the macromarkets that Shiller envisions do not yet exist. Today's financial markets facilitate capital flows and permit the trading of claims against capital income. For a quantitative perspective, note that the US States capital stock is about 225 percent of GDP, net foreign liabilities are about 25 percent of GDP, direct investments and equity holdings abroad are 36 percent of GDP, and foreign direct and equity investment into the USA total 43 percent of GDP (2003). Domestic residents thus retain a 190 GDP-percent exposure to domestic asset valuation risk (=226−36), almost equal to their 200 GDP-percent net wealth (=225−25). The low ratio of foreign assets to net worth (43/200) suggests that international assets are a smaller source of risk than any of the aggregate risks discussed earlier. While uncertainty about the return on foreign assets is a source of risk that might be shared across generations, it is unclear why international risk-sharing is so incomplete.

Endogenous Growth

A promising area for future research is intergenerational risk-sharing in an endogenous growth context, though most of the literature to date assumes exogenous growth. It has been noted that intergenerational risk-sharing could have much greater welfare benefits if it also affects economic growth. For instance Obstfeld (1994) posits that individuals can choose between low-risk, low-return and higher-risk, higher-return technologies. Under autarchy, risk-averse individuals choose relatively low-return investments. When risk are shared and thus reduced, individuals choose higher-return investments, leading to an increase in the *average* rate of growth. Applied in a multigenerational setting, the same argument would suggest that better intergenerational risk-sharing may encourage savers to select higher-risk, higher-return technologies, which would lead to an increase in average growth rates. The Obstfeld model suggests that growth effects could magnify the gains from risk-sharing by an order of magnitude.

Conclusions

This chapter has examined the allocation of major aggregate risks from an intergenerational perspective. Such risks cannot be eliminated by insurance, but they can be managed through risk-sharing. Government has a key role in this endeavor, because it can oblige future generations to participate in risk-sharing arrangements. Many fiscal institutions and practices can be interpreted as beneficial risk-sharing arrangements in this sense, but intergenerational risk-sharing is far from perfect. More specifically, we have reviewed risks related to productivity growth and to asset prices, demographic risks due to changes in fertility and longevity, and medical-expense risks created by changing health care needs and by innovations in medical technology.

With regard to macroeconomic risks, the message is to focus on productivity growth and not be distracted by uncertain asset values. Though uncertain asset values are indeed a risk for retirement savers and other asset holders, productivity growth is a much greater source of long run uncertainty. Fiscal institutions in the USA are well suited to provide safe claims to retirees via social security and government bonds, and asset valuation risk is shared via income taxes. Growth uncertainty has received comparatively little attention. Compared to a benchmark allocation with perfect risk-pooling, the retiree generation appears underexposed to productivity risk, though still overexposed to asset valuation risk. With regard to baby-boom and baby-bust phenomena, the key insight is that DB pensions and other intergenerational transfers have an important risk-sharing function. In an economy without such transfers, large cohorts are worse off than small cohorts. A large cohort's labor supply tends to depress wages and its supply of retirement savings tends to depress asset returns. DB pensions impose relatively lighter burdens on larger cohorts and thereby help share demographic risk.

Fiscal policy has a similar risk-sharing role with regard to longevity. Longevity insurance is awkward from a distributional perspective, however. To share the financial risk of longevity, cohorts suffering from low-life expectancy have to make transfers to cohorts that enjoy a longer life. It is important therefore to condition risk-share on a trend path of rising longevity (e.g. by linking normal retirement to the longevity trend). If one focuses on deviations from the trend, one finds that annuitized pensions with defined benefits help share longevity risk across generations.

Uncertain health care expenses create similarly awkward insurance problems as longevity. Full insurance against medical innovations (say, though Medicare or Medicaid) mean that cohorts receiving relatively inferior care would have to transfer resources to cohorts that benefit from medical innovations. Such transfers would be implied, for example, by the fiscal balance rule of generational accounting. Efficient risk-sharing does not support full coverage for retirees' unexpected medical needs. We address this issue from two perspectives. One view is that medical needs are inelastic and separable from other consumption. In this case, efficient risk-sharing calls for the retiree generation's unexpected medical needs to be financed, in part, by taxes on future generations and, in part, by reduced nonmedical consumption. A different view is that medical care may be seen as a substitutable component of normal consumption; in this case, increased expenditures would be seen as driven by declining quality-adjusted prices and more than unit-elastic demand. In this case, efficient risk-sharing calls for the retiree generation to self-finance the impact of unexpected medical innovations, even for intergenerational transfers to decline a little. These results are, to reemphasize, macroeconomic and, therefore, disregard potentially challenging issues of cross-sectional distribution. They nonetheless provide a macroeconomic starting point for the design of health care policies.

Endnotes

1. Bernheim and Bagwell (1988) suggest an even stronger result: with intermarriage between dynasties, not even idiosyncratic risk would be an issue because altruistically motivated transfers from more fortunate to less fortunate family members would eliminate idiosyncratic risk. Barro's and Bernheim and Bagwell's papers specifically examine idiosyncratic taxes, but their insights apply equally to family responses to other idiosyncratic shocks.

2. The model abstracts from overlap between work status and income types. Much of the capital income during working age accrues in retirement funds or as housing wealth that is rarely liquidated before retirement. The economics of retirement savings is therefore not much distorted if one pretends that the return on working-age savings accrues at the time of retirement.

3. A temporary productivity shock would require a period of high growth to be followed by an offsetting period of low growth—a somewhat implausible scenario. Even then, consumption smoothing is insufficient under plausible assumptions to correct the overexposure of working-age cohorts to productivity risk (see Bohn (2004) for details).

4. Readers with a finance background may question this argument because up-front incentives imply a proportionally higher account balance at the individual level. If invested entirely in equities, this implies the same risk-exposure as an investment in an account without up-front incentives but tax-exempt earnings. The equivalence is invalid at the aggregate level, however, because up-front exemptions must be financed. *Ceteris paribus*, they imply a greater share of government debt in capital markets and hence in the average retiree's (enlarged) portfolio. On aggregate, savers must hold the capital stock and therefore cannot hold more equities in a system with up-front incentives than in a system with after-tax saving.

5. This uses the preferred error-corrections specification that exploits the stationarity of the dividend yield and the dividends/GDP ratio.

6. It is an open question to what extent estimates for the S&P500 generalize to other financial assets used for retirement savings. One may suspect that diversification into other asset classes would yield a lower valuation risk. The results for the S&P500 provide at least a starting point for thinking about long-run risks.

7. The main macroeconomic assumptions are a 30 percent capital share in production, an elasticity of intertemporal substitution of 0.5, a 25 percent share of old capital in the total return on retirement savings, an inelastic labor supply, a trend path with 1 percent annual population growth, 1.5 percent annual productivity growth, a 4.5 percent real return on capital, and a length of the retirement equal to one-third of work-life (15:45 years).

8. To be specific, bequests are modeled as 'accidental' due to stochastic mortality and imperfect annuitization. The latter is discussed below in the section on longevity risk.

9. See Bohn (1990), Shiller (1993), and Borensztein et al. (2005) for more discussion of GDP indexing.

10. Because stochastic inflation would create new risks, the point of this caveat is more to distinguish wage- and GDP-indexing from inflation-indexing than argue for nominal debt.

11. Note that variable immigration would have the same impact on cohort size as a variable fertility. The macroeconomic implications would be identical. My interpretation focuses on fertility mainly to avoid questions about whose preferences count, for the welfare analysis.

12. The factor two is conservative, to avoid overstating the differences. The ratio was 2.67 in 1999 for public and private health care expenses and about 5.7 for government-funded care. The overall value is relevant for welfare calculations. These ratios and the 65 percent coverage value below are computed from US Department of Health and Human Services, Centers for Medicare and Medicaid Services, National Health Care Expenditure Tables, online at *http://www.cms.hhs.gov/statistics/nhe/historical* downloaded 3/17/2005.

13. This percentage is about halfway between the Social Security Administration's intermediate cost and high-cost estimates for Hospital Insurance in 2035. It may be interpreted as standard deviation if one views the high- and low-cost estimates as 2-σ confidence bands.

References

Altonji, Joseph, Fumio Hayashi, and Laurence Kotlikoff (1996). 'Risk Sharing Between and Within Families', *Econometrica*, 64(2): 261–94.

Auerbach, Alan J., Lawrence J. Kotlikoff, and Willi Leibfritz (eds.) (1999). *Generational Accounting around the World.* Chicago, IL: University of Chicago Press.

Barro, Robert (1974). 'Are Government Bonds Net Wealth?' *Journal of Political Economy*, 82(6): 1095–117.

—— (1979). 'On the Determination of Public Debt', *Journal of Political Economy*, 87(5): 940–71.

Bernheim, Douglas and Kyle Bagwell (1988). 'Is Everything Neutral?' *Journal of Political Economy*, 96(2): 308–38.

Bohn, Henning (1990). 'Tax-Smoothing with Financial Instruments', *American Economic Review*, 80(5): 1217–30.

—— (1999). 'Should the Social Security Trust Fund Hold Equities? An Intergenerational Welfare Analysis', *Review of Economic Dynamics*, 2(3): 666–97.

—— (2001). 'Social Security and Demographic Uncertainty: The Risk-Sharing Properties of Alternative Policies', in John Campbell and Martin Feldstein (eds.), *Risk Aspects of Investment Based Social Security Reform.* Chicago, IL: University of Chicago Press, pp. 203–41.

—— (2004). 'Intergenerational Risk Sharing and Fiscal Policy', Unpublished paper, University of California at Santa Barbara.

Borensztein, Eduardo, Marcos Chamon, Olivier Jeanne, Paolo Mauro, and Jeromin Zettelmayer (2005). 'Sovereign Debt Structure of Crisis Prevention', IMF Occasional paper #237.

Diamond, Peter (1965). 'National Debt in a Neoclassical Growth Model', *American Economic Review*, 55: 1126–50.

Gokhale, Jagadeesh and Kent Smetters (2003). *Fiscal and Generational Imbalances.* Washington, DC: American Enterprise Institute Press.

Kotlikoff, Laurence and Scott Burns (2004). '*The Coming Generational Storm.*' Cambridge, MA: MIT Press.

Lucas, Robert and Nancy Stokey (1983). 'Optimal Fiscal and Monetary Policy in an Economy without Capital', *Journal of Monetary Economics*, 12: 55–93.

Obstfeld, Maurice (1994). 'Risk-Taking, Global Diversification and Growth', *American Economic Review*, 84(5): 1310–29.

Shiller, Robert (1993). *Macro Markets.* Oxford: Oxford University Press.

—— (1999). 'Social Security and Institutions for Intergenerational, Intragenerational and International Risk Sharing', *Carnegie-Rochester Conference Series on Public Policy*, 50: 165–204.

Smetters, Kent (2001). 'The Effect of Pay-When-Needed Benefit Guarantees on the Impact of Social Security Privatization', in John Campbell and Martin Feldstein (eds.), *Risk Aspects of Investment Based Social Security Reform.* Chicago, IL: University of Chicago Press, pp. 91–105.

United States Department of Health and Human Services, Centers for Medicare and Medicaid Services (2005). *National Health Care Expenditure Tables, http:// www.cms.hhs.gov/statistics/nhe/historical* downloaded 3/17/2005.

Welch, Finis (1979). 'Effects of Cohort Size on Earnings: The Baby Boom Babies' Financial Bust', *Journal of Political Economy*, 87(5): S65–97.

Chapter 3

The Role of 401(k) Accumulations in Providing Future Retirement Income

Sarah Holden and Jack VanDerhei

At year-end 2004, in aggregate, some 43 million 401(k) plan participants held more than \$2 trillion in 401(k) plan assets.[1] Nevertheless, today's retirees do not tell us about the future status of workers having had 401(k) plans available over a full career. This is because the 401(k) plan is just now turning twenty-five years old, which means that even the oldest current participants could have only saved in a 401(k) plan for at most, a little over half of their careers. Thus, the EBRI/ICI 401(k) Accumulation Projection Model[2] was developed to project the proportion of an individual's preretirement income that *might* be replaced by 401(k) plan accumulations at retirement after a full career with availability of 401(k) plans under many scenarios.

The question of retirement income adequacy involves examining the potentially several sources of income in retirement: (*a*) Social Security benefits, (*b*) income from defined benefit (DB) and/or defined contribution (DC) retirement plans and individual retirement accounts (IRAs), (*c*) income from other individual savings (possibly including housing equity), and (*d*) income from continued employment.[3] The model in this chapter only focuses on the income stream future retirees are projected to receive from 401(k) accumulations, which are the sum of 401(k) balances at all employers and rollover IRA assets, in the first year of retirement.

Growth of 401(k) Plans

The past quarter century has witnessed a shift in the US pension landscape. About twenty-five years ago, 401(k) plans had only just come into existence, DB plans held the bulk of the pension asset base, with over \$444 billion, while DC plans, which were usually supplemental, held \$185 billion.[4] Today, by contrast, DC plans control \$2.7 trillion in assets, and DB plan assets total \$1.8 trillion.[5] Significantly, IRAs are also very substantial, amounting to \$3.5 trillion;[6] these benefited not only from contributions and investment returns over time but also from rollover assets from employer-sponsored plans.[7]

This dramatic change in the pension landscape has shifted some responsibility for retirement security from plan sponsors to individual participants. Further, while 401(k) plans have great potential, individual workers must now take the important steps of participating when offered a plan, preserving assets while working and on job change, and spending down assets responsibly in retirement. As a result, it is natural to reflect on where participation in 401(k) plans might be leading future retirees. This chapter weaves together two recent trends in pension research[8] to examine whether 401(k) plans will be able to provide retirees with substantial retirement income under a range of scenarios. In addition, following Holden and VanDerhei (2002), the chapter assesses the role that plan design plays in shaping the different outcomes. We begin by briefly describing the EBRI/ICI 401(k) Accumulation Projection Model and then present baseline results reflecting continuous employment, continuous coverage by 401(k) plans, and historical market returns (based on the performance of US financial markets from 1926 through 2001). Next we modify the model to explore the impact of catch-up contributions, contributing to IRAs if a worker is not offered a 401(k) plan, and changing the retirement age.

Methodology

The key elements of the EBRI/ICI 401(k) Accumulation Projection Model are sketched in Figure 3-1.[9] The starting point for the model is to collect data on 401(k) plan participants' account balances at their current employers, asset allocations, loan balances, and annual incomes (at year-end 2000) using the EBRI/ICI database.[10] The model then projects participants' plan activity over the remainder of their careers, which varies as a function of personal characteristics and typical behaviors observed among millions of 401(k) participants at different ages, tenures, and income levels (based on our analysis of the EBRI/ICI database). For example, asset allocations are adjusted as participants age, because in the cross-sectional data we see that older participants tend to hold lower percentages of their account balances in equities compared with younger ones. However, individuals' risk profiles vary. Thus, those with more of their accounts in equities at year-end 2000 relative to others in their age group are assumed to continue to hold higher equity allocations over their careers, albeit with some rebalancing away from equities as they age. Further, the group of 401(k) participants also engages in behaviors typical at job change. If a job change is predicted to occur, the model determines whether the individual leaves his balance in his employer's plan, cashes it out, or rolls it over into an IRA. If a rollover IRA is created, then typical IRA behaviors are modeled including asset allocation decisions and IRA withdrawal activity.

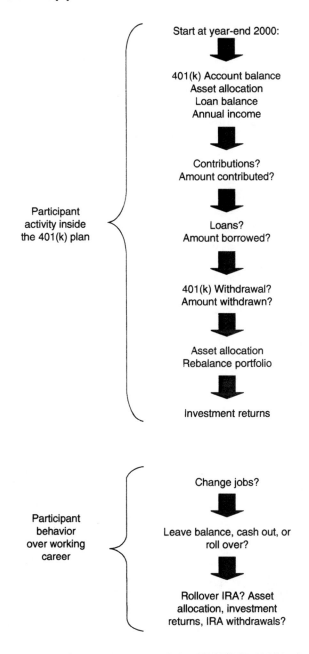

Figure 3-1. Diagram of basic elements of the EBRI/ICI 401(k) Accumulation Projection Model.
Source: EBRI/ICI 401(k) Accumulation Projection Model (see Holden and VanDerhei 2002).

To evaluate a full career with exposure to 401(k) plans, we first present results for participants born 1965–74 (age 26–35 in 2000); they will turn age 65 between 2030 and 2039. The 401(k) accumulation value at the end of each individual's career represents the sum of all 401(k) balances at all employers as well as IRA balances resulting from the 401(k) experience. We also convert the accumulations into an income stream—an annuity or set of installment payments—using current life expectancies at the retirement age indicated (in most cases, age 65) and projected discount rates. Finally, replacement rates are calculated to compare benefit payments in the first year of retirement to each worker's projected final five-year average preretirement income.[11]

Baseline Results

In the model's baseline run we move participants through a career with continuous employment, continuous 401(k) plan coverage, and financial market returns as characterized by the experience in US financial markets from 1926 through 2001.[12,13] In this case, 401(k) accumulations are projected to replace a significant fraction of projected preretirement income. For example, Figure 3-2 shows that the median retiree in the lowest income quartile attaining age 65 between 2030 and 2039 (based on projected final five-year average preretirement salary) will have a 401(k) payout

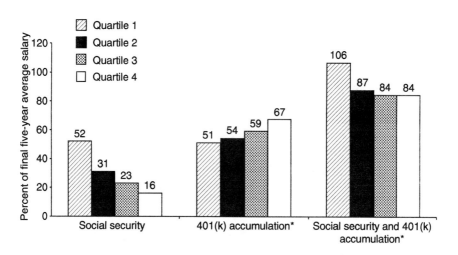

Figure 3-2. Median replacement rates for participants turning 65 between 2030 and 2039, by income quartile at age 65.
*The 401(k) accumulation includes 401(k) balances at employer(s) and rollover IRA balances.
Source: EBRI/ICI 401(k) Accumulation Projection Model.

in the first year of retirement that replaces about half of preretirement earnings. The median retiree in the highest income quartile at age 65 is projected to replace about two-thirds of projected preretirement income using 401(k) accumulations.[14]

For comparison, the median individual in the lowest income quartile would anticipate projected social security benefits worth 52 percent of projected preretirement income at age 65, if the current benefit structure were maintained.[15] Social security replacement rates decline with income, by design, so the median highest income quartile worker would have social security replace only 16 percent of projected preretirement income (if the current benefit structure is maintained). As mentioned earlier, 401(k) accumulation replacement rates tend to rise with income.

Alternative Simulations

The Economic Growth and Tax Relief Reconciliation Act of 2001 (EGTRRA) increased contribution limits and also permitted catch-up contributions by individuals age 50 or older. Specifically, workers age 50 or older who were already at the tax-deferred contribution limit were now allowed to make additional catch-up contributions. The first simulation examines the impact of this increased saving opportunity, in addition to having already included the legislated limit increases. We also evaluate scenarios where workers contribute to IRAs as they would have to their 401(k) plans during times when they do not find 401(k) coverage, following suggestions in the literature (Ippolito 1997; Pence 2002) that 401(k) plan participants may differ from other workers in that they are 'savers'.[16] An additional projection simulation combines the IRA contribution scenario and catch-up contributions in both IRAs and 401(k) plans. Finally, we allow some flexibility in selecting a retirement date, by exploring the impact of retiring at 60, versus postponing retirement until age 67 or 70.

Impact of the Catch-Up Provisions. In part because life-cycle analysis has suggested that older individuals are able to save more,[17] EGTRRA created catch-up contributions for individuals age 50 or older to allow them additional contributions if they had already reached the tax-deferred participant contribution limit.[18] The model assumes that any individual age 50 or older who would have contributed at the limit in the simulation in any given year (after 2001), will also make a catch-up contribution of the entire amount allowed, as seen in Figure 3-3.[19]

Holden et al. (2005) find that households taking advantage of IRA catch-up contributions, did so to the limit.[20] Thus, we assumed that 401(k) plan participants making catch-up contributions contribute the entire amount allowed;[21] we do not account for participants constrained from reaching the 402(g) limit by either plan design or nondiscrimination testing and

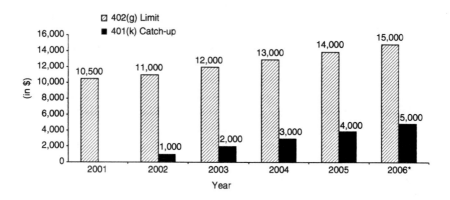

Figure 3-3. Internal Revenue Code deferred contribution limits in 401(k) plans, 2001–2006.
*After 2006, these limits are indexed for inflation in $500 increments.
Source: Authors' Summary of US Internal Revenue Code.

thus do not recognize them as eligible to make catch-up contributions.[22] In reality, such individuals would be eligible for catch-up.

As one would expect, because highly compensated employees are more likely to be at contribution limits, higher replacement rates are primarily observed among the fourth income quartile when catch-up contributions are modeled. As shown in Table 3-1, this boosts the projected replacement rate of the median individual in the fourth income quartile by 3.1 percentage points. The impact on the median individual in the other income quartiles is indistinguishable from zero.[23]

Impact of Saving in IRAs When 401(k) Plan Not Available. The baseline case assumes that workers always have a 401(k) plan, but replacement rates fall significantly if this assumption is relaxed. For example, as seen in Figure 3-4, the baseline replacement rate from 401(k) accumulations for the median lowest income quartile worker is about 51 percent of projected preretirement income, which falls to 25 percent if 401(k) coverage is not continuous and no other plan is allowed to take its place. Table 3-1 shows that the reduction in replacement rates rises with income, reaching 37 percentage points among the highest income quartile.

Next we examine the impact of modeling saving through IRAs, if employees find that their employers do not offer a 401(k) plan. Because workers are assumed to use the IRA only when a 401(k) plan is unavailable, the model uses the 401(k) contribution decision variables to determine whether a contribution will be made to an IRA when the individual does not have access to a 401(k) plan. We assume that each individual tries to contribute to the IRA what would have been contributed to the 401(k) plan by the employee and

TABLE 3-1 Change in Median Replacement Rates from 401(k) Accumulations[*]

	Income Quartile			
	1	2	3	4
Assuming always have contributions to 401(k) plan account	9.1	8.9	6.5	4.6
Assuming all 50+'s contributing at the 402(g) limit take advantage of catch-up	(***)	(***)	(***)	3.1
Assuming loans are never taken from 401(k) plan account	0.4	0.3	0.4	0.3
Assuming preretirement withdrawals are never taken from 401(k) plan account	6.7	6.0	6.0	3.8
Assuming do not always have 401(k) plan coverage	−25.7	−29.1	−32.6	−37.1
Assuming contribute to IRAs when don't have 401(k) coverage	−0.1	−3.7	−11.9	−23.6
Assuming catch-up in IRA and 401(k) plans	−0.1	−2.6	−10.3	−21.5
Assuming never cash out balance at job change	13.3	9.1	6.8	4.7
Assuming preretirement withdrawals are never taken from IRA balances	11.1	12.8	14.8	18.4
Memo: Median replacement rates for typical 401(k) participant**	50.7	54.0	59.5	67.2

Source: Authors' computations using the EBRI/ICI 401(k) Accumulation Projection Model.

Notes: Relative to baseline model assumptions for participants reaching age 65 between 2030 and 2039, by income quartile at age 65 (percentage points)

* Change in median replacement rate for 401(k) accumulations relative to final five-year average salary. This is the first-order difference and does not take into account changes in participant behavior that might occur as result of changing the activity in question.
** The ratio of the income generated in the first year of retirement from 401(k) accumulations to final five-year average salary (in percent) for the baseline model.
(***) Indistinguishable from zero.

employer combined, taking into account the lower IRA contribution limits, which are shown in Figure 3-5. Thus, individuals will be constrained to contribute the minimum of what would have been contributed in a given year in a 401(k) and what they are allowed to contribute to an IRA.

Interestingly, contributing to an IRA if an employer plan is not available almost moves workers in the lowest income quartile back to baseline results. This is because the 401(k) plan contribution amounts among lower income quartiles are closer to the IRA limits, and thus these individuals are better able to replicate their 401(k) contribution activity in an IRA, as seen in Figure 3-4. For those in the higher income quartiles, lower

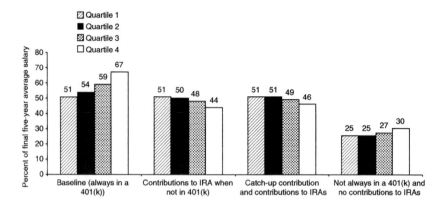

Figure 3-4. Median replacement rates from 401(k) accumulations* for participants turning 65 between 2030 and 2039, by income quartile at age 65.
*The 401(k) accumulation includes 401(k) balances at employer(s) and rollover IRA balances
Source: EBRI/ICI 401(k) Accumulation Projection Model.

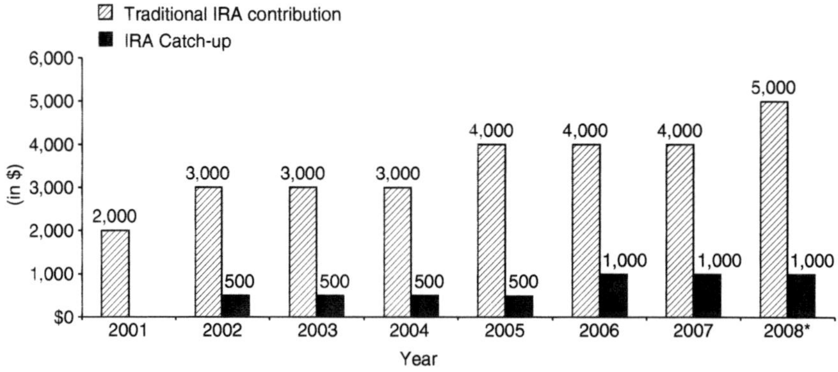

Figure 3-5. Internal Revenue Code traditional IRA contribution limits, 2001–2008.
* After 2008, traditional IRA contributions are indexed for inflation in $500 increments. IRA catch-up contributions are not indexed for inflation.
Source: Authors' Summary of US Internal Revenue Code.

IRA limits prevent them from replicating their 401(k) contributions; for example, the median replacement rate for the highest earning group improves by about 14 percentage points, to 44 percent of preretirement income, but it does not attain the baseline result. Allowing catch-up contributions in addition to the availability of IRAs moves the projected replacement rate among higher income participants up a bit.

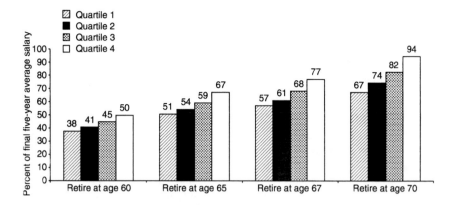

Figure 3-6. Median replacement rates from 401(k) accumulations* for participants born between 1965 and 1974 at the retirement age indicated, by income quartile at retirement age indicated.
*The 401(k) accumulation includes 401(k) balances at employer(s) and rollover IRA balances.
Source: EBRI/ICI 401(k) Accumulation Projection Model.

Impact of Changing Retirement Date. Participants in 401(k) plans have flexibility in selecting a retirement age;[24] furthermore, when employer contributions are provided, working longer is often a financially attractive proposition. Accordingly, we vary the retirement age from the baseline model, which assumes retirement occurs for everyone at age 65. By varying retirement across ages 60, 67, and 70, we find that the compounding of investment returns at the end of an individual's career produces important differences in replacement rates.

For instance, Figure 3-6 shows that working two extra years from age 65 to age 67 increases the projected replacement rate in the first year of retirement of the lowest income quartile by about 6 percentage points, from 51 percent of preretirement income to 57 percent. The projected replacement rate of the highest income quartile rises by about 10 percentage points. Working until age 70 increases replacement rates even more dramatically. On the other hand, retiring five years earlier reduces projected replacement rates.

Conclusions

Current retirees' 401(k) accumulations are not representative of what a full career with exposure to 401(k) plans might generate for retirees. Thus, the EBRI/ICI 401(k) Accumulation Projection Model simulated several projected retirement scenarios for a group of 401(k) plan participants born between 1965 and 1974 after essentially a full career's exposure to 401(k) plans. The simulations suggest that catch-up contributions, which are available to participants who are age 50 or older and already contributing at the limit, primarily help higher income participants increase their replacement rates, while use of IRAs during lapses in 401(k) coverage is more successful at making lower income participants whole. Postponing retirement tends to increase replacement rates.

Endnotes

1. At year-end 2004, IRAs held $3.5 trillion in assets, with some of those monies coming from employer-sponsored retirement plans including 401(k) plans (as rollovers). See Investment Company Institute (ICI 2005). Estimate of number of 401(k) plan participants from Cerulli Associates (2004).

2. The EBRI/ICI 401(k) Accumulation Projection Model was developed as part of an ongoing collaborative effort between the Employee Benefit Research Institute (EBRI) and the Investment Company Institute (ICI). In this ongoing research effort, known as the EBRI/ICI Participant-Directed Retirement Plan Data Collection Project, EBRI and ICI have gathered data from some of their members that serve as plan recordkeepers. The data include demographic information, annual contributions, participant account balances, asset allocations, and loan balances. The year-end 2003 EBRI/ICI database contained information on 15 million 401(k) plan participants, in 45,152 plans, holding $776 billion in assets (Holden and VanDerhei 2004).

3. Here we do not address the issue of retirement income adequacy. For a recent summary of changes in consumption and income in retirement, see Hurd and Rohwedder (2005). There is an extensive research literature that analyzes whether DC plans will be able to provide workers with significant retirement income. Many of these research papers find favorably for 401(k) plans in many instances. For example, Poterba (2004) finds that although retirement wealth in 401(k) accounts is reduced by the deferred tax liabilities, a 401(k) with an employer match consistently has a higher rate of return than any other type of account considered. Samwick and Skinner (2004) conclude that 401(k) plans are as good or better than DB plans in providing for retirement. Chernozhukov and Hansen (2004) find that 401(k) plan participation has a positive effect on wealth. Other research recognizes the potential of the DC plan structure, but points to human foibles and mistakes that prevent workers from reaching the most beneficial outcome. For example, Munnell and Sundén (2004) emphasize the practical changes in workers' participation, contribution, asset allocation, loan, and withdrawal decisions that must be made to ensure the potential of 401(k) plans is realized. While Hurst (2003) concludes that households who entered retirement with lower-than-predicted wealth generally engaged in near-sighted consumption during their working lives. Scholz et al. (2004) conclude that fewer than 20 percent of households have less retirement wealth accumulated than their optimal targets. Other related research includes: VanDerhei and Copeland (2004); Butrica and Uccello (2004); Engen et al. (1999, 2004a, 2004b); US Social Security Administrations Modeling Income in the Near Term (MINT) projections (Butrica et al. (2003/2004) and Toder et al. (2002)); Shackleton (2003); Fore (2003); Poterba et al. (2003); Poterba et al. (2001);

Scholz (2001); Uccello (2001); Steuerle et al. (2000); Montalto (2000); Moore and Mitchell (2000); Yuh et al. (1998); and Smith (1997).

4. See US Department of Labor, Employee Benefits Security Administration (2004).
5. See Board of Governors of the Federal Reserve System (2005).
6. See Investment Company Institute (2005).
7. For a history of IRAs, see Holden et al. (2005).
8. For a summary of recent retirement saving research, see Holden and VanDerhei (2004).
9. For a complete description of the model, see Holden and VanDerhei (2002 and Appendix).
10. See Holden and VanDerhei (2002 and Appendix) for references on the EBRI/ICI 401(k) Accumulation Projection Model.
11. The 401(k) distributions are not indexed to inflation over retirement, while social security payments are. In addition, if the individual elects a set of install-ment payments rather than an annuity, the amount that may be reasonably withdrawn each year after the first year may vary as future market fluctuations affect the account going forward.
12. In the projection model, the future equity returns are assumed to be similar to historical returns experienced by the S&P 500 between 1926 and 2001 (see 'large company stocks total returns' in Ibbotson 2002). Between 1926 and 2001, about two-thirds of the time, equity returns in any given year have fluctuated between −7 and 33 percent. The total return used for bonds, GICs, money market funds, and other investments in the projection was based on 'long-term government bonds total returns' from the beginning of 1926 to the end of 2001 (Ibbotson 2002). Historically, about two-thirds of the time, these returns in any given year have fluctuated between −1 and 14 percent.
13. Holden and VanDerhei (2002) also consider projections for many different investment return scenarios including: the worst 50-year return period for US equities (1929–1978); a bear market (three consecutive years of −9.3 percent annual returns on equities) at the beginning, middle, or end of individuals' careers; and a bull market (three consecutive years of +31.2 percent annual returns on equities) at the beginning, middle, or end of individuals' careers.
14. Among participants reaching age 65 between 2030 and 2039, the real (in 2000 dollars) cut-off points for the income quartiles are: first quartile—$36,700; second quartile—$56,400; and third quartile—$87,200. Thus, individuals in the highest income quartile at age 65 have a real income of $87,200 or more.
15. Technically, this is called the primary insurance amount (PIA). The PIA was calculated for the individual participant's earnings history and did not consider the possibility of a spousal benefit, which can be substantially larger than an individual's own benefit in some cases. The PIA calculated for each individual is the sum of three separate percentages of portions of their average indexed monthly earnings (AIME). The portions depend on the year in which the worker reaches retirement. For example, for 2005 the PIA was 90 percent of the first $627 of their AIME plus 32 percent of their AIME over $627 and through $3,779 plus 15 percent of their AIME over $3,779 (see the Social Security Administration's website for benefit formulas).

16. Pence (2002) finds that 401(k) plan participants have greater interest in saving compared with other workers, and Ippolito (1997) argues that firms that offer DC plans attract workers who are savers.
17. The life-cycle pattern of saving suggests that older individuals are able to save at higher rates because they no longer face the expenses of raising children or buying a home. An augmented version of the life-cycle theory predicts that the optimal savings pattern increases with age. For a summary discussion of life-cycle models, see Browning and Crossley (2001). For a more detailed discussion, see Engen et al. (1999). In addition, Mitchell and Utkus (2004) discuss life-cycle savings and behavioral finance models in the context of retirement plan design considerations.
18. See Mitchell et al. (this volume) and Holden and VanDerhei (2001) for discussions of nondiscrimination and other contribution limits.
19. The model assumes that all 401(k) plans allow catch-up contributions. Profit Sharing/401(k) Council of America (PSCA 2004) reports that nearly all member plans allowed catch-up contributions in 2003. Utkus and Mottola (2005) report that 86 percent of 401(k) plans in Vanguard's recordkeeping system offered catch-up contributions in 2004.
20. On the other hand, Utkus and Mottola (2005) report an estimated average 401(k) catch-up contribution of $2,207 in 2004 (out of $3,000 possible), derived from total employee 401(k) contributions.
21. While assuming full catch-up contributions may overstate the impact, limiting the catch-up contributions to participants already contributing at the 402(g) limit reduces the modeled impact. This is because many 401(k) plan participants wanting to contribute at the 402(g) limit are prevented from doing so. For example, in 1999, only 11 percent of participants making contributions were at the 402(g) limit, but, among those not contributing at the limit, 52 percent could not have done so because of formal plan-imposed limits; see Holden and VanDerhei (2001).
22. PSCA (2004) reports that 8.6 percent of their member plans limit the contributions of highly compensated participants by plan design; 9.3 percent of plans limited contributions of highly compensated employees when contributions reached the maximum allowed by the nondiscrimination tests; and another 18.8 percent of plans returned excess contributions to participants after the plan year ended.
23. Utkus and Mottola (2005) also find that participants with higher income are more likely to take advantage of catch-up contributions, although they identify catch-up contribution activity across participants who are 50 or older in all income groups.
24. Munnell et al. (2003) and Friedberg and Webb (2003) explore how the shift in pension coverage toward DC plans may be a factor that affects the timing of retirement. Chan and Stevens (2003) examine the influence of financial factors on the timing of retirement.

References

Board of Governors of the Federal Reserve System (2005). 'Flow of Funds Accounts of the United States', Federal Reserve Statistical Release. First Quarter 2005.

Browning, Martin and Thomas F. Crossly (2001). 'The Life-Cycle Model of Consumption and Saving', *Journal of Economic Perspectives*, 15(3): 3–22.

Butrica, Barbara and Cori Uccello (2004). *How Will Boomers Fare at Retirement?* Washington, DC: AARP Public Policy Institute.

—— Howard M. Iams, and Karen E. Smith (2003/2004). 'The Changing Impact of Social Security on Retirement Income in the United States', *Social Security Bulletin*, 65(3): 1–13.

Cerulli Associates. 'Retirement Markets 2004.' *Cerulli Quantitative Update*. Boston, MA: Cerulli Associates.

Chan, Sewin and Ann Huff Stevens (2003). 'What You Don't Know Can't Help You: Pension Knowledge and Retirement Decision Making', NBER Working Paper 10185: 1–43.

Chernozhukov, Victor and Christian Hansen (2004). 'The Effects of 401(k) Participation on the Wealth Distribution: An Instrumental Quantile Regression Analysis', *The Review of Economics and Statistics*, 86(3): 735–51.

Engen, Eric M., William G. Gale, and Cori E. Uccello (1999). 'The Adequacy of Household Saving', *Brookings Papers on Economic Activity*, 2: 65–188.

—— —— —— (2004a). 'Effects of Stock Market Fluctuations on the Adequacy of Retirement Wealth Accumulation', CRR Working Paper 2004-16: 1–38.

—— —— —— (2004b). 'Lifetime Earnings, Social Security Benefits, and the Adequacy of Retirement Wealth Accumulation', CRR Working Paper 2004-10: 1–23.

Fore, Douglas (2003). 'Do We Have a Retirement Crisis in America?' *Research Dialogue*, 77, TIAA-CREF Institute.

Friedberg, Leora and Anthony Webb (2003). 'Retirement and the Evolution of Pension Structure', NBER Working Paper 9999: 1–43.

Holden, Sarah and Jack VanDerhei (2001). 'Contribution Behavior of 401(k) Plan Participants', *ICI Perspective*, 7(4): 1–20 and *EBRI Issue Brief*, 238: 1–20.

—— —— (2002a). 'Can 401(k) Accumulations Generate Significant Income for Future Retirees?' *ICI Perspective*, 8(3): 1–20, and *EBRI Issue Brief*, 251: 1–28.

—— —— (2002b). 'Appendix: EBRI/ICI 401(k) Accumulation Projection Model', *ICI Perspective*, 8(3A): 1–12.

—— —— (2004). '401(k) Plan Asset Allocation, Account Balances, and Loan Activity in 2003', *ICI Perspective*, 10(2): 1–16, and *EBRI Issue Brief*, 272: 1–24.

—— Kathy Ireland, Vicky Leonard-Chambers, and Michael Bogdan (2005). 'The Individual Retirement Account at Age 30: A Retrospective', *ICI Perspective*, 11(1): 1–24.

Hurd, Michael and Susann Rohwedder (2005). 'The Retirement-Consumption Puzzle', RAND Labor and Population Working Paper WR–242: 1–33.

Hurst, Erik (2003). 'Grasshoppers, Ants, and Pre-Retirement Wealth: A Test of Permanent Income', NBER Working Paper 10098: 1–52.

Ibbotson Associates (2002). *SBBI (Stocks, Bonds, Bills, and Inflation) 2002 Yearbook: Market Results for 1926–2001.*

Ippolito, Richard A. (1997). *Pension Plans and Employee Performance: Evidence, Analysis, and Policy.* Chicago, IL: University of Chicago Press.

Investment Company Institute (2005). *2005 Investment Company Fact Book*, 45th edn.

Mitchell, Olivia S. and Stephen P. Utkus (2004). 'Lessons from Behavioral Finance for Retirement Plan Design', in Olivia S. Mitchell and Stephen P. Utkus (eds.), *Pension Design and Structure: New Lessons from Behavioral Finance.* Oxford: Oxford University Press, pp. 3–41.

Mitchell, Olivia S., Stephen P. Utkus and Stella Yang (2006). 'Determinants of 401(k) Design: A Plan-Level Analysis', this volume.

Montalto, Catherine P. (2000). 'Retirement Savings of American Households: Asset Levels and Adequacy', *Report to the Consumer Federation of America and DirectAdvice.com*, Columbus, OH: Ohio State University, pp. 1–11.

Moore, James F. and Olivia S. Mitchell (2000). 'Projected Retirement Wealth and Savings Adequacy', in Olivia S. Mitchell, P. Brett Hammond, and Anna M. Rappaport (eds.), *Forecasting Retirement Needs and Retirement Wealth*. Philadelphia, PA: University of Pennsylvania Press, pp. 68–94.

Munnell, Alicia H. and Annika Sundén (2004). *Coming Up Short: The Challenge of 401(k) Plans*. Washington, DC: Brookings Institution Press.

—— Kevin E. Cahill, and Natalia A. Jivan (2003). 'How Has the Shift to 401(k)s Affected the Retirement Age?' *CRR Issue in Brief*, 13: 1–8.

Pence, Karen M. (2002). 'Nature or Nurture: Why Do 401(k) Participants Save Differently than Other Workers?' Finance and Economics Discussion Series Paper. Washington, DC: Board of Governors of the Federal Reserve System.

Poterba, James M. (2004a). 'Saving for Retirement: Taxes Matter', *CRR Issue in Brief*, 17: 1–8.

—— (2004b). 'Valuing Assets in Retirement Saving Accounts', NBER Working Paper 10395: 1–39.

—— Steven F. Venti, and David A. Wise (2001). 'The Transition to Personal Accounts and Increasing Retirement Wealth: Macro and Micro Evidence', NBER Working Paper 8610: 1–94.

—— Joshua Rauh, Steven Venti, and David Wise (2003). 'Utility Evaluation of Risk in Retirement Saving Accounts', NBER Working Paper 9892: 1–49.

Profit Sharing/401(k) Council of America (PSCA) (2004). *47th Annual Survey of Profit Sharing and 401(k) Plans: Reflecting 2003 Plan Year Experience*. Chicago, IL: Profit Sharing/401(k) Council of America.

Samwick, Andrew A. and Jonathan Skinner (2004). 'How Will 401(k) Pension Plans Affect Retirement Income?' *The American Economic Review*, 94(1): 329–43.

Scholz, John Karl (2001). 'Can Americans Maintain Pre-Retirement Consumption Standards in Retirement?' Working Paper. Madison, WI: University of Wisconsin, Department of Economics and the Institute for Research on Poverty.

—— Ananth Seshadri, and Surachai Khitatrakun (2004). 'Are Americans Saving "Optimally" for Retirement?' NBER Working Paper 10260: 1–64.

Shackleton, Robert (2003). 'Baby Boomers' Retirement Prospects: An Overview', *A CBO Study*, Washington, DC: The Congress of the United States, Congressional Budget Office.

Smith, James P. (1997). 'The Changing Economic Circumstances of the Elderly: Income, Wealth, and Social Security', *Maxwell School of Citizenship and Public Affairs, Center for Policy Research, Policy Brief*, 8/1997: 1–29.

Social Security Administration (2005). 'Primary Insurance Amount', July, *http://www.ssa.gov/OACT/COLA/piaformula.html*

Steuerle, Eugene, Christopher Spiro, and Adam Carasso (2000). 'Measuring Replacement Rates at Retirement', *Straight Talk on Social Security and Retirement Policy*, 24: 1–2.

Toder, Eric, Lawrence Thompson, Mellisa Favreault, Richard Johnson, Kevin Perese, Caroline Ratcliffe, Karen Smith, Cori Uccello, Timothy Waidmann, Jillian

Berk, Romina Woldemariam, Gary Burtless, Claudia Sahm, and Douglas Wolf (2002). *FINAL REPORT Modeling Income in the Near Term—Projections of Retirement Income Through 2020 for the 1931–60 Birth Cohorts.* Washington, DC: The Urban Institute.

Uccello, Cori E. (2001). 'Are Americans Saving Enough for Retirement?' *CRR Issue in Brief,* 7: 1–12.

US Department of Labor, Employee Benefits Security Administration (EBSA) (2004). 'Abstract of 1999 Form 5500 Annual Reports', *Private Pension Plan Bulletin* 12, Summer 2004. US Department of Labor, Employee Benefits Security Administration.

Utkus, Stephen P. and Gary R. Mottola (2005). 'Catch-Up Contributions in 2004: Plan Sponsor and Participant Adoption', *The Vanguard Center for Retirement Research and The Vanguard Group,* April 2005.

VanDerhei, Jack and Craig Copeland (2004). 'ERISA at 30: The Decline of Private-Sector Defined Benefit Promises and Annuity Payments? What Will It Mean?' *EBRI Issue Brief,* 269: 1–36.

Yuh, Yoonkyung, Sherman Hanna, and Catherine Phillips Montalto (1998). 'Mean and Pessimistic Projections of Retirement Adequacy', *Financial Services Review,* 7(3): 175–93.

Chapter 4

Changing Risks Confronting Pension Participants

Phyllis C. Borzi

The only section of the Internal Revenue Code that most Americans can immediately recognize is 'Section 401(k)'. Furthermore, in contrast to the typical reaction to tax law, the mention of a Section 401(k) plan is often greeted with approval and even excitement, as people think about how this wonderful nest egg will help carry them through retirement. Nevertheless, the average 401(k) account balance currently stands at only about $77,000 (Holden and VanDerhei 2004), which, given improvements in longevity, means that these assets may fail to produce enough assets to support the average person in retirement.

It is well known that 401(k) account balances depend on annual contributions by the participant and/or the employer, investment returns on account balances (which, of course, is related to the performance of the financial markets and the allocation of assets within the participant's account), and leakage, which involves withdrawals, borrowing, and loan repayments. Participant age and job tenure as well as the allocation to equity funds in the plan enhance the chances that any individual will be on the higher end of the account balance spectrum. This chapter explores some of the consequences of the US shift in employer-sponsored pension plans over the last decade. We shall argue that the shift from traditional employer-sponsored defined benefit (DB) plans to individual defined contribution (DC) plans has profound implications for retirement security. Specifically the new model no longer rests on group saving arrangements; rather, the norm emphasizes individual responsibility. This represents a fundamentally different way to think about and plan for retirement. We begin by examining the challenges to participants' retirement income security and then identify policy options that might enable participants to handle shifting pension risk.

The Stampede to Self-Directed 401(k) Plans

In 1992, some 40 percent of all American families had a participant enrolled in a traditional DB pension plan only, while 38 percent had someone enrolled in only a DC plan.[1] A decade later, the number of families with individuals in only a DB plan had fallen by half, to 20 percent, while those enrolled in only a DC plan ballooned to 58 percent. The number of families with individuals enrolled in both DB and DC plans during this period remained relatively constant at approximately 22 percent. Further, the total value of assets in individual retirement accounts (IRAs) at $3 trillion were much greater than assets in DB plans ($1.1 trillion) and DC plans ($1 trillion).

This process substantially altered risks borne by pension plan participants. In the DB framework, participants are generally offered an annuity payment at retirement in the form of periodic payments for life. These benefits are paid for primarily through employer contributions (employee contributions to private sector DB plans are rare) and investment income generated by these assets. The federal Employee Retirement Income Security Act of 1974 (ERISA) requires that DB plan assets be held in trust. Some of the key design characteristics of a DB plan may be summarized as follows (Zelinsky 2004): (*a*) deferred income is provided at retirement, not before;[2] (*b*) retirement income is provided in periodic annuity-type payments, rather than a lump sum; (*c*) employer contributions are pooled in a common trust fund from which all participants' benefits are paid; and (*d*) legal responsibility to fund the benefits promised rests on the employer so that if the funds are not adequate to fulfill those promises, the employer is responsible for making up the shortfall.

In contrast, DC plans usually distribute the plan assets to the employee when he terminates employment irrespective of his age, and typically pays benefits in the form of a lump sum. In addition, DC plans do not pool participants' assets but rather provide each participant with an individual account to which contributions (plus investment earnings or losses on those assets) are allocated.[3] At retirement, DC participants are only entitled to receive the balance in their accounts; employers are not required to supplement the participant's account if it is inadequate to provide necessary retirement income.

Today, 401(k) plans make up the largest component of all DC plans, and generally take the form of a profit-sharing plan with a salary-reduction 401(k) feature. Three quarters of DC participants were enrolled in 401(k) plans in 1999 (Munnell and Sundén 2004). And as a rule, 401(k) plan assets are selected by individual participants, not the plan's fiduciary. For example, the US Department of Labor, Bureau of Labor Statistics (USBLS) notes that 81 percent of 401(k) participants may choose how their funds are invested (2005).

The trend toward participant self-direction of investments has been fueled by several factors.[4] These include employer interest in minimizing liability for investment decisions, and the belief by some participants that by taking charge of investing their pension contributions they can better control their financial security in retirement. Further, the mutual fund industry has persuaded employers to take advantage of the opportunity to shift fiduciary responsibility to participants, and fiduciaries also find relief under ERISA from shareholder lawsuits, if participants incur investment losses when they are permitted to exercise investment control over their accounts. In any event, the idea that participants can be empowered to decide how their retirement assets are invested represents a powerful statement of confidence by employers in the ability of their employees to manage their own future.

Those expressing concern that some employees might not be able to make wise choices, because they lack the interest or experience in financial management and investment, tend to be cast as paternalists and out of step with the times. Often those urging a more cautious approach have been accused of not being willing to trust employees' competence and good judgment. For instance, in 2005, President George W. Bush spoke in Iowa saying to the crowd, 'Why is Congress afraid to let you control your own money?'[5] Overlooked in the rhetoric, however, is the fact that DC plans, by their very nature and design, require participants to bear substantially more risk than under traditional DB plans and that self-directed investments within a 401(k) plan do impose a burden on employees. The fact remains, therefore, that challenges facing employees are daunting and the potential for mistakes substantial. Further, depending when mistakes occur, there may be little chance to correct prior missteps. [6]

Risks and Rewards of Retirement Saving in Self-Directed 401(k) Plans

The reallocation of various risks and rewards from the plan sponsor to the employee poses serious challenges to many participants.

Risk of Inadequate Saving. Even the best-designed 401(k) plan in the most favorable of investment climates cannot produce adequate retirement income when the participant fails to contribute a significant amount to the plan on a regular basis. Lack of continuous access to a 401(k) plan, financial inability to make annual contributions because of low wages, competing economic priorities, life and family changes, and unexpected major expenses all contribute to this problem. Obviously, when an eligible participant makes no or low contributions to the 401(k) account, account assets at retirement will fall short of what is required in retirement.

Part of the problem is that participation in 401(k) plans is voluntary. Currently, only a meager 8 percent of eligible participants make the maximum contribution each year, and about one quarter of eligible workers choose not to participate (Smith et al. 2004). To remedy this situation, proposals have been advanced to create 'automatic 401(k)' plans, by establishing certain default options to facilitate employee participation such as making participation automatic unless the employee affirmatively opts out of coverage, and providing for automatic contributions through payroll deduction.[7] These proposals may reduce the number of nonparticipants and boost saving somewhat, but they are incomplete solutions because they primarily address nonenrollment that results from inertia of eligible participants. Some participants also make a deliberate choice to forgo 401(k) participation because of cost (they feel they cannot afford to contribute) or fear (they are intimidated by having to assume the responsibility for making investment choices that will determine their ultimate financial future). This is particularly a concern for low and moderate wage workers who lack the financial resources. Most studies show that contribution rates and amounts increase with age, earnings, and income, though even middle-class workers face the risk of failing to accumulate sufficient assets to meet retirement income needs (Smith et al. 2004).

Compounding the problem, employers generally do not contribute to a 401(k) plan unless the worker contributes. Employer matching contributions are generally predicated on prior employee elective deferrals because, as a plan design matter, participation in a 401(k) plan is initiated by an election by the employee to enroll and make a contribution. Mitchell et al. (this volume) review prior research supporting the view that employee savings rates are strongly influenced by employer matching contributions, although the extent of this effect depends on whether one is focusing on introducing a match or increasing an existing match. The underlying premise for this research is a typical 401(k) plan design where the employer contribution is used as an enticement for the individual to contribute; if the individual does not participate in the plan, no employer contribution is made. In this case, failure of the participant to contribute in a given year may have a far more significant impact on the retirement account balance than an employee may realize.

A related point is that workers may not be able to make 401(k) contributions in all working years if they are not continuously employed by companies which offer these plans. VanDerhi and Holden (this volume) conclude that replacement rates are much lower if individuals are not offered a 401(k) plan. Moreover, workers in the highest income quartile who decide to save in an IRA instead, would see their replacement rate decline since IRA limits are lower than those of 401(k) plans. For those in the lowest income quartile, however, replacement rates hold steady if IRA saving is substituted for 401(k) contributions. Naturally, moving from job to job creates risk for participants, even when 401(k) coverage is available on both jobs, because assets from a worker's initial plan may be made available at employment termination; unless the funds are rolled over, 401(k) distributions may be spent on other things rather than saved for retirement.[8] Moreover, interruptions in contribution patterns, particularly if frequent, may seriously undermine even the most diligent saver's ability to accumulate a sufficient amount of assets in a 401(k) plan.

Failure to Roll over Distributions. One long-standing criticism of 401(k) plans is that the balance in participants' accounts can be distributed at termination of employment, also known as 'leakage'. Although participants who receive pension distributions prior to attaining retirement age, death, or disability are taxed on those distributions unless they are rolled over, some see this as a relatively small price to pay for access to the money. To counteract this leakage, Congress in 2001 required plans to establish mandatory direct rollovers of eligible rollover distributions in excess of $1,000 as a default option (in the Economic Growth and Tax Relief Reconciliation Act or EGTRRA). The distribution must be automatically rolled over to a designated IRA of the plan sponsor's choice unless the participant affirmatively elects to have the distribution transferred to a different IRA (or another qualified retirement plan), or elects to receive it directly. Since this new provision has only recently been implemented, its effect on retirement savings will not be measurable for several years.

The decision to roll over a lump sum is closely linked to the individual's age and the size of the distribution. Moore and Muller (2002) note that only 17 percent of individuals who received lump-sum distributions at ages 25–29 rolled them over. By contrast, 56 percent of individuals who were older than 60 when they received a distribution rolled it over.[9] We note that this problem of leakage is not necessarily limited to DC plans but instead can apply to any plan that pays benefits in a lump sum such as a cash balance plan.[10]

Because the legality of cash balance plans has been challenged (particularly those that converted from traditional DB plans), few employers are establishing new cash balance plans or converting their current DB plans. Among other things, these plans have been challenged as age discriminatory because disagreement exists over whether they discriminate against older workers in the rate of benefit accrual (Purcell 2003). But at some point, the cloud over their legality will be lifted either by the courts or Congress, and the numbers of cash balance plan adoptions or conversions will rise again.

Leakage via Loans and Hardship Withdrawals. Workers are more likely to participate in 401(k) funds when they know they can have access to them in an emergency through plan loans[11] and provisions allowing for hardship withdrawals (Munnell et al. 2003).[12] Mitchell et al. (this volume) find that the incentive effect of these features is relatively small. Nonetheless, giving the participant access to retirement assets through plan loans or hardship withdrawals clearly creates a tension between retirement savings and savings for other worthy purposes. Even those who have a consistent saving plan may find the plans disrupted by unexpected consumption needs or unexpected declines in income. These disruptions occur most frequently around key lifestyle changes, including medical crisis, marriage, the birth of a child, the purchase of a home, or educational expenses, leading to loans or hardship withdrawals from the 401(k) plan. And even if the participant repays a loan in accordance with plan terms (as opposed to failing to repay the loan and having the amount offset against the participant's account balance when he or she terminates employment), earnings are still lost during the loan period because the participant's account balance may be considerably smaller than it was prior to the loan.

Investment Risk. While many studies and reports have discussed this problem, a few key points bear repeating. In a DB benefit plan, employer and employee contributions are pooled in a trust and invested professionally. When investment results fall short of what is necessary to pay promised benefits, the plan sponsor must make up the shortfall (as long as the sponsor has not filed for bankruptcy). The plan sponsor also bears administrative and transaction costs associated with investments, including those incurred for commissions and investment advice, and these costs are spread over the commingled asset pool.

By contrast, in a DC plan, just as the investment risk is transferred to the plan participant, so too are administrative and transaction costs. Although from the plan sponsor's point of view the administrative costs of a DC plan may be less than those of a DB plan,[13] participants in 401(k) plans do bear these costs directly as they are often allocated on an account-by-account basis, reducing participant account balances. Further, the cost to the participant is inversely related to the size of the account balance (ICI 2004). In addition, large DC plans (and nonself-directed DC plans such as a money purchase pension plan that uses centralized asset management), and mutual funds, have the potential for higher returns as compared to an individual employee investing own 401(k) assets, because the relative size of the participant's account balance is significantly smaller.

Maximizing investment performance is key to assuring that a self-directed 401(k) plan yields adequate retirement income. But the ability to invest wisely is not an innate skill—it must be learned and/or delegated. Even if delegated, some understanding of basic investment, insurance, and risk management principles is necessary. If pension assets are concentrated in a single pooled trust, the plan fiduciary can hire professional advisors to provide this expertise. By contrast, DC plan participants may not have access to the same level of expertise at comparable cost.

Another important advantage that DB plan sponsors have, as compared to DC plan participants, is the longer and more stable time horizon that the former enjoys for asset investment. When retirement benefits are being paid from a single pool of assets and the call on those assets occurs over a long period, DB plan investors can better diversify their portfolios and select investments with a longer time horizon and/or greater risk (and greater concomitant returns).[14] This subcategory of investment risk has been called 'temporal risk' (Zelinsky 2004).

Studies have shown that many 401(k) participants tend to invest their assets more conservatively and in a less diversified manner than professional asset managers do, thus leading to lower overall returns (Gale et al. 2004). This may be a function of what funds are offered as well as participant age (Holden and VanDerhi 2004; Medill 2003). In addition, as Mitchell and Utkus (2003) observe, DC plans often allow participants to invest in employer stock because plan sponsors see this as an obvious way to encourage and enable their employees to become investors; they may also believe that employer stock investments improve productivity and enhance shareholder value. Yet this type of investment may not be beneficial to employees; a high level of concentration in this one investment type generally poses a substantially greater investment risk than a more diversified portfolio would. Participants in self-directed 401(k) plans who do not understand risk and return strategies are unlikely to be successful in maximizing return.

Currently about half the participants in 401(k) plans elect to invest in employer stock when given the option; of those offered, more than half held 20 percent or less stock, and about 13 percent had more than 80 percent of their account balances invested in employer stock (Holden and VanDerhei 2004). Over a fifth of participants in large companies have 401(k) assets invested in employer stock (Spence 2005). It is true that some employers, through their 401(k) vendors, offer online pension educational resources and advice, including interactive programs to assist in creating profiles of the participant's risk tolerance and needs. This is intended to assist them in determining asset allocation and perhaps even helping them select specific investment vehicles; furthermore, online pension calculators can help participants gauge what their financial needs will be in retirement and what concrete steps they must take to meet those needs. Yet these programs have their limitations.[15] Not all participants have access to or are capable of using computers. Some participants prefer dealing with humans rather than machines or need old-fashioned printed documents instead of accessing or downloading those online, and for them the process is demanding, cumbersome, and confusing. Therefore, a system in which every worker bears the investment risk for all or most of the assets he or she will have in retirement may not be effective, efficient, and sensible, if the pension plans covering them are to promise adequate retirement income.

Risk of Retiring Earlier Than Planned. According to the 2005 Retirement Confidence Survey,[16] many workers are planning to work beyond the age at which current retirees retired; this means they have longer to continue their earnings stream and save for retirement. But though retirement ages are rising, nearly 40 percent of retirees still leave the workforce earlier than planned, often citing health problems or disability (41 percent) or changes at their company including downsizing (34 percent) as causes for early retirement (Helman et al. 2005). Of course, in the past, workers may have retired early because of generous early retirement packages and the promise of retiree medical benefits, both of which are being cut back. In the future, early retirees forced to stop work due to health, disability, or downsizing may therefore enter retirement with fewer monetary benefits and less coverage in the form of retiree medical benefits.

The literature suggests that those who retire earlier than planned are also more likely to express concern about having sufficient retirement resources. For instance, Helman et al. (2005) report that fewer than four of ten workers believe they are on track to save enough for retirement. Almost one quarter (23 percent) of workers describe themselves as 'a little behind schedule' and one-third (32 percent) say they are 'a lot behind schedule'. Only 7 percent of workers describe themselves as 'ahead of schedule' for retirement savings.

Longevity Risk. One component of investment risk that some participants may have difficulty in estimating is how long they are likely to live in retirement and therefore how long the assets they have accumulated for retirement will last. Hurd and McGarry (1997) found that HRS respondents age 46–65 had a realistic expectation of how long they would live; follow-up interviews showed that they also modified those expectations based on new information such as the onset of a disease. Interestingly, they also found that men tended to overestimate their survival probability, while women tend to underestimate it. Helman et al. (2005) came to a similar conclusion using data from the 2005 Retirement Confidence Survey.[17]

Traditional DB plans typically paid benefits in the form of an annual benefit for life. Distributions were made directly from a single pooled trust or through an annuity purchased by trust assets for the participant and his or her spouse, if any. Participants would therefore not face the risk of outliving retirement assets (although the benefit would often diminish over time with inflation). By contrast, most DC plans, including self-directed 401(k)s, make distributions in a single sum. Accordingly, the challenge for the participant is to determine what to do with the lump-sum distribution so that it will last through retirement. Initially many participants roll their distributions into an IRA, so as to avoid immediate taxation of the distributed amounts. While participants can then purchase an annuity, most appear to be unaware of or skeptical of this option. Partly as a consequence, the current level of annuitization is low (Ameriks and Yakoboski 2003) and many participants receiving lump-sum distributions decide to self-annuitize.

Even if the retiree has a realistic expectation of his life expectancy, people tend to underestimate how much money they will need on an annual basis to live comfortably in retirement (Helman et al. 2005). This problem is compounded by the fact that most workers have not even tried to calculate how much they need to save for retirement. Only 42 percent report that they (or their spouse) have done so, and of those who made the calculation, only 44 percent state that their saving patterns changed as a result of that information.[18]

Recent research suggests that many people do anticipate that their consumption needs will fall in retirement, in part because they no longer have work-related expenses (Hurd and Rohwedder 2005). Indeed, these expectations are often realized, which suggests that these people may have a reasonably realistic view of retirement needs. Yet the fact remains that many do not fully appreciate the effect of inflation on their projected income and expenses, and many fail to realize that half will live beyond their life expectancy. And not surprisingly, the lower is preretirement income and the worse is one's health status, the more likely one is to expect to struggle during retirement.

Risk of Irrational Behavior. Much of America's retirement policy rests on the fundamental economic assumption that individuals will behave rationally and make choices that are in their economic best interests. This assumption is sometimes incorrect. For example, despite the problems illustrated by the Enron debacle where individuals lost their jobs and a substantial amount of their pension investments in employer stock due to corporate malfeasance, participants continue to allocate a disproportionate share of their investments in employer stock.

Enhancing Retirement Income Security. This discussion suggests some premises from which pension policy experts might work to improve retirement income security. For one thing, no one plan type will be superior to all others for all employees over their working lives. Because of different work, family, saving, and spending patterns, as well as the variety of decisions that must be made both during the working career and after retirement, it appears that many people may not accumulate adequate retirement assets that will cover them throughout retirement, in a DC type retirement system. Such workers would likely be better off having both DB and DC plans, as each helps assure asset accumulation at different stages of the worklife. Nevertheless, fewer than one quarter of all employers offering pension plans today provide both a DB and a DC plan, and it seems unlikely that this number will rise much in the near future (Copeland 2005). Alternatively, proposals to permit default options in 401(k) plans could make contributing and investing less burdensome and risky for participants. If consensus emerges around the adoption of particular default mechanisms, it would be important to minimize any legal impediments to implementing the idea.

Policymakers concerned that not all employees want or are able to handle critical investment decisions would do well to reassess the current structure of self-directed 401(k) programs. For instance, participants might be allowed to choose between self-direction of their assets in a 401(k) plan and entrusting those decisions to professional asset managers. Amounts in the individual accounts of participants who choose the latter approach could be placed in a common investment trust and earnings and losses in the common fund could be ratably allocated among all participants in the trust.

Many participants would probably also benefit from assistance when making investment decisions with their retirement assets, yet employers are concerned about liability if they were to offer investment advice. Congress could encourage employers with 401(k) plans to offer investment advice by implementing a statutory safe harbor protecting fiduciaries who facilitate this process. Conditions could be attached to that fiduciary protection, such as requiring that the advice be given only by an independent financial organization willing to assume fiduciary responsibility for the advice provided. At the same time, and consistent with ERISA requirements, a plan fiduciary would still have to prudently select and monitor the independent organization offering the investment advice. If policymakers were concerned about avoiding potential conflicts of interest, investment advice provided by the plan's current 401(k) vendors could be excluded from safe-harbor treatment.

Finally, to better protect against the risk of outliving retirement assets, plan participants could be offered advice about the relative merits of annuities versus lump sums, as well as an annuity option in addition to the lump-sum distribution. In addition, assistance estimating ongoing financial needs and monitoring expenditures could be provided to those who elected the lump sum. Furthermore, many retirees would benefit from continued access to the types of investment advice that active employees also need.

Conclusions and Future Research

Retirement security experts in the past referred to US retirement system as a 'three-legged stool', with the legs representing employer-sponsored pensions, social security, and private saving. The transformation of workplace pensions into much more individually oriented plans means that some workers now face a future where their pension has, in effect, been merged with individual saving, since in both cases workers rather than employers now bear investment risk. Accordingly, the challenge for policy experts is to identify and build on past successes with the employer-sponsored pension system and recognize and learn from past mistakes. As long as the US approach to retirement security relies on a variety of public and private programs, it is useful to ensure that these fairly allocate risks among individual retirees, their employers, and taxpayers.

Several areas require additional research. If providing investment advice to 401(k) plan participants is to be pursued as a legislative goal, additional research will be required on consumer literacy. Recent analysis has helped to crystallize the discussion,[19] but it will be necessary to do more with interactive focus groups and small group discussions to test participants' understanding and response to advice and information provided. More must be also learned about the effectiveness of online consumer tools such as pension calculators, summary plan descriptions, and other written communications on pension plan decision-making would also enhance understanding. Another question deserving of attention is why eligible participants so often fail to enroll and contribute to 401(k) plans. Some may think they cannot afford to contribute; others may lack motivation or suffer from inertia; and still others may not want to assume investment responsibility. If the latter were true, 401(k) participation could be enhanced by giving participants given the option to receive professional investment advice. There is much opportunity for policy response.

Endnotes

1. These data are from Copeland (2005).
2. Many DB plans do offer participants a lump-sum option; employers with cash balance or other hybrid arrangements also usually provide lump-sum benefits as the normal form of distribution, with periodic payments as an optional form of benefits (Munnell et al. 2004). For an extensive discussion of cash balance and other hybrid plans, see Clark and Schieber (2004), and Schieber (2003).
3. Although DC plan assets may be held in trust, increasingly they are not managed by professional asset managers but are invested by the participants themselves through a self-directed process that, under ERISA, may be structured to relieve the plan fiduciary (typically the employer or other plan sponsor) of the fiduciary duty to invest plan assets prudently and other fiduciary responsibilities.
4. For a general discussion of the development, structure and implications of self-direction under ERISA § 404(c), see Perun and Steurle (2005).
5. President Bush's views on people's ability to manage their own investments were expressed in many speeches on his plan to incorporate personal accounts into social security. Edited transcripts of these speeches appear at *http://www.whitehouse.gov/infocus/social-security/map.html*. For example, in Pensacola, Florida on March 18, 2005, the President said: '...everybody has got a chance—should have a chance to be an investor. Investing is not limited to a certain class of person. ...And yet, I think the attitude of some, you know, we can't let certain people maybe invest their own money...' Similarly, on April 15, 2005 in Kirtland, Ohio, the President said 'One of the key principles is government has got to trust people. The more government trust people, trust people with their own money, the more content, the more prosperous our society will be.'
6. We recognize that to focus on the 401(k) plan alone is incomplete, since many retirees also have social security, personal saving, and other real property assets. Nevertheless, it is valuable to explore retirement saving in 401(k) plans inasmuch as many employers offer these as the sole retirement plan.

7. These proposals are designed to make contributing to a 401(k) plan and investing those assets less burdensome for participants by creating a series of default options that have the effect of increasing savings. For instance, Gale et al. (2005) propose a system of automatic enrollment where employees who fail to sign up are enrolled automatically at a designated contribution level deducted from their paychecks through payroll deduction, automatic escalation of contributions as a percentage of earnings, automatic investment in broadly index funds or professionally managed programs unless the employee chooses otherwise, and automatically rolled over when the employee terminates employment to an IRA, a 401(k) or other retirement plan offered by the new employer. Recognizing that default options have a significant impact on participant choices under a 401(k) plan, many others have advanced proposals with similar features, including Utkus and Young (2004), Thaler and Bernartzi (2004), and Mitchell and Utkus (2003).

8. For instance, Moore and Muller (2002) report that nearly two-thirds of individuals who received lump-sum distributions were under 40 years of age, and the amount of their distribution was slightly over $14,000. More than half of the individuals who received a lump-sum distribution reported saving those funds in a tax-deferred vehicle (35 percent) or another savings vehicle (17 percent). Of those who spent their distribution, most used the funds to pay bills, buy other items, or finance everyday expenses; only 1 percent reported using the money for education or medical expenses. Relatively little is known about whether distributions not rolled over to another qualified retirement plan or an IRA ultimately erode retirement wealth. Englehardt (2002) uses Health and Retirement Study data (HRS) to examine this question and concludes that there is not much evidence that consumption of distributions has resulted in significant pension leakage. However, one quarter of the households that spent distributions could have increased their pension and social security wealth by 25 percent had the distributions been rolled over.

9. The amount of the distribution is one of the strongest predictors of whether it will be rolled over or otherwise saved. Moore and Muller (2002) found that the mean distribution in 2000 dollars was $13,999 and the median distribution was $4,860. However, with respect to distributions that were rolled over, the mean cash-out in 2000 dollars that was rolled over was $22,839 and the median was $10,611.

10. As employers shifted from DB to DC plans, there has also been a shift within the DB universe toward cash balance plans; in fact, Munnell and Sundén (2004) report that nearly 15 percent of all participants in DB plans are in cash balance plans. Legally, cash balance pensions are treated like DB plans (e.g. the employer bears the risk for paying promised benefits), but they are structured to resemble DC plans. A hypothetical account is established for each employee with an opening balance. Each month, pay credits (a percentage of salary) and interest credits are credited to each participant's hypothetical account. Upon termination of employment or retirement, the participant can withdraw the hypothetical account balance as a lump sum or convert the hypothetical account balance into an annuity payable at normal retirement age. Clark and Schieber (2003) further describe the history and key design, operation, and policy issues surrounding cash balance and other hybrid plans.

11. Loans are permitted from tax-qualified pension plans under certain legal conditions; if these requirements are not satisfied, the loan will be treated as a taxable distribution. Generally, this means that the loan cannot exceed the lesser of: (*a*) $50,000 (less other outstanding loan balances), or (*b*) the greater of one-half of the present value of the amount in the participant's account or $10,000. The loan must be repaid within five years; the payments must be substantially level, not less than quarterly. The five-year repayment rule does not apply to loans used to acquire the participant's principal residence.

12. A 401(k) plan may allow hardship withdrawals from the plan even while the employee is still working as long as the appropriate conditions and accompanying Treasury regulations are satisfied.

13. Hustead (2000) concluded that the cost of a DC plan was less than the cost to the plan sponsor of a DB plan on a per participant basis, while Freeman and Brown (2001) concluded that mutual funds costs are higher than investment management costs in public sector DB plans. Recent work by the ICI (2003, 2004, and Collins 2003) disputes that conclusion, finding that total costs for mutual funds are actually lower than DB costs.

14. One way to deal with temporal risk is through the purchase of a variable annuity. Ameriks and Yakoboski (2003) describe the role of annuities in protecting against longevity and temporal risk.

15. Bodie (2003) examined the major websites offered by a number of prominent financial institutions and concluded that the educational materials and investment advice offered were 'often dangerously misleading' for those individuals who lack the knowledge and training to handle investment risk.

16. The RCS is described at *http://www.ebri.org/surveys/rcs/*

17. Helman et al. (2005) note that the average worker expects to retire at age 65 and spend 20 years in retirement. More than one quarter (27 percent) plan to spend between 20 and 24 years retired; 9 percent believe they will spend between 25 and 29 years; and 17 percent believe that they will spend more than 30 years in retirement.

18. Eighteen percent of workers think that they will need less than 50 percent of their preretirement income to live comfortably in retirement, while 23 percent believe they will need 70–85 percent of preretirement income, and 3 percent expect that 85–95 percent of preretirement income will be necessary. Only 4 percent believe they will need the same preretirement income and 6 percent think they will need greater income in retirement than their working years for a comfortable retirement. Most financial planners recommend that workers plan to save enough to assure a stream of retirement income that is at least 70 percent of preretirement income.

19. See for instance by Nyce (2005), Arnone (2004), Bodie (2003), Clark and Schieber (1998), and Moore and Mitchell (2000).

References

Ameriks, John and Paul Yakoboski (2003). 'Reducing Retirement Income Risks: The Role of Annuitization', *Benefits Quarterly*, Fourth Quarter 2003: 13–24.

Arnone, William J. (2004). 'Educating Pension Plan Participants', *PRC Working Paper*, No. 2004-7: 1–16. Philadelphia, PA: University of Pennsylvania.

Bodie, Zvi (2003). 'An Analysis of Investment Advice to Retirement Plan Participants', in Olivia S. Mitchell and Kent Smetters (eds.), *The Pension Challenge: Risk Transfers and Retirement Income Security*. Oxford: Oxford University Press, pp. 19–32.

Clark, Robert. L. and Sylvester J. Schieber (1998). 'Factors Affecting Participation Rates and Contribution Levels in 401(k) Plans', in Olivia S. Mitchell and Sylvester J. Schieber (eds.), *Living With Defined Contribution Plans*. Philadelphia, PA: University of Pennsylvania Press, pp. 69–97.

—— —— (2004). 'Adopting Cash Balance Pension Plans: Implications and Issues', in *Journal of Pension Economics and Finance*. Special Issue on US Hybrid Pension Plans 3(3): 271–95.

Collins, Sean (2003). 'The Expenses of Defined Benefit Pension Plans and Mutual Funds', *Investment Company Institute Perspective*, 9(6): 1–20.

Copeland, Craig (2005). 'Changes in Wealth for Americans Reaching or Just Past Normal Retirement Age', *EBRI Issue Brief*, 277: 1–36.

Englehardt, Gary V. (2002). 'Pre-Retirement Lump Sum Pension Distributions and Retirement Income Security: Evidence from the Health and Retirement Study', *National Tax Journal*, 55(4): 665–85.

Freeman, John P. and Stewart Brown (2001). 'Mutual Fund Advisory Fees: The Cost of Conflicts of Interest', *The Journal of Corporation Law*, 26(3): 609–73.

Gale, William G., J. Mark Iwry, Alicia H. Munnell, and Richard H. Thaler (2004). 'Improving 401(k) Investment Performance', *CRR Issue Brief*, 26: 1–8.

—— —— and Peter R. Orszag (2005). 'The Automatic 401(k): A Simple Way to Strengthen Retirement Saving', *Tax Notes*, March 7: 1207–14.

Helman, Ruth, Dallas Salisbury, Variny Paladino, and Craig Copeland (2005). 'Encouraging Workers To Save: The 2005 Retirement Confidence Survey', *EBRI Issue Brief*, 280: 1–32.

Holden, Sara and Jack VanDerhei (2004). '401(k) Plan Asset Allocation, Account Balances and Loans', *EBRI Issue Brief*, 272: 1–24.

Hurd, Michael D. and Kathleen McGarry (1997). 'The Predictive Validity of Subjective Probabilities of Survival', NEBR Working Paper 6193.

—— and Susann Rohwedder (2005). 'The Retirement-Consumption Puzzle: Anticipated and Actual Declines in Spending at Retirement', Rand Labor and Population Working Paper WR-242: 1–33. Santa Monica, CA: RAND.

Hustead, Edwin (2000). 'Determining the Cost of Public Pension Plans', in Olivia S. Mitchell and Edwin Hustead (eds.), *Pensions in the Public Sector*. Philadelphia, PA: University of Pennsylvania Press, pp. 218–40.

Investment Company Institute (2004). 'The Cost of Buying and Owning Mutual Funds', *Fundamentals: Investment Company Institute Research in Brief*, 13(1): 1–24.

Medill, Colleen E. (2003). 'Challenging the Four "Truths" of Personal Social Security Accounts: Evidence From the World of 401(k) Plans', 81 N.C.L.Rev. 901, 932.

Mitchell, Olivia S. and Stephen P. Utkus (2003). 'The Role of Company Stock in Defined Contribution Plans', in Olivia S. Mitchell and Kent Smetters (eds.), *The Pension Challenge: Risk Transfers and Retirement Income Security*. Oxford: Oxford University Press, pp. 33–70.

Mitchell, Olivia S. (2004). 'Lessons from Behavioral Finance for Retirement Plan Design', in Olivia S. Mitchell and Stephen P. Utkus (eds.), *Pension Design and Structure: New Lessons From Behavioral Finance*. Oxford: Oxford University Press, pp. 3–41.

—— —— and Tongxuan (Stella) Yang (2006). 'Determinants of 401(k) Design: A Plan-Level Analysis', this volume.

Moore, James H. and Leslie A. Muller (2002). 'An Analysis of Lump-sum Pension Distribution Recipients', *Monthly Labor Review*, 125(5): 29–46.

—— and Olivia S. Mitchell (2000). 'Projected Retirement Wealth and Saving Adequacy', in Olivia S. Mitchell, P. Brett Hammond, and Anna M. Rappaport (eds.), *Forecasting Retirement Needs and Retirement Wealth*. Philadelphia, PA: University of Pennsylvania Press, pp. 68–94.

Munnell, Alicia H. and Annika Sundén (2004). *Coming Up Short: The Challenge of 401(k) Plans*. Washington, DC: Brookings Institution Press.

—— —— and Catherine Taylor (2003). 'What Determines 401(k) Participation and Contributions?' *Social Security Bulletin*, 64(3): 64–75.

—— James Lee, and Kevin B. Meme (2004). 'An Update on Pension Data', *CRR Issue Brief*, 20: 1–12.

Nyce, Stephen A. (2005). 'The Importance of Financial Communication for Participation Rates and Contribution Levels in 401(k) Plans', PRC WP 2005-3. Philadelphia, PA: Pension Research Council, The Wharton School, University of Pennsylvania.

Perun, Pamela and C. Eugene Steurele (2005). 'From Fiduciary to Facilitator: Employers and Defined Contribution Plans', Forthcoming in William G. Gale, John B. Shoven, and Mark J. Warshawsky (eds.), *The Evolving Pension System: Trends, Effects and Proposals for Reform*. Washington, DC: The Brookings Institution.

Purcell, Patrick J. (2003). *Pension Issues: Cash Balance Plans*. Washington, DC: CRS Report for Congress. Washington, DC: Congressional Research Service, The Library of Congress.

Schieber, Sylvester (2003). 'A Symposium on Cash Balance Pensions: Background and Introduction', PRC WP 2003-21. Philadelphia, PA: Pension Research Council, The Wharton School, University of Pennsylvania.

Smith, Karen E., Richard W. Johnson, and Leslie Muller (2004). 'Deferring Income in Employer-Sponsored Retirement Plans: The Dynamics of Participant Contributions', Working Paper, CRR WP-2004-20. Boston, MA: Center for Retirement Research at Boston College.

Spence, John (2005). '401(k) Investors Lack Diversification', *MarketWatch Inc. http:// cbs.marketwatch.com/news/print_story.asp?print=1&guid={022E1F06-D0B-3C0-F*

Thaler, Richard H. and Shlomo Benartzi (2004). 'Save More Tomorrow℠: Using Behavioral Economics to Increase Employee Saving', *Journal of Political Economy*, 112(1) Part 2: 164–87.

US Department of Labor, Bureau of Labor Statistics (USBLS) (2005). *National Compensation Survey: Employee Benefits in Private Industry in the United States, 2002–2003*. Bulletin 2573.

Utkus, Stephen P. and Jean A. Young (2004). 'Lessons from Behavioral Finance and the Autopilot 401(k) Plan', Valley Forge, PA: The Vanguard Group, the Vanguard Center for Retirement Research.

VanDerhi, Jack and Sara Holden (2006). 'The Role of 401(k) Accumulation in Providing Future Retirement Income', this volume.

Zelinsky, Edward A. (2004). 'The Defined Contribution Paradigm', 114 *Yale L.J.*, 451: 455–59.

Part II
Pooling Pension Risks and Rewards

Chapter 5

A Regulatory Framework for Strengthening Defined Benefit Pensions

Mark J. Warshawsky, Neal McCall, and John D. Worth

In the USA, recent financial market and pension events have exposed serious structural flaws in the regulatory system governing single employer defined benefit (DB) plans. Evidence of such problems includes substantial unfunded liabilities in the pension system, estimated at approximately $450 billion, and very large insurance claims for unfunded pension liabilities as the result of the restructuring or liquidation of major companies. At US fiscal year-end 2004 (September 30), the Pension Benefit Guaranty Corporation (PBGC)—government corporation that insures pension benefits—had only $39 billion in assets to meet $62 billion in liabilities (the present value of future benefit payments owed to participants of failed pension plans). The PBGC's net position fell from a surplus of $7.7 billion in 2001 to a deficit of $23.3 billion in 2004. In addition, billions of dollars in benefits earned by thousands of workers, retirees, and their beneficiaries were lost as a result of the termination of underfunded plans. In response to these problems, the Administration of President Bush proposed a plan to strengthen funding for single-employer DB pensions (hereafter, the Administration Proposal), and Congress has moved to consider a comprehensive regulatory reform for these plans.

This chapter discusses four principles that must be recognized in order to design effective regulations for the DB pension system. After outlining these principles, we provide examples of how they can be implemented, by drawing on the recent Administration proposal that is designed to correct the structural deficiencies in the DB regulatory system. If DB pensions are to remain a viable, self-financing, retirement option for employers and employees, the entire system must be placed on a sound financial footing.

In what follows, we briefly describe the regulatory background and then discuss the motivation for government pension regulation. Then, we highlight some salient characteristics of the 'traditional actuarial view' as reflected in the current pension funding regime. Next, we outline principles for a well-designed pension funding and guaranty regulatory regime and provide examples of implementation. The last section concludes.

The Regulatory Background

Although DB pensions have existed in the USA since the late nineteenth century, comprehensive pension regulatory oversight did not exist prior to the passage of the Employee Retirement Income Security Act of 1974 (ERISA). Before this law, regulation was piecemeal: plans funded through insurance companies were subject to state regulation of insurance company solvency and regulation, while plans managed by banks were subject to general trust law. The Internal Revenue Code (IRC) was first modified to make explicit reference to pension plans in 1921, when contributions to employer-based stock bonus profit sharing plans were exempted from the corporate income tax. But it was not until 1942 that the legal code was modified to provide some general guidelines on plan design and operation. Disclosure problems were first addressed in the Federal Welfare and Pensions Disclosure Act of 1958 and 1962 amendments. The objectives of these laws, however, were limited: they were designed only to provide participants with enough information to detect malfeasance on the part of the plan administrator or other interested parties to enable participants to bring actions against the plan under existing law. Many deemed the regulatory environment largely ineffective (McGill et al. 1996).

Regulatory shortcomings became evident to the general public with the closing of the Studebaker plant in South Bend Indiana and the termination of its employee pension plan in 1963. Although retirees and active workers over the plan's retirement age of 60 received full benefits in the form of annuities, other participants were far less fortunate. Participants between 40 and 59 with 10 years of service under the plan received lump sum payments equal to about 15 percent of earned benefits while other vested employees received nothing. Many cite this termination as the event that set in motion the reform process that led to the passage of ERISA in 1974 (Jefferson 1993).

Today, ERISA and the IRC provide a general framework for private sector pension regulation. Current rules set minimum plan funding standards, standardize the computation of a plan's financial status, require certain financial disclosures to participants, and govern the pension insurance system. Pension regulation is motivated by a number of considerations including information asymmetries between the pension plan sponsor and the plan participants, the noncompetitive nature of employer-sponsored pension plans, and the tax-favored treatment of pension contributions and investments as will be discussed later. Though ERISA and the Tax Code have been revised to strengthen plan funding standards and improve the insurance system on several occasions, most notably in 1987 and 1994, the DB regulatory system continues to suffer from a number of structural flaws.

Motivations for Pension Regulation

It is sometimes argued that pension plan sponsors have inherent informational advantages over plan participants as the sponsors invest assets, monitor returns, and compare assets to future payment obligations. Absent reporting requirements, many plan sponsors would lack the incentive to disclose adequately the financial position of the pension fund to participants. Because of these informational asymmetries, some firms might mislead participants by under- or not funding the DB plan while acting as if the plan was well protected. The concern is that this could result in retirees not receiving the retirement income they anticipated, at a time in their lives when it would be impossible to remedy the breach. Accordingly, DB plan regulation seeks to minimize this type of outcome.

One might argue that concern over loss of reputation would temper such plan sponsor behavior and discourage pension defaults. In practice, however, defaults on pension plans are typically associated with the reorganization or liquidation of the sponsoring firm. Because a sponsor that defaults on its pension obligations has also defaulted on other financial obligations and because its pension customers are limited to its own employees, reputational effects can fail to constrain sponsor behavior. Also, from the employee's viewpoint, the pension contract is a one-shot commitment not subject to renegotiation. That is, employees have one career and sometimes one or two employers over which to prepare for retirement; as such, they lack an effective recourse if their pension promises are defaulted on. The possibility that a sponsoring firm will default on the contract at some future date, therefore, is believed to provide a strong basis for DB plan funding regulation. Minimum funding rules are designed to ensure that a threshold level of financial backing exists for accrued pension benefits at all times.

Defined benefit pension plans are noncompetitive: that is, employee participation—which includes deferral of income—is mandatory with employment at a firm providing a DB plan, and employees do not have a choice of retirement assets, outside the pension trust managed by the plan sponsor. The plan sponsor and plan participants may also have different assessments of the appropriate priority for plan funding, relative to other uses of working capital. This is another reason for the establishment of laws and regulation governing minimum funding requirements: the appropriate segregation of assets and prudent and diversified investments.

The existence of a government guarantee for DB plan benefits, as in the US pension insurance system, introduces an additional concern for government, namely, that of moral hazard.[1] When participants are guaranteed to receive pension payments, in whole or in part, irrespective of their pension plan's performance and its sponsor, they will have less incentive to be vigilant in monitoring the plan. Further, benefit guarantees in employer-sponsored plans provide a greater incentive for workers to ex-change future promises of pension payments for current wages.

The Traditional Actuarial View

One assumption appears to have motivated the traditional actuarial ap-proach to pension regulation: namely, that pension sponsors and pension plans should be thought of as 'living' over a very long, indeed, indefinite time horizon. ERISA rules reflecting this view tend to focus on funding and measurement of the ultimate pension commitment—pension obligations that participants will be entitled to at retirement. The accrued benefit commitment, which measures pension obligations earned to date using current market values, is thought to be relevant only when a sponsor intends to terminate a plan.

A good example of how the concept of long-lived plans motivates current pension regulation and actuarial practice is seen in the area of asset and liability measurement. Current law views pension liabilities as long-run in nature and unlikely to be settled in the short-run because (it is implicitly assumed) pension sponsors are unlikely to be compelled to terminate their plans. Therefore, ERISA rules allow plan actuaries to choose plan discount rates that reflect an estimate of the pension funds long-run investment returns. McGill et al. (1996) argues that the actuarial present value of future benefits is defined as today's value of future benefits, taking into account future investment earnings. This implies that the value of the pension liability is not determined using the *current* market value of a reference security with the same characteristics as those of accrued bene-fits, but rather by the asset allocation choices and the actuary's estimate of expected returns. This approach is clearly focused on long-run results, since only 'by coincidence' will actual results conform to expected ones (McGill et al. 1996). Basing measures of pension liabilities using returns on risky assets clearly implies that the plan sponsor will be both willing and able to make good on any unanticipated investment shortfalls when pen-sion obligations come due in the future. Using smoothed values of assets comports with this same long-run view.

Another good example has to do with ERISA plan funding rules. Plan funding rules are designed to satisfy the ultimate pension commitment over the long run, rather than to ensure that a plan will have sufficient assets at any given point in time to meet accrued liabilities (where both are measured on a current market basis). The ERISA funding rules reflect this view, for example, by allowing long-amortization periods for new benefits, even though they are immediately accrued, for investment losses, and for changes in actuarial assumptions. These long-amortization periods are motivated by the belief that the plan actuary's assumptions will be realized in the long run.

As these examples suggest, the traditional actuarial approach to pension regulation as codified in the law treats DB plan sponsors as ongoing and long-lived entities. This view has influenced how pension regulation has been structured. Next, we discuss the shortcomings of this view and introduce some important principles for a new approach to pension regulation.

Principles for a Pension Funding and Regulatory Regime

A well-designed pension regulatory system should take into account four principles, each of which we take up in turn.

Principle 1: Pension Plans Are Financial Intermediaries. Sponsoring firms take deferred compensation from employees and contribute it on their behalf to pension plans. This money, in turn, is made available to the capital markets when the plan invests in stocks, bonds, and other financial instruments. In exchange, the pension plan promises participants a stream of future annuity payments or, in some cases, the lump-sum equivalent of such payments, in accordance with the plan's design. Although the DB plan is an independent entity under the law, its financial well-being is wholly dependent on contribution and investment decisions made by the sponsoring firm.

As financial intermediaries, it seems sensible to hold pension plans to the standards of reporting transparency and market value discipline that apply in other financial markets. For example, most financial regulators require that assets be valued at current and not past prices. Yet ERISA allows pension assets values to not be marked-to-market, but rather to reflect 'smoothed' values based on past prices. Following Bader and Gold (2003), we identify three standards of financial practice that are the basis for the reporting transparency and market value discipline that regulators enforce for most financial intermediaries and can be applied to pension funds. These are (*a*) employee exchanges of current for future compensation and valuations of pension assets and liabilities must be conducted at market prices or values; (*b*) because pension liabilities are not traded in a market there are generally no observable prices; accordingly, pension liabilities should be valued using prices for similar liabilities trading in liquid markets; and (*c*) all involved parties have a right to timely and complete information about the current market-based values of assets and liabilities.

Voluntary financial trades do not generally take place at nonmarket values or in the absence of current information on prices. When employers and employee bargain (formally or informally) over compensation, one dimension of the negotiation is the form that compensation will take— cash wages or salaries, or deferred postretirement pension benefits. In the case of formal negotiations under collective bargaining agreements, the trade is often explicit, though in other cases the exchange is implicit. If the assets backing the promise of deferred compensation or the pension liabilities (the discounted value of the future pension benefit payments) are not accurately valued because of smoothing, the transaction itself does not use market prices.

For example, assume that an employee has computed the expected value of receiving promised future benefits based on the degree to which those benefits are backed by assets, i.e. are funded. Based on this expected value and his preferences, he will decide on an optimal rate of substitution between current wages and future benefit payments in determining the composition of compensation package. If available information on plan funding is based on smoothed asset values and liabilities, however, the employee's choice will be distorted. His optimal mix of current and deferred compensation would change if his decision were based on market prices for assets and liabilities. Similarly, smoothed asset and liability measures do not provide shareholders, potential investors, and others with a true picture of a pension plan's financial status. Under ERISA, the actuarial value of DB plan assets may differ from the fair market value of plan assets because it may be determined under a formula that smoothes fluctuations in market value by averaging the value over a period of up to five years (US Treasury 2005). In a similar manner, pension liabilities are computed using a discount rate that is either a long-run assumed rate of return on investments or a four-year smoothed Treasury bond rate.

Another concern applies to the appropriate method for valuing pension liabilities. Pension benefit payments are similar to debt and therefore, it can be argued, should be discounted at rates applicable to that debt. In this case, liabilities would be discounted using interest rates that are matched to the timing of the future benefit payment cash flows. Such matching can be accomplished through the use of a yield curve of zero coupon bonds. Generally, higher interest rates would be used to discount benefit payments expected to be made further in the future, with lower interest rates applying for benefit payments made in the near term. Discount rates used for establishing funding requirements would then be based on current returns on bonds with the same credit quality that pension obligations are assumed or are deemed to have and that mature on the same dates as the future benefit payment obligations come due.

An economically coherent approach, and one that provides the most meaningful measure of liabilities, recognizes that once pension promises are made and backed by assets there is a high probability that they will be kept. Accordingly a consistent approach to pension liability discounting would adopt high-quality corporate bonds as the appropriate source of rates. This contrasts with current law, where two discount rates are used—one selected by the actuary as part of the actuarial valuation and calculation of the original minimum funding requirement, and another set by law and used in the computation of the plan's current liability. The latter is a measure that is defined as part of a set of backstop minimum funding rules put in place in 1987 to require poorly funded plans to improve their funding. Regardless of the minimum funding requirement computed by the actuary, if a plan's funding as measured by current liability falls below certain thresholds, then supplemental deficit reduction contributions (DRCs) are required.

The discount rate used in current actuarial pension plan valuations is based on the actuary's best estimate of anticipated investment experience in the plan—the best estimate of the long-run future earnings on plan assets (US Treasury 2005). This approach is at odds with standard financial practice. The present value of a debt is unrelated to expected earnings on the assets that are used to secure the debt. As Bader and Gold (2003) note, corporate debt is not discounted using a firm's projected return on corporate assets, therefore, it is inappropriate to discount pension liabilities at that rate. Moreover, the discount rate used as part of the actuarial valuation is typically a single rate rather than a yield curve as would be necessary for accurate valuation of the liabilities.

The discount rate used in computing current liability is not based on actuarial judgment, but is a standardized assumption set in law. In the past, the discount rate has been based on a four-year weighted average of the rate of interest on the thirty-year Treasury bond. The Pension Funding Equity Act of 2004 specified that the interest rate used to determine current liability be based on the weighted average of interest rates on long-term corporate bonds. These standardized assumptions are inaccurate both because they do not use current market rates and because they do not reflect the timing of future cash flows.

These flaws in liability measurement along with permitted smoothing of assets cause traditional measures of assets and liabilities to be inaccurate and misleading. Two recent real-world examples provide evidence of just how misleading these values can be. In its last filing prior to termination, Bethlehem Steel Corporation reported that its pension plan was 84 percent funded on a current liability basis. At termination, however, the plan proved to be only 45 percent funded on a termination basis, with underfunding totaling $4.3 billion. Similarly, in its last filing prior to termination, the US Airways Pilots plan was reported to be 94 percent funded on a current liability basis; at termination, it proved to be only 33 percent funded (Kandarian 2003a).

The regulatory changes embedded in the Administration proposal take the position that market values of assets, along with correctly and accurately measured pension liabilities, are sensible. Further, the proposal requires that all pension plan liabilities be measured on an accrual basis using consistent rules and standards, and it requires the use of current market values of assets. The plan also requires that the discounted value of pension liabilities be determined using a series of interest rates drawn from a yield curve for high-quality zero-coupon corporate bonds. Finally, it also stipulates that pension plan participants, regulators, and investors should receive timely and accurate information about pension plan assets and liabilities.

Principle 2: Plan Sponsors and Pension Plans Are Not Always Long-Lived. A pension plan termination may be coincident with the dissolution or reorganization of a financially distressed sponsor, or it may be terminated at the sponsor's option at an earlier date. This fact has important implications for the design of pension regulations because failing firms will default on any existing unfunded obligations at the time of their failure. In particular, it suggests that, even abstracting from fairness issues, private pensions are ineffective intermediaries for intergenerational transfers. Pay-as-you-go (PAYGO) private pension systems guarantee future defaults. To the extent that pension funding rules allow for accrued liabilities to be unfunded, pension plans operate on a partial PAYGO basis.

Table 5-1 shows the average cumulative default rates of corporate bond issuers as computed by Moody's Investor Service (2005). This table indicates that, over time, even some of the highest-rated companies experience significant financial difficulties and ultimately some of them default on obligations. For example, 2 percent of firms with the highest credit ratings at the beginning of the sample (1970) defaulted over a twenty-year period. Looking at companies with a Moody's rating of Ba, the table indicates that 10.72 percent default within 5 years and 37 percent within 20 years. For firms in the Caa-C rating, nearly four-fifths, 78.53 percent, default within 20 years.

Defaults on US pension sponsor commitments result in claims on the government-chartered guarantor, the PBGC. During the economic

TABLE 5-1 Average Cumulative Default Rate by Credit Rating, 1970–2004

Years	Moody's credit rating						
	Aaa	Aa	A	Baa	Ba	B	Caa-C
1	0.00	0.00	0.02	0.19	1.22	5.81	22.43
3	0.00	0.03	0.22	0.98	5.79	19.51	46.71
5	0.12	0.20	0.50	2.08	10.72	30.48	59.72
7	0.30	0.37	0.85	3.12	14.81	39.45	68.06
10	0.63	0.61	1.48	4.89	20.11	48.64	76.77
15	1.22	1.38	2.74	8.73	29.67	57.72	78.53
20	1.54	2.44	4.87	12.05	37.07	59.11	78.53

Source: Moody's Investor Services (2005).

downturn in the early 1990s, the pension insurance program absorbed large claims—$600 million for the Eastern Airlines plans and $800 million for the Pan American Airlines plans. More recently, the PBGC has taken in steel and airline plans with extremely large unfunded liabilities. Steel plan claims—resulting from plan sponsor defaults on obligations—have included $1.3 billion for National Steel, $1.9 billion for LTV Steel, and $3.9 billion for Bethlehem Steel. Airline claims have included a $600 million claim for the US Airways pilots' plans in February 2003 and a $2.3 billion claim for the terminated US Airways plans covering flight attendants, machinists, and other ground employees in January 2005. The largest claim against the single-employer insurance fund to date occurred in April 2005 when PBGC agreed to the termination of United Airline's four major pension plans. The total claim of these four plans against the insurance fund is expected to be $6.6 billion. Participants are expected to lose $3.2 billion in unfunded nonguaranteed benefits. Figure 5-1 shows the time series of dollar claims on the PBGC, clear evidence that plan sponsors can and do default on pension obligations due to failing financial health, bankruptcy, and liquidation. The figure indicates that (in nominal terms) claims in 2002, 2003, or 2004 were, by far, the largest claims in PBGC's history.

Firms generally have a below investment grade (BIG) credit rating for several years prior to defaulting on pension obligations triggering a PBGC claim. After studying twenty-seven large claims, the PBGC found that most

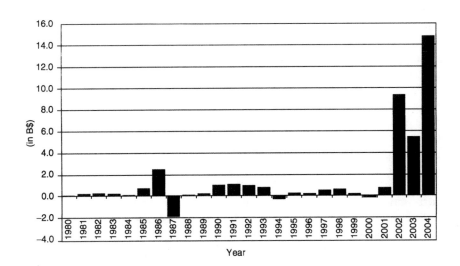

Figure 5-1. PBGC losses from terminations 1980 to 2004 (billions of dollars).
Source: Authors' calculations based on data from PBGC Annual Reports (PBGC, various years).

of the plan sponsors had been BIG for several years prior to termination; none of the plans had been BIG for less than three years prior to termination (Kandarian 2003*b*). This suggests that, while defaults are certainly not easily predictable far in the future (many other plans with BIG credit ratings did not default), a low credit rating for a plan sponsor is a clear warning sign that any responsible set of laws and regulations should take into account.

The list of companies whose financial difficulties have resulted in defaults on pension obligations and, in claims against the PBGC, is enlightening. It includes many companies, who, in their day, were industry leaders and undoubtedly considered excellent credit risks with strong futures. Sponsoring firms that have defaulted on their pension obligations includes former retailers such as Bradlees, Caldor, Grand Union, and Payless Cashways; steelmakers including Bethlehem, LTV, National, Acme, Empire, Geneva, and RTI; other manufacturers, such as Singer, Polaroid, Harvard Industries, and Durango; and airlines, such as United Airlines, TWA, Pan American, Eastern, and US Airways. This list underscores the fact that the future is uncertain, and almost any company, regardless of how secure it appears today, can face significant financial hardships in the future that might result in plan termination and pension obligation default due to either individual and secular circumstances.

Most discussion on losses from plan terminations centers on claims against the government pension guarantor; however, these are best thought of as a proxy for the total losses arising from the default on unfunded pension liabilities. Even though plan participant benefits are backed by a limited guarantee, underfunded pension plan terminations can lead to significant worker benefit reductions. In many cases, these benefit reductions have been significant. When pension benefits are insured by a government entity, defaults raise the risk that taxpayers will be asked to pay for broken promises. Under the current government guarantee system, the pension insurer is required to be self-financing; it does not have full faith and credit backing of the USA. Despite this mandate, however, the insurer has no authority to set premium rates or to reject coverage for plans that pose a very high risk of filing a claim. It is not surprising that under these circumstances the insurer has run a substantial deficit for most of its existence. Because the insurer is a government corporation with a limited line of credit to the Treasury, the insurer's deficit is not viewed as a major problem by plan sponsors who, along with participants, seem to count on the existence of an implicit guarantee of private pension obligations. A financially unsound government insurance system clearly puts the taxpayer at risk.

Recognition of the finite lives of pension plans and their sponsors implies that a sensible set of pension funding rules would do well to:

(1) Set a plan funding goal for plans to maintain assets sufficient to meet an accurate measure of accrued liabilities. Funding ratios should be computed using assets and liabilities that are measured accurately and meaningfully as described earlier. When assets fall short of plan liabilities, sponsors should be required to remedy that shortfall by funding up in a timely manner;

(2) Set a higher funding target for plans with sponsors in financial difficulty or that reflects both accrued liabilities and other costs incurred when a plan is terminated; and

(3) Prohibit plans from incurring additional liabilities when they are significantly underfunded, particularly plans that are sponsored by financially troubled firms. Restrictions on the addition of new benefits limit liability growth as a plan becomes progressively underfunded relative to its funding target.

Each of these elements is applied in a meaningful manner in the Administration's proposed reforms. In addition to the requirements to mark assets to market and use an accurate and meaningful method for discounting plan liabilities, the proposal sets accrual-based funding targets based on these measures. The funding target for any plan reflects the financial health of the plan sponsor.

Current pension funding rules focus on prescribing annual contributions that move plans gradually toward a long-term funding target. This approach has resulted in plans being significantly underfunded for long periods. A regulatory regime that allows significant long-term underfunding does not, in our opinion, reflect the principle of that pension plan sponsors and, therefore, pension plans are not always very long lived. One need only look at recent examples from the steel and airline industries to recognize the basic unfairness and human cost resulting from not recognizing and incorporating this principle into pension regulation. The Administration proposal requires sponsors that fall below minimum funding targets to fund up toward their target in a timely manner and imposes benefit restrictions on significantly underfunded plans, especially those sponsored by companies in poor financial health. Allowing permanent underfunding virtually guarantees that participant and pensions insurer losses stemming from sponsor default at from the time of reorganization or liquidation will be larger than necessary.

Thus far we have discussed the termination of pension plans coincident with the reorganization or dissolution of the sponsoring firm—typically when the plan sponsor defaults on obligations. However, the termination of a pension plan at the sponsor's discretion can also occur if sponsors freeze a plan and pay benefit obligations fully as they come due; or, when a sponsor ends a plan through a standard termination and meets all its obligations immediately. Sponsors have the right, except when constrained by collective bargaining agreements, to either freeze a plan or take it through a standard termination at any time. Of course in the case of a standard termination, the plan must have sufficient assets to satisfy all benefits through an annuity insurance contract. Historically most plans have ended by way of a freeze or a standard termination.

This means that employers are obligated to provide participants benefits only for past service. However, participants may believe that there is an implicit contract to continue such plans in order to enable them to earn future benefits until they reach retirement. Continuation of service until retirement is especially valuable to participants in back-loaded final pay plans. This characteristic of DB plans has two important implications for pension funding policy. First, minimum funding targets cannot obligate sponsors to maintain funding above that level needed to satisfy close out costs for accrued benefits. As discussed later, prefunding of anticipated benefit increases, through either amendments in flat dollar plans or salary increases in final pay plans, could be permitted and even encouraged but not required. Funding targets in the Administration proposal are directly related to accrued benefits.

Further, setting minimum funding targets below the level of accrued benefits is problematic. Some have argued that rules allowing perennial underfunding are beneficial to participants, because plan sponsors will need to make large payments in order to exit the system, thus encouraging them to stay. Clearly, this is not a responsible regulatory approach, as it implicitly assumes that pension plan sponsors are very long-lived. It seems more appropriate to design funding rules so they do not 'trap' sponsors into underfunding. When plans exit the system responsibly by way of standard terminations, satisfying all their pension obligations immediately, or by way of plan freezes, satisfying all outstanding obligations as they come due, participants receive all benefits they are owed and there are no claims against the guaranty program.

Principle 3: Plan Sponsors and Participants Are Economic Agents and Therefore Respond to Incentives in Predictable Ways. An effective pension regulatory regime is one where plan sponsors and participants are seen as economic agents that respond to incentives in predictable ways. In the context of a pension regulatory regime, this takes the form of providing incentives for plans to make contributions sufficient to maintain adequate funding levels.

Four components of current practice would provide plan sponsors with adequate incentives to fund pension obligations. These four mechanisms are: (*a*) funding rules that require plans to make up funding shortfalls (relative to a meaningful funding target) in a timely manner, (*b*) benefit restrictions that limit liability growth as a plan becomes progressively underfunded relative to its funding target, (*c*) a meaningful system of insurance premiums that reflects the risk that a plan imposes on the guaranty system (in systems that include a pension benefit guarantor or guaranty mechanism), and (*d*) tax incentives that encourage plans sponsors to contribute more than the minimum required contribution. These mechanisms would induce firms to fund up quickly, reduce the rate at which new obligations accrue, and compensate the insurance fund for risk; also they would provide incentives for rational, forward-looking managers to ensure that plan assets are closely matched with plan obligations on an ongoing basis.

The current pension regulation regime has failed to ensure adequate plan funding, in part because current rules give sponsors inadequate incentives to fund accrued liabilities adequately. The interaction of inadequate plan funding rules with a pension guaranty system in which premiums do not reflect the risk of loss from such underfunding creates incentives for financially weak plan sponsors to make generous pension promises rather than increase wages. Employees have an incentive to agree to this arrangement because the PBGC provides a guaranty of many of these pension benefits. Figure 5-2 shows the result of a system with such weak and perverse funding incentives.

Plans are generally not required to make up funding shortfalls in a timely manner under current law. Under the ERISA rules, amortization periods vary depending on the source of the unfunded accrued liability: if an unfunded accrued liability is attributable to an actuarial loss, the amortization

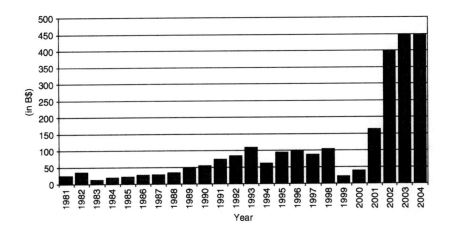

Figure 5-2. Underfunding of underfunded single-employer pension plans (billions of dollars).
Source: Belt (2005).
Note: 2004 data are estimated.

period is five years, but if it is due to a plan amendment, the amortization period is thirty years. If the plan is subject to DRC rules, the minimum required contribution for the year is based on a complex formula that includes a contribution related to current underfunding that generally amortizes that shortfall over a period of four to seven years. The DRC, however, has been ineffective in ensuring adequate plan funding because it is based on a liability measure that is inaccurate and plans do not become subject to the DRC sufficiently quickly when they become underfunded. The DRC applies only when the actuarial value of the plan's assets is less than 90 percent of current liability. In addition, the DRC rules do not apply if the actuarial value of the plan's assets is between 80 and 90 percent of current liability, provided that the plan's assets were at least 90 percent of current liability in 2 consecutive years out of the last 3 years. The lack of a consistent requirement to make-up funding shortfalls in a timely manner reduces the incentive to keep plans well funded.

Benefit restrictions are critical because they limit liability growth as a plan becomes progressively underfunded relative to its funding target. It is important to arrest the growth of liabilities when plans become dangerously underfunded in order to ensure that plan participants collect benefits that they accrue. Under current law, sponsors of underfunded plans can continue to provide for additional accruals and, in many situations even make benefit improvements. For this reason, companies have an incentive to provide generous pension benefits rather than increase current wages, and employees may go along because of the PBGC guaranty. If a company's plan is poorly funded, the company should be precluded from adopting further benefit increases unless it fully funds them, especially if it is in a weak financial position. Accordingly, the Administration proposal included a set of benefit limitations reflecting both the plan sponsors financial health and degree of underfunding relative to their funding target.

Finally, when a pension regulatory system includes a pension benefit guarantor or guaranty mechanism, it is critical to have premiums reflect the risk that each plan imposes on the insurance system; failure to do so encourages irresponsible behavior by both plan sponsors and plan participants. The absence of proper risk-based pricing creates a system subject to moral hazard because the guarantor bears the risks associated with negotiated agreements between employers and employees. In this situation, both the employer/plan sponsor and plan participants have an incentive to increase levels of unfunded accrued benefits up to the guaranty limit of the guarantor.

The current PBGC premium structure relies heavily on flat-rate, rather than risk-based, premiums and does not reflect the risk of plan termination. Accordingly, existing 'variable' premiums embody only part of the PBGC's exposure to each pension plan, as the current exposure measure is a poor measure of the plan's underfunding. The system's weakness is exacerbated by rules that exempt underfunded plans from paying variable premiums in many situations. For instance, variable premiums are charged at a fixed rate per dollar of unfunded vested liability as defined in statute. As a result, plans can be substantially underfunded and still pay no variable premiums. Despite substantial underfunding, only about 10 percent of participants were in plans that paid *any* risk-based premium in 2003.

The Administration has sought to make premiums better reflect the risks that underfunded plans pose to the system. Risk-based premiums would be set as a fixed charge per dollar of plan underfunding, as previously, but unlike current law, underfunding is to be measured against each plan's funding target. The idea is that plans sponsored by financially weak firms have higher funding targets than those sponsored by healthy firms. Consequently underfunding charges will reflect the higher risk of plan termination posed by a weak company on the system.

Principle 4: Governments Cannot Provide a Financial Guaranty to Protect One Group from Risk Without Exposing Itself and Taxpayers to Risk. Financial economics shows that risks do not disappear, simply by shifting them among parties. Earlier we have argued that current pension rules permit, indeed encourage, sponsors to underfund their plans over long periods. At the same time, premium revenues are artificially restricted at levels well below those needed to meet contingent liabilities and are structured in a way that is largely unrelated to the insured risk. These practices transfer the risks associated with terminations of poorly funded plans to other plan sponsors, participants, and perhaps ultimately the taxpayer. Tighter funding rules which require plans to maintain assets equal in value to accrued liabilities can significantly reduce the risk that underfunded plans pose to the system. To ensure that residual idiosyncratic risks are borne by the insurance system rather than by participants and taxpayers, PBGC premiums must be adjusted regularly to reflect such risk. A pension regulatory system that allows plan sponsors to shift risk does not reduce the amount of risk; rather, it simply exposes other parties to that risk. Figure 5-3 shows the net position of the PBGC's single-employer insurance fund. It has posted record deficits recently, in 2004, reporting a deficit of more than $23 billion. This large negative net position reflects PBGC's assumption (and likely future assumptions) of obligations of pension plans whose sponsors defaulted on their liabilities.

Conclusions

Defined benefit pensions can be a valuable means for providing retirement income, but without reform, the US system is not likely to survive. Existing rules fail to take into account principles of sound pension regulation; this,

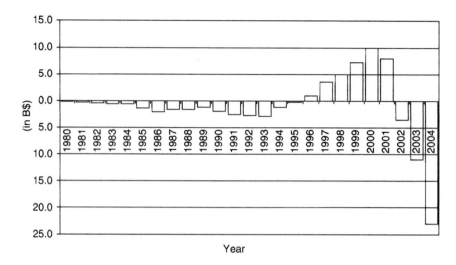

Figure 5-3. Net position, US Pension Benefit Guaranty Corporation (billions of dollars).
Source: PBGC Annual Reports (various years).

in turn, led to widespread pension plan underfunding and a large and growing deficit in the pension guaranty fund. Although well-designed pension funding rules can do little to avert sponsor bankruptcies and accompanying plan terminations, this chapter argues that they can limit losses to participants and remaining sponsors.

The DB pension system can continue to be a source of retirement income for participants far into the future, if the fundamental principles of financial economics are integrated into pension regulation. The Administration's proposed reform of the single-employer DB system can lead to better funded plans, with fewer claims from termination than under current law (PBGC 2005). Ignoring these issues can ultimately lead to larger losses for participants, large premium increases for remaining plan sponsors, the possible insolvency of the government guarantor, and conceivably political pressure for bailout.

Endnote

1. This is also an issue in other countries; see McCarthy and Neuberger (this volume) on the recently adopted UK pension insurance scheme.

References

Bader, Lawrence N. and Jeremy Gold (2003). 'Reinventing Pension Actuarial Science', *The Pension Section of the Society of Actuaries*, 14(2): 1–13.

Belt, Bradley D. (2005). *Testimony before the Committee on Finance, United States Senate*, July 7, 2005. *http://www.pbgc.gov/media/news-archive/ExecutiveTestimony/tm13061.html*

Jefferson, Regina T. (1993). 'Defined Benefit Plan Funding: How Much is Too Much?' *Case Western Reserve Law Review*, 44(1): 1–74.

Kandarian, Steven A. (2003a). *Testimony before Governmental Affairs Committee, Subcommittee on Financial Management, the Budget and International Security*, United States Senate, September 15, 2003, *http://www.pbgc.gov/media/news-archive/ExecutiveTestimony/tm1168.html*

—— (2003b). *Testimony before Special Committee on Aging*, United States Senate, October 14, 2003, *http://www.pbgc.gov/media/news-archive/ExecutiveTestimony/tm1167.html*

McCarthy, David and Anthony Neuberger (2006). 'The UK Approach to Insuring Defined Benefit Pension Plans', this volume.

McGill, Dan M., Kyle N. Brown, John J. Haley, and Sylvester J. Scheiber (1996). *Fundamentals of Private Pensions*, 7th edn. Oxford: Oxford University Press.

Moody's Investor Services (2005). *Default and Recovery Rates of Corporate Bond Issuers, 1920–2004*. Global Credit Research. New York: Moody's, January.

Pension Benefit Guaranty Corporation (various years). *Annual Report*. Washington, DC: PBGC, *http://www.pbgc.gov/workers-retirees/about-pbgc/content/page13176.html*

Pension Benefit Guaranty Corporation (2005). *Impact of the Administration's Pension Reform Proposal*. Washington, DC: PBGC, *http://www.pbgc.gov/publications/white_papers/wp_040605.pdf*

US Department of Treasury (US Treasury) (2005). *General Explanations of the Administration's Fiscal Year 2006 Revenue Proposals*. Treasury Blue Book. Washington, DC: USGPO, *http://www.ustreas.gov/offices/tax-policy/library/bluebk05.pdf*

Chapter 6

The Influence of PBGC Insurance on Pension Fund Finances

Julia Coronado and Nellie Liang

The funding position of the Pension Benefit Guaranty Corporation (PBGC), the US government enterprise that insures accrued benefits in private pension plans, has deteriorated steadily in the past few years to its worst levels in its history. Many proposals for reforming the public insurance system for defined benefit (DB) plans attempt to move toward more stringent funding requirements and will possibly depend on the credit ratings of the sponsors. In general, these proposed requirements would give firms less incentive to take on equity risk in their pension portfolios. Stressing the need for reform, Director Bradley Belt has opined that the PBGC's current predicament was the result of flexible funding standards combined with moral hazard incentives, permitting weak firms to less-than-fully fund their plans and take more risk with their portfolios prior to bankruptcy.

This chapter makes use of recently enacted Financial Accounting Standards Board (FASB) requirements for enhanced disclosure of pension fund finances, to explore the degree to which firms have, in fact, responded to the incentives for risk-taking built into the current system. Risk-taking is encouraged because insurance premiums and funding requirements do not reflect sponsor bankruptcy risk nor the riskiness of the pension plan portfolio. Because funding requirements have been fairly flexible, firms have been able to maintain underfunded plans, in which the value of DB assets fell below projected obligations over an extended horizon. We combine firm-specific expected default probabilities with data on funding and newly available information on the allocation of DB assets to determine whether firms with higher expected bankruptcy risk fund their pension plans less generously and take more risk with their pension portfolios through higher allocations to equity. This analysis provides insight into the degree to which flexible funding standards and the absence of risk-based PBGC insurance premiums have distorted pension finances, and thus will be useful in considering the ramifications of possible reforms.

Our results provide support for the notion that moral hazard brought about by the current structure of private pension insurance has had a significant influence on the financing choices of corporate DB pension sponsors. Moral hazard manifests itself mainly through reduced contributions leading to significant underfunding. This result is not just driven by struggling firms facing liquidity constraints: even after controlling for cash availability, we find that firms closer to bankruptcy have funded their plans much less generously. On the other hand, we find no evidence that the share of DB assets invested in equities is related to firm bankruptcy risk or the plan's contingent claims on the PBGC.

Private Pension Insurance and Moral Hazard

The PBGC was established by the Employee Retirement Income Security Act of 1974 (ERISA) to insure the benefits of participants in private-sector DB pension plans in the event that (a) the sponsoring firm declares bankruptcy and (b) the value of plan assets is insufficient to cover plan liabilities. When assets fall short of projected obligations at an insolvent sponsor, the PBGC assumes the assets and liabilities of the pension plan and pays participant benefits according to plan provisions subject to a cap.[1] As a result of its insurance activities over the previous three decades, the PBGC is now the trustee and administrator of nearly 3,500 terminated DB pension plans covering over 1 million participants. Yet premium and investment revenue have not kept pace with the net liabilities assumed from terminated, underfunded plans. As shown in Figure 6-1, the net position of the insurance program has fallen deeply into the red in recent years.

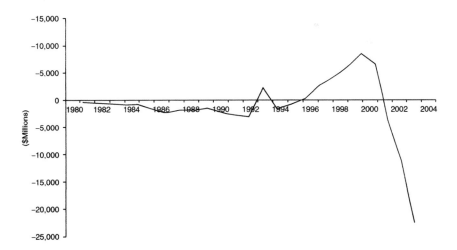

Figure 6-1. Net position of the PBGC single-employer program 1980–2004.
Source: PBGC 2004 Annual Report, Pension Benefit Guaranty Corporation.

The deterioration in the PBGC's position reflects a steep acceleration in claims. As shown in Figure 6-2, claims put to the PBGC—defined as liabilities minus assets for plans taken over by the PBGC—rose sharply, beginning in 2001. Indeed, roughly two-thirds of both the total dollar value of claims and the total number of current and deferred PBGC payees have come from claims since 2001. The amount of these claims is determined by firm's amount of underfunding at the time of bankruptcy.

The most important factors driving the PBGC's risk exposure are sponsor bankruptcy and plan underfunding, but pension funding rules and the insurance premium structure do not in any way take into account sponsor bankruptcy risk. For firms nearing insolvency, the lack of consideration of bankruptcy risk in combination with flexible funding standards introduces moral hazard into the system. Flexibility in pension funding standards is built into the system in order to allow firms who are assuming financial market risk on behalf of their employees to manage that risk. Sponsors have some limited ability to overfund their plans, when either their core business and/or asset returns are favorable, and they are allowed to fall below full funding in recognition that there will be times when sponsors will find it difficult to make large cash contributions to the pension plan.

This flexibility in funding standards does not translate into significant increased risk to the PBGC for sponsors with solvent and profitable core

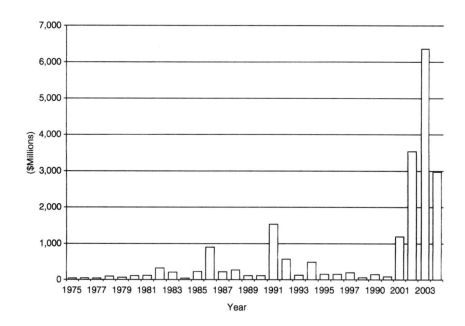

Figure 6-2. PBGC claims for the single-employer program 1975–2004.
Source: 2004 Annual Report, Pension Benefit Guaranty Corporation.

operations. But for firms at elevated risk of bankruptcy, there is considerable flexibility in exploiting the PBGC put option. This is because rising bankruptcy risk, either because of unanticipated changes in competitive or regulatory environments or because of poor management choices, tends to unfold over a period. Companies which perceive that revenues are faltering and prospects slipping have significant leeway under the current system to fund their existing benefit promises at a slower pace, and they may continue to promise new benefits without funding them. In addition, sponsors nearing bankruptcy have the incentive to take more risks with their pension portfolio, since funding problems arising from poor asset returns can be put to the PBGC.

Analysts have long recognized the incentives inherent in PBGC insurance. Both Sharpe (1976) and Treynor (1977) showed, in theoretical papers, that the guarantee provided by the PBGC creates a put option that firms can maximize by reducing funding and investing in risky assets. Marcus (1987) was modeled on the value of the PBGC guarantee to a firm by incorporating the fact that the guarantee had value only if the firm entered bankruptcy. His model, however, did not recognize the asymmetry in the PBGC's loss function. In particular, the PBGC loses when a firm goes bankrupt and the DB pension plan is underfunded, but it does not receive any surplus when DB plans are overfunded. Pennacchi and Lewis (1994) modeled the PBGC obligation as a put option held by the firm, where the exercise price of the option is the value of the fund's liabilities and a stochastic maturity date equal to the date of the firm's bankruptcy. Their model assumed processes for firm market value and firm liabilities, which together determine firm bankruptcy, and values of pension fund assets and liabilities. In recent work by Neuberger and McCarthy (2005), stochastic bankruptcy probabilities are evaluated. These theoretical approaches illustrate that firms can increase the value of the pension put option in the DB case by reducing contributions, increasing the volatility of fund assets, and increasing pension plan liabilities.

Several factors offset the incentives for moral hazard. First, companies with high value as ongoing entities would rather remain solvent than go bankrupt. Second, there are strong tax-based incentives to fund a pension plan. Pension contributions are tax-deductible, and investment returns accumulate on a tax-free basis, leading Black (1980), Tepper (1981), and Feldstein and Seligman (1981) to note that that sponsors can maximize firm value through full funding of their pension liabilities. These authors have also suggested that plan sponsors should invest in the most heavily taxed assets, usually bonds. Third, there are deadweight losses associated with bankruptcy or underfunded pension plans. These costs include interferences by the PBGC and pension plan participants, legal expenses from law suits, and poor management–labor relations (Bicksler and Chen 1985). The higher expected cost of plan termination implies a lower net value of pension insurance from the PBGC to the firm.

Empirical work on pension finances has generally supported the idea that firms manage their DB plans as part of their overall corporate balance sheet.[2] Yet measuring the moral hazard incentives directly has been difficult, and various studies have yielded mixed results. Bodie et al. (1987) found that lower credit ratings and a lower return on firm assets were associated with lower levels of pension funding. By contrast, Friedman (1983) and Thies and Sturrock (1988) find no significant relationship or even a negative relationship between return on assets and funding. Hsieh et al. (1997) ask whether firms with underfunded pension funds exhibited riskier asset allocation strategies relative to overfunded pension funds. Using a database of 176 firms with DB pension plans in 1989, they report no significant differences in the percentage of assets allocated to equities, bonds, real estate, Treasury bills, or other asset categories based on funding status. That is, they find no support for the claim that pension funds invest in riskier assets such as equities, when they are worse funded. Yet none of these empirical studies considers the firms' likelihood of bankruptcy, so the analysis below advances the literature by directly measuring the effects of moral hazard.

Evidence of moral hazard from deposit insurance has been found in studies of the bank and thrift industries. For instance, Hooks and Robinson (2002) found that, after deposit insurance was introduced in Texas in the 1920s, state-chartered insured banks increased loan concentrations following declines in equity capitalization, but uninsured banks exhibited no such behavior. Similarly, Cole et al. (1995) showed that savings and loans (S&Ls) with lower capital ratios in 1982 had riskier portfolios several years later, as measured by a higher share of nontraditional assets and greater reliance on purchased funds. Buser et al. (1982) recognized that the risk-taking incentives associated with deposit insurance are mitigated by a bank's charter value, the value of the bank that would be lost if it failed. Firms with greater ongoing charter value would find it more costly to take on additional risks to increase the value of the put option because the loss in charter value would be greater if the firm were to fail.

In what follows, we attempt to evaluate the extent to which moral hazard is prevalent in funding and investment policies of DB plans and expand previous research by explicitly incorporating firm bankruptcy risk and firm charter value.

Data and Sample Characteristics

Evidence consistent with moral hazard would imply greater costs to the PBGC when a firm declares bankruptcy and turns over its DB plan, and would suggest that the PBGC would benefit by addressing sponsor bankruptcy risk in the structure of its funding requirements and premiums in order to limit claims. To determine how much influence the incentives embedded in PBGC insurance have on pension funding and asset allocation decisions, we combine data-sets from three sources. First, we use data on cash contributions, funded status, and asset allocation for pension plans sponsored by Fortune 1000 firms, from Watson Wyatt's database on FASB disclosures collected from the sponsor's 10-k filings with the Securities and Exchange Commission for 2003. Funded status on the 10-k statements is based on market values of assets and liabilities, and these reports may differ from measures filed with the PBGC based on actuarial values of assets and liabilities. The marked-to-market values in the 10-k filings are more relevant to our analysis as they represent the current position of the plan, whereas the actuarial values smooth in the effects of market movements over time. In addition, the funded status in the financial statements is for all DB plans sponsored by the firm on a combined basis, and may also include some nonqualified executive pension plans, as well as foreign plans that are not insured by the PBGC. For qualified plans, the consolidated funding figures are the measure of interest because it represents the total net pension position of the firm. We will control for the presence of nonqualified plans in our analysis and, while we cannot control for the presence of foreign plans, these plans represent a small minority of the total assets.

As a second datasource, to capture sponsor risk, we use firm-specific measures of the probability of bankruptcy from Moody's KMV that combine detailed financial data from balance sheets and income statements with a firm's stock price and its volatility. These measures are commonly referred to as the expected default frequency (EDF) in the coming year. We eliminate from the sample any firms for which an EDF was unavailable, essentially firms that are not publicly traded, as well as those firms that had already declared bankruptcy before 2003. This process leaves us with 523 firms, roughly 85 percent of Fortune 1000 DB sponsors. The third datasource is Standard & Poor's (S&P) Compustat database, containing plan sponsor assets, operating income, pretax income, interest expenses, capital expenditures, market value, and bond ratings. Our ultimate sample is of 468 firms.

The distribution of funding ratios in the DB plans sponsored by these firms is shown in Figure 6-3 (for the fiscal year-end 2003). The funding ratio is defined as the mark-to-market value of plan assets divided by the projected benefit obligations. Most of these plans were underfunded in 2003, with the mean and median funding ratios at almost 80 percent. These figures are very similar to those reported for DB sponsors among firms in the S&P 500 Composite (Zion and Carache 2005). Overall, the financial condition of DB plans in 2003 reflected some recovery from the three preceding years, during which falling interest rates had increased the present value of liabilities while falling equity prices punished their asset values.

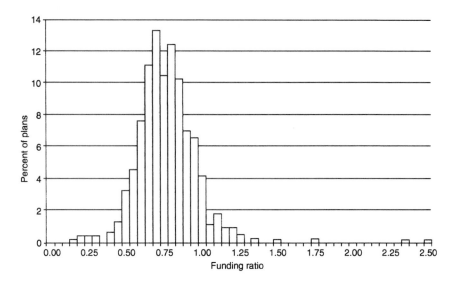

Figure 6-3. Funding ratios 2003.
Source: Authors' calculations from data collected from company 10-k reports.

The vast majority of firms made cash contributions to their pension plans in 2003, but most did not get their plans to a fully funded status. Employer contributions relative to underfunding at the beginning of the plan year are shown in Figure 6-4. Contributions of the median firm were only 23 percent of underfunding, and over three quarters of the firms contributed less than half of the amount of underfunding at the beginning of the year. Only 17 percent made contributions that equaled or exceeded underfunding in the year before (ignoring new costs incurred in 2003), and another 6 percent of firms made contributions even though the plan at the start of fiscal year 2003 was not underfunded. The high degree of variation in contributions and funding ratios is an indication that firms are able to pursue a wide array of funding strategies with respect to their DB pensions.

There is considerably more uniformity in DB plan asset allocation patterns than funding ratios. As seen in Figure 6-5, about two-thirds of the firms allocated between 60 and 75 percent of their DB assets to equity securities. Similarly, two-thirds of the firms allocated between 20 and 35 percent of the portfolio to fixed income securities. On average, about 5 percent of DB portfolios were split between real estate and other assets. Yet there are a handful of firms with very high allocations to equity. Table 6-1 lists the ten firms with the highest stock allocations. The moral hazard that arises from the put option available through PBGC insurance implies that firms closest to bankruptcy should take more risks with their portfolios suggesting high allocation to equity should be associated with poor credit

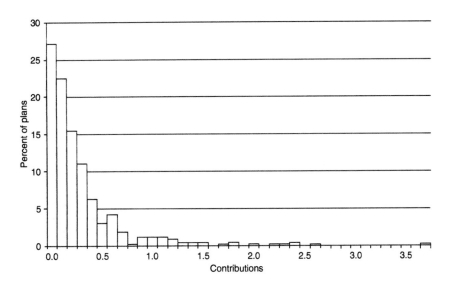

Figure 6-4. Contributions 2003.
Source. Authors' calculations from data collected from company 10-k reports.
Notes. Excludes four observations where contributions is greater than four times the underfunding at the beginning of 2003.

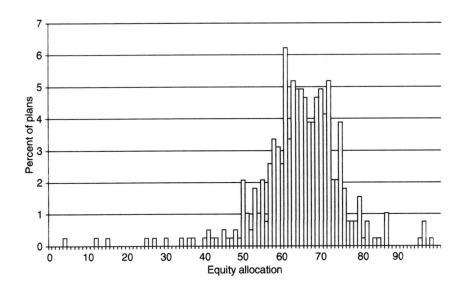

Figure 6-5. Equity allocation.
Source: Authors' calculations from data collected from company 10-k reports.

TABLE 6-1 Companies with the Highest Allocation to Equity

Company name	Equity allocation	Proxy for duration	Funding ratio 2003	S&P bond rating
1. Intel Corporation	100	0.78	0.61	A+
2. United Defense Industries, Inc.	97	0.30	0.96	BB+
3. U.S. Bancorp	97	0.34	1.10	A+
4. Cincinnati Financial Corp.	97	0.50	0.83	A
5. General Dynamics Corp.	96	0.32	0.97	A
6. Autoliv, Inc.	87	0.63	0.57	BBB+
7. Masco Corp.	87	0.29	0.72	BBB+
8. R. R. Donnelley and Sons Co.	87	0.31	0.95	A−
9. Electronic Data Systems Corp.	87	0.45	0.75	BBB−
10. Federal National Mortgage Assn.	86	0.51	0.64	AAA
Sample average	65	0.33	0.82	

quality. Yet despite the fact that our sample includes a number of firms estimated to be very close to default, all on this list but one had an above investment-grade bond rating. Given equity market declines since 2000, it is not surprising that most plans on the list are in a poorer-than-average funding position.

In our test for moral hazard, the key independent variable is firm risk, as measured by the firm's EDF. Data on EDFs are produced by Moody's KMV, in which bankruptcy is deemed likely to occur when a firm's asset value falls below its liabilities. Bankruptcy risk rises with the distance between the value of a firm's assets and liabilities and also depends on the volatility of its asset values, which is based on stock prices. The EDFs are a continuous measure of bankruptcy risk and more forward looking than bond ratings which adjust more slowly. To smooth through monthly fluctuations caused by stock price volatility, we measure the likelihood of bankruptcy using a twelve-month average of EDFs. These are depicted in Figure 6-6.

We are also concerned with reverse causation, that is, that unfunded pension liabilities may be reflected in the capital market prices used to calculate the EDFs. There is mixed evidence that stock market investors appropriately value unfunded pension liabilities; for instance, Coronado and Sharpe (2003) find that equity investors inappropriately focus on accounting measures, while Jin et al. (2004) show that stock prices do reflect risk to a firm from its pension plan. There is also evidence that bond prices incorporate unfunded pension liabilities (Cardinale 2005). In order to control for this potential endogeneity, we use the EDFs over the twelve months before the beginning of the firm's fiscal year 2003.

The data show that the distribution of bankruptcy probability was concentrated at low levels in 2003. Most firms (72 percent) had only a negligible expected default probability in the year ahead, and another 19

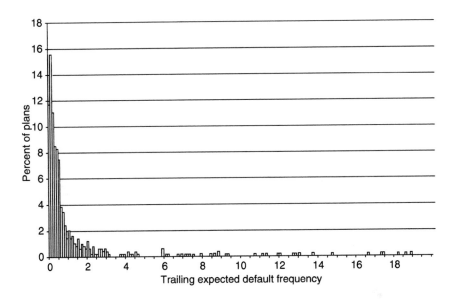

Figure 6-6. Distribution of default probabilities.
Source: Moody's KMV Corporation.

percent had an EDF of between 1 and 5 percent, a still moderately low rate. About 9 percent of the firms would be considered high risk: that is, they had a likelihood of default in the coming year of more than 5 percent. The Moody's KMV probabilities are truncated at 20 percent, implying that the true distribution is even more skewed than indicated in Figure 6-6. This skewness highlights the strong potential for moral hazard under the current system of pension insurance: specifically, the PBGC's contingent liabilities are more dependent on the likelihood of default than underfunding and yet variable premiums and funding standards are based solely on underfunding. As firms enter the tail of the distribution of default probabilities, the value of their put option expands rapidly.

Another way of measuring the influence of moral hazard is to measure the current value of the contingent claim on the PBGC, or expected losses of the PBGC based on the firm's EDF. Expected losses can be estimated by multiplying the EDF by the amount of underfunding if the plan is underfunded. The distribution of this expected loss measure is also skewed, and even more so than the distribution of EDFs because underfunding is more pronounced for high-risk firms.

In addition to expected bankruptcy or expected losses to the PBGC, the empirical model controls on several other firm-specific variables that proxy for the willingness and ability of firms to make contributions and fund their DB pension plans. To measure a firm's ability to fund its pension plan, we use excess cash flow, defined as operating income before depreciation less interest expenses and capital expenditures, relative to assets. Firms with greater excess cash flow would likely be less financially constrained from making contributions to an underfunded pension plan.[3] Firms that face higher corporate tax rates will have a greater incentive to keep their plans fully funded because contributions are tax-deductible. To estimate a firm's corporate tax rate, we adopt a method proposed by Plesko (2004) that uses information on both taxable income and the availability of tax loss carryforwards to separate firms that face a high marginal tax rate from other firms. Firms that have both positive taxable income and do not have tax loss carryforwards are considered to face high-tax rates, while firms with negative taxable income or both positive taxable income and tax-loss carryforwards are considered to face a zero or uncertain marginal tax rate. Because our sample of firms is based on Fortune 1000 firms, it is not surprising that 59 percent of the firms are determined to face the highest marginal tax rate.

Firm charter value is measured by a firm's market-to-book value of assets; a value greater than 1 suggests ongoing value that exceeds its replacement cost. As for bankruptcy risk, we measure a firm's market-to-book ratio at the beginning of 2003, so as to reduce endogeneity with the financial status of the pension plan. The average value is 1.5, again consistent with relatively successful firms. In addition to firm charter value, we include variables to measure the financial viability of the industry that may affect the ability of all firms in the industry to offer a DB pension plan. For example, firms in declining industries may be less willing to bear the costs of contributing to or fully funding their pension plans if competitors have already failed and put their plan to the PBGC.

Finally, we include in the model characteristics related to the DB plan that might affect funding decisions. These include an indicator variable for whether the firm has a nonqualified plan embedded in its consolidated pension finance measures. Since nonqualified plans are rarely funded, the presence of such a plan should lead to lower funding ratios for firms with these plans. An indicator is also included if new obligations reflect a merger of the sponsoring firm in the previous year, since this could imply movements in funding ratios and portfolio allocation not reflective of specific pension funding decisions. Finally, we control on whether the firm sponsors a cash balance or other hybrid plan. We would expect this to be particularly important in the asset allocation regressions as these plans allow for more preretirement lump-sum payout and therefore have a greater need for liquidity.

Tests for Moral Hazard

The empirical analysis first tests for evidence of moral hazard behavior in direct funding decisions, specifically cash contributions, changes in net obligations, and funding ratios. Next, we test for moral hazard in asset allocation decisions. The low degree of dispersion in asset allocations might be thought to indicate that moral hazard would not be apparent in DB plan portfolio choices, a conclusion verified in the multivariate framework. We also find compelling evidence of moral hazard in direct funding decisions, suggesting that regulatory reform efforts should recognize that this behavior may impose costs on the PBGC.

Funding Decisions. Analysis of contributions and funding ratios appears in Table 6-2. As noted, contributions refer to the firm's cash contributions to the DB plan in fiscal year 2003, scaled by the amount of underfunding at the beginning of the year. This variable is a direct measure of how aggressively the firm funds its pension plan in that year. For the 6 percent of firms that made cash contributions when the plan was not underfunded, we reset the contribution value to the 95th percentile of the distribution, signifying that contributions are largely relative to what might be required.

To test for moral hazard, we estimate regressions of contributions on measures of firm risk. Firm risk is measured at the beginning of the period to reduce the potential endogeneity problem that high-firm risk could reflect that a firm's DB plan is underfunded and represents a financial drain on the firm.[4] As shown in Column 1, the EDF estimated coefficient is negative and statistically significant. The magnitude of the coefficient suggests that the EDF effect is substantial for very risky firms, but small for most firms with a very low probability of bankruptcy in the near term. Were the EDF to increase from the 25th to 75th percentile, from 0.19 to 1.07, the estimated coefficient of -0.017 indicates that contributions at the median plan would fall by 1.5 percentage points (from 23 percent). But if the EDF were to rise from the 90th to 99th percentile, from roughly 3 to 17, the coefficient indicates that a firm with a 17 percent chance of default would make excess contributions of 23 percentage points less than a firm with a 3 percent chance of default.

Because the majority of firms in our sample face only a minimal chance of default in the near-term horizon, it may be difficult to discern moral hazard for the average firm. To capture the subset of companies more likely to value the put option on the PBGC, we identify firms with both an EDF in the top 10 percent of the distribution of EDFs and whose DB plans are underfunded, about 8 percent of the sample. Column 2 reveals that the coefficient on this new interaction variable is negative and significant, and larger than the EDF coefficient, consistent with the skewed distribution for EDFs. An alternative risk variable is the expected dollar losses to the PBGC, a continuous measure of high risk and an underfunded DB plan, which is the product of the EDF and the amount of underfunding in the DB plan. As with the other two measures of risk, the estimated coefficient on expected losses in Column 3 is significant and negative. These findings provide strong empirical support that moral hazard is at play and that firms

TABLE 6-2 Regressions of Cash Contributions and Funding Ratios on Firm Risk

	Contributions				Funding ratio			
	(1)	(2)	(3)	(4)	(5)	(6)	(7)	(8)
EDF	-0.017**	—	—	—	-0.007***	—	—	—
	(2.54)				(2.40)			
EDF*under	—	-0.219***	—	—	—	-0.092***	—	—
		(3.61)				(3.43)		
Expected loss to PBGC	—	—	-0.059***	0.059***	—	—	-0.041***	-0.042***
			(2.99)	(2.97)			(-6.37)	(6.37)
Excess cash flow	1.08**	1.09**	1.05**	—	0.345***	0.345**	0.269***	—
	(1.96)	(2.01)	(1.93)		(3.07)	(3.10)	(2.49)	
High tax	0.059	0.056	0.057	0.073	0.022	0.020	0.015	0.020
	(0.77)	(0.72)	(0.74)	(0.97)	(1.14)	(1.05)	(0.81)	(1.05)
DB assets	0.026	0.025	0.025	0.025	0.028***	0.028***	0.026***	0.026***
	(0.79)	(0.76)	(0.73)	(0.73)	(4.84)	(4.76)	(4.55)	(4.49)
Market-to-book	—	—	—	0.156***	—	—	—	0.019**
				(2.63)				(2.08)
N	468	468	468	460	468	468	468	460
R^2	0.07	0.07	0.07	0.08	0.19	0.19	0.22	0.22

Source: Authors' calculations.

Notes: The table presents coefficients (robust t-statistics) from regressions of cash contributions on measures of firm risk, using a White correction for heteroskedasticity. Cash contributions to the DB plan in 2003 are scaled by the excess of PBO and the value of DB assets at the beginning of the period; when PBO is less than DB assets (plan is overfunded), the value is reset to equal to the 95th percentile value to signify high contributions. Funding ratio is the DB assets to PBO from 10-k filings. EDF is an average of monthly values for EDFs from KMV Corp. in 2002; EDF*under is an indicator variable for firms with an EDF in the top 5th percentile and an underfunded pension plan; Expected loss is EDF multiplied by the amount of underfunding. Excess cash flow is operating income less interest expenses and capital spending; high tax is an indicator variable that firm has positive taxable income and no tax loss carryforwards, and market-to-book is the ratio of the market value of assets to the book value of assets. All regressions include indicator variables for whether the DB plan is a nonqualified plan and if the firm was acquired or merged in 2002, and eight broad industry dummy variables.

with a higher chance of default respond to the risk-taking incentives in the system and systematically underfund their DB pensions.

We also include a direct measure of cash-flow constraints in these regressions to address a potential interpretation problem. It is possible that firms with high probability of bankruptcy may reduce contributions—not to exploit the PBGC insurance, but because they do not have the financial resources to boost plan funding levels. Thus we include excess cash flow, measured as the ratio of operating income less capital spending and interest expenses to assets, in the regressions to proxy for financial constraints. As predicted, the coefficients on excess cash flow are positive and statistically significant in all of the regressions. In other words, companies with greater excess cash flow are indeed more likely to make greater cash contributions relative to their underfunding.[5] The important implication is that, after controlling for financial constraints, coefficients on the expected default rates remain negative and significant, consistent with moral hazard.

High excess cash flow is also positively related to a firm's charter value and so may reflect management's interest in preserving the firm as an ongoing entity as well as financial constraints. In Column 4, we replace excess cash flow with the market-to-book value of assets, and the estimated positive coefficients indicate that firms with greater charter value more aggressively fund their DB plans, consistent with our hypothesis that these firms have considerable value to lose before they can exploit the put option on the PBGC. The coefficients on expected loss to the PBGC are unaffected and remain significant. Other control variables are also of interest. Firms that face a higher corporate tax rate will receive a higher tax deduction for the DB plan contributions. The variable indicating that the firm faces a high marginal corporate tax rate is positive though not significant in the contribution regressions. Coefficients on an indicator variable for whether the DB plan is nonqualified or a variable for if the plan sponsor was acquired or merged are not significant in any specification.[6]

Contributions are only part of the story: companies can also promise additional benefits to employees without funding those promises. To capture this broader concept of underfunding, we define a net increase in obligations as the increase in obligations less the increase in assets, both in 2003, again scaled by the amount of underfunding at the beginning of the period. We find no statistical relationship between the net increase in obligations and bankruptcy risk or expected losses to the PBGC (results not shown), although additional work is needed to control for differences in discount rates that may vary with firm risk. While these results do not provide evidence of moral hazard as suggested by results for contributions and excess contributions, we also find no evidence that firms in weak financial condition take actions to reduce their net pension obligations.

The results for funding ratios at fiscal year-end 2003 are also shown in Table 6-2, in Columns 5 to 8. This variable can be viewed as a good summary measure of the various funding decisions, since it reflects the net effect of contributions and increased obligations. Consistent with results supporting moral hazard in the contribution outcomes, here we again find that the coefficient on EDF is negative and significant. This suggests that a firm with an EDF of 1 will have a funding ratio that is 7 percentage points higher than a firm with an EDF of 11, an economically significant difference. As with excess contributions, however, the difference in the funding ratio for most firms with low risk is small. Significant coefficients on an indicator of high default probability and DB underfunding and the variable measuring expected losses to the PBGC are also consistent with moral hazard.

In addition, as found in the contribution regressions, the coefficients on excess cash flow are positive and statistically significant, indicating that firms not facing financial constraints are more likely to have better-funded DB plans. The positive coefficient on market-to-book, when used in place of excess cash flow, also suggests that firms with high ongoing charter value see little gain from exploiting the put option. The coefficient on DB assets is positive and significant, suggesting larger plans are more likely to be better funded. This could reflect that management at firms with large and thus more prominent plans find it in their interest to avoid the costs of underfunding such as more interference by pension plan participants or the PBGC. The indicator for whether the firm faces a high marginal tax rate is positive, but not significant. Finally, nonqualified DB plans tended to have lower funding ratios.

In summary, the results for the funding ratios are consistent with the view that riskier firms underfund their DB plans by a greater amount, but not because they lack the financial resources to boost funding. The underfunding at riskier firms stems from lower contributions and not greater unfunded promises to workers. To try to parse out the effect that lower contributions have on reduced funding ratios at riskier firms, we perform some comparative static exercises. As illustrated earlier, estimated coefficients on the risk measures we consider imply large changes in funding ratios due to increased firm risk when firm risk is high, but only small changes at the majority of firms that have a low probability of default. For low-risk firms, estimated contingent claims on the PBGC are minimal and their behavior is mostly unaffected by the put option. For high-risk firms, if the expected probability of default rises from the 90th to 99th percentile, from 3 to 17, the funding ratio would be predicted to fall by 10 percentage points. Holding the amount of dollar obligations constant, this implies a drop of $64 million dollars in assets at the median plan (with DB assets of $542 million). In this same scenario, if the EDF rises from 3 to 17, we estimate that contributions would fall from their median rate of 0.23 to about 0. At the median plan, this fall would imply that about 40 percent of the lesser funding at high-risk firms would come from lower current cash contributions. The contributions regression captures only a year of funding choices. The fact that the dollar amount of underfunding from an increase in risk is so much larger than the estimate from one year of contributions suggests that the lower contribution behavior may persist over a number of years. It is also possible that some of the underfunding may be due to different returns on assets owing to risk-taking in the pension portfolio.

Asset Allocation Decisions. A different channel through which firms might display moral hazard is by choosing to take greater risks with their pension assets as they move closer to bankruptcy. Hsieh et al. (1994) found no effect of DB underfunding on pension equity allocations, but no studies have looked at whether equity allocations are systematically related to plan sponsor risk. Our newly available data from disclosures in company financial statements on equity allocations allow us to assess this issue directly.

In considering the influences of risk on asset allocation, we need to consider some other factors as well. As noted earlier, one factor much discussed in the theoretical literature is that firms with higher marginal tax rates can create value for shareholders by investing more of their DB assets in bonds as they are the most highly taxed security, implying a negative relationship between high-tax status and allocations to equity. In addition, finance theory predicts that firms should mitigate the risk on their balance sheet by immunizing their pension liabilities through bond investments. A corollary of this hypothesis is that plans with shorter duration liabilities should be more inclined to immunize their portfolios, implying a larger allocation to fixed investments. Since we do not observe actual liability duration, we develop a proxy by taking the service cost, which is the value of benefits earned by employees as a result of their work during the current year, divided by the sum of service cost and interest cost, which is the cost of losing a year of discounting and is calculated by multiplying the discount rate by the present value of liabilities. The larger is this fraction, the greater is the share of increased benefits that is due to current service and, therefore, the longer the duration of liabilities. The average value of our duration proxy is 33 percent for firms in our sample. Finally, we include an indicator for whether the plan is a cash balance plan in our equity share regressions. Cash balance plans generally have a greater need for liquidity and could therefore hold less equity.

Regression results linking the equity share of the DB assets to firm risk and other variables appear in Table 6-3. The coefficients on the three measures of firm risk are not statistically significant, providing no evidence that riskier firms systematically put a greater share of their DB assets in equities. We find similar results, not reported here, when we add the share held in 'other' assets, primarily venture capital and other private equity funds, to the equity share. Nor do we find a relationship when firm risk

TABLE 6-3 Regressions of Equity Allocation on Firm Risk

	Equity share of DB assets		
	(1)	*(2)*	*(3)*
EDF	−0.038	—	—
	(0.26)		
EDF*under	—	−0.82	—
		(0.47)	
Expected loss to PBGC	—	—	−0.351
			(−1.14)
Excess cash flow	8.35	8.16	7.27
	(1.13)	(1.13)	(1.00)
High tax	3.31***	3.26***	3.22***
	(2.86)	(2.82)	(2.83)
DB assets	−0.75	−0.76	−0.78
	(0.89)	(0.90)	(0.92)
Duration	13.02**	12.99***	13.32***
	(2.44)	(2.43)	(2.48)
DB assets-to-firm assets	8.88*	8.81*	8.88*
	(1.67)	(1.67)	(1.67)
Cash balance plan	−1.84	−1.80	−1.80
	(1.22)	(1.20)	(1.23)
N	363	363	363
R^2	0.13	0.13	0.13

Source: Authors' calculations.

Notes: The table presents coefficients (robust *t*-statistics) from regressions of the share of DB assets in equities on measures of firm risk, using a White correction for heteroskedasticity. Equity share of DB assets is disclosed in the footnotes of company financial statements. EDF is an average of monthly values for EDFs from KMV Corp. in 2002; EDF*under is an indicator variable for firms with both an EDF in the top 5th percentile and an underfunded pension plan; Expected loss is EDF multiplied by the amount of underfunding. Excess cash flow is operating income less interest expenses and capital spending, high tax is an indicator variable that firm has positive taxable income and no tax loss carryforwards, and market-to-book is the ratio of the market value of assets to the book value of assets. Duration is the ratio of service cost to the sum of service cost and interest cost. All regressions include indicator variables for whether the DB plan is a nonqualified plan and if the firm was acquired or merged in 2002, and eight broad industry dummy variables.

lagged an additional year is added, to allow for a longer adjustment period to higher risk. Thus, while riskier firms appear to reduce contributions and have underfunded pension plans, they do not invest more of the DB assets in higher-risk assets, at least as measured by the share of the portfolio allocated to equity. Another possibility is that while the allocation to all equities is not affected, weaker firms are investing in equities with higher risk, but our data are unable to capture that.

Even if there is no relationship of firm risk and risk-taking in the pension portfolio, these results do not imply that the high share of assets held in equities cannot explain a good portion of PBGC losses. In fact, because firm bankruptcies and general stock market returns are procyclical and both tend to be low at the same time (Neuberger and McCarthy 2005), high equity allocations are likely a big contributor to PBGC losses. Instead, our results merely reflect that firms tend to congregate around an equity share of between 60 and 75 percent, and the limited variation is not related to the risk of the firm. It is possible that as firms grow riskier and their plans are underfunded, they may face greater pressure from participants or the PBGC to hold more liquid assets and thus less equity. But when we estimate similar regressions of the cash share, or the combined cash and fixed-income securities share of the pension portfolio, the coefficient on firm risk is insignificant. This suggests that equity allocations are more likely to be explained by nonrisk factors.

An alternative hypothesis for equity allocations is the higher expected returns to equities receive favorable treatment from both actuaries and accountants. Actuaries tend to smooth the value of assets, thereby suppressing the volatility of equities. Current accounting standards under FAS 87 allow firms to reduce their stated pension costs by offsetting benefit accruals with an expected return on assets that include an equity premium unadjusted for risk. Firms are then allowed to smooth actual returns that deviate from this expected return, effectively obscuring the realizations of risk in stated earnings. To the degree that investors fail to 'see through' pension accounting, the value of this apparent cost reduction will be greater for firms with larger pension plans. In order to write down a higher expected return, in general firms must allocate a higher fraction of their portfolio to equity. The positive coefficient on the size of the DB plan relative to the firm is consistent with this hypothesis. A related hypothesis, but one that cannot be tested with our data, is that pension fund managers do not want to deviate greatly from other pension funds in terms of asset allocations so that returns do not deviate, because managers who fail to match benchmark returns to pension assets might be fired. The costs of underperformance might help explain the concentration of equity assets at between 60 and 75 percent. In terms of other variables, the coefficient on duration is positive and significant as predicted, indicating that plans with longer durations invest more in equity. The coefficient on the high-tax rate, however, has the opposite sign of what would be predicted by tax efficiency.

In summary, these results provide support for the hypothesis that moral hazard brought about by the current structure of private-pension insurance has a significant influence on the finances of corporate DB pensions. It appears that this moral hazard manifests itself mainly through reduced contributions which lead to lower funding among very high-risk firms. We do not find evidence that firms nearing bankruptcy allocate a greater fraction of their portfolio to risky assets, although the risk-taking may occur within the broad stock portfolio, and the equity share can still account for a large part of PBGC losses since firm bankruptcies and low-equity prices tend to correlated. As illustrated here, lower contributions likely occur over a number of years and imply substantially lower funding levels for firms nearing bankruptcy.

Conclusions

Firms' actions as they approach bankruptcy influence the pension claims put to the PBGC, a topic not explored in previous empirical work. While some previous literature seems to suggest that most of these claims can be explained by the high share of plan assets in equities, we suggest the behavioral channel is quite important. We find that riskier firms tend to make lower cash contributions to their DB plans and have lower funding ratios, even after controlling for excess cash flow. Our estimates suggest that reduced current contributions at high-risk firms can account for about 40 percent of the lower funding ratios at these firms. On the other hand, we do not find evidence that firms closer to bankruptcy invest more of their DB assets into equities.

This is not to say that the PBGC does not bear a substantial amount of risk from equity investments, since bankruptcies tend to increase at times when stock prices are low. However, the fact that pension insurance does not account in any way for firm insolvency risk combined with our evidence of moral hazard among riskier firms suggests that attempts to shore up the insurance system need to provide strong incentives for weaker enterprises to make different choices with their pension fund finances.

Endnotes

1. If an insolvent sponsor has sufficient assets to meet obligations, the PBGC is involved only in overseeing compliance with ERISA requirements through the termination process. Likewise, if a solvent sponsor decides to terminate the PBGC oversees the termination but the company is responsible for fully funding promised benefits.
2. See Orszag (2005) for a comprehensive review of the literature.
3. We also included a firm's debt-to-asset ratio, in that less-leveraged firms could raise debt to fund their pension plan, but this variable was not statistically significant and is not reported.
4. Although it is possible that an underfunded DB plan could cause a firm's bankruptcy risk to increase, we find in a simple regression model that a firm's expected default frequency is not significantly related to its current period or previous period DB funding ratio.
5. We also include firm debt-to-asset ratios, to proxy for the ability to issue bonds or secure a bank loan to fund the DB plan, but this variable is not significant in any regressions, and so was excluded in the regressions that we report.

6. We also examined a variable of two-digit industry market-to-book values to distinguish declining industries from growth industries and interest in offering a DB plan, but it was not significant in any of the regressions, and so is not included. Instead, industry dummy variables appear to pick up industry effects.

References

Bicksler, James L. and Andrew H. Chen (1985). 'The Integration of Insurance and Taxes in Corporate Pension Strategy', *Journal of Finance*, 40(3): 943–55.

Black, Fischer (1980). 'The Tax Consequences of Long-run Pension Policy', *Financial Analysts Journal*, 36 (July–August): 1–28.

Bodie, Zvi, J. O. Light, Robert Morck, and R. A. Taggart, Jr. (1987). 'Funding and Asset Allocation in Corporate Pension Plans: An Empirical Investigation', in Zvi Bodie, John B. Shoven, and David A. Wise (eds.), *Issues in Pension Economics*. Chicago, IL: University of Chicago Press, pp. 15–47.

Buser, Stephen, Andrew Chen, and Edward J. Kane (1981). 'Federal Deposit Insurance, Regulatory Policy, and Optimal Bank Capital', *Journal of Finance*, 36(1): 51–60.

Cardinale, Mirko (2005). 'Corporate Pension Funding and Credit Spreads'. London: Watson Wyatt Technical Paper.

Cole, Rebel, J. McKenzie, and Lawrence White (1995). 'Deregulation Gone Awry: Moral Hazard in the Savings and Loan Industry', in A. Cottrell, M. Lawlor, and J. Wood (eds.), *The Causes and Consequences of Depository Institution Failures*. Amsterdam: Kluwer Publishing, pp. 29–57.

Coronado, Julia L. and Steven Sharpe (2003). 'Did Pension Plan Accounting Contribute to a Stock Market Bubble?' *Brookings Papers on Economic Activity*, 1: 323–59.

Feldstein, Martin S. and Stephanie Seligman (1981). 'Pension Funding, Share Prices and National Savings', *Journal of Finance*, 36(4): 801–24.

Hooks, Linda M. and Kenneth J. Robinson (2002). 'Deposit Insurance and Moral Hazard: Evidence from Texas Banking in the 1920s', *The Journal of Economic History*, 62(3): 833–53.

Hsieh, Su-Jane, Kenneth R. Ferris, and Andrew H. Chen (1997). 'Evidence on the Timing and Determinants of Overfunded Pension Plan Termination', *Review of Quantitative Finance and Accounting*, 8(2): 129–50.

Jin, Li, Robert C. Merton, and Zvi Bodie (2004). 'Do a Firm's Equity Returns Reflect the Risk of its Pension Plan?' NBER Working Paper No. W10650.

Marcus, Alan J. (1987). 'Corporate Pension Policy and the Value of PBGC Insurance', in Zvi Bodie, John B. Shoven, and David A. Wise (eds.), *Issues in Pension Economics*. Chicago, IL: University of Chicago Press, pp. 49–79.

Neuberger, Anthony and David McCarthy (2006). 'The UK Approach to Insuring Defined Benefit Pension Plans', this volume.

Pennacchi, George G. and Christopher M. Lewis (1994). 'The Value of Pension Benefit Guaranty Corporation Insurance', *Journal of Money, Credit and Banking*, 26(3): 735–53.

Plesko, George A. (2003). 'An Evaluation of Alternative Measures of Corporate Tax Rates', *Journal of Accounting and Economics*, 35(2): 201–26.

Sharpe, William F. (1976). 'Corporate Pension Funding Policy', *Journal of Financial Economics*, 3(3): 183–93.

Tepper, Irwin (1981). 'Taxation and Corporate Pension Policy', *Journal of Finance*, 36(1): 1–13.

Thies, Clifford F. and Thomas Sturrock (1988). 'The Pension-Augmented Balance Sheet', *Journal of Risk and Insurance*, 55(3): 467–80.

Treynor, Jack L. (1977). 'The Principles of Corporate Pension Finance', *Journal of Finance*, 32(2): 627–38.

Zion, David and Bill Carache (2005). *The Magic of Pension Accounting*, Part III. Credit Suisse First Boston Equity Research.

Chapter 7

The UK Approach to Insuring Defined Benefit Pension Plans

David McCarthy and Anthony Neuberger

The UK government recently established a Pension Protection Fund (PPF) to protect members of private sector defined benefit (DB) occupational pension schemes[1] whose firms become insolvent (Pensions Act 2005). Some of the details of the way the fund will operate have still to be finalized. The purpose of this chapter is to identify and roughly quantify some of the main policy issues involved in the establishment of such a fund.

One key issue is the future solvency of the PPF, and possible claims on the public purse. The largest and best established exemplar of a Protection Fund is the Pension Benefit Guaranty Corporation (PBGC) of the USA. After a run of years of very low claims—claims over the period 1980–99 averaged $300 m/year—the PBGC has now faced some very large claims. In the period 2000–4, shortfalls amounted to some $21 billion in total. Its 2004 accounts show a deficit of $23.3 billion, taking account of probable claims from currently insured plans. The total underfunding of US pension plans covered by the PBGC increased from less than $30 billion in 1999 to more than $450 billion in 2004, as a result of interest rate changes and poor equity market performance (PBGC 2004). With premium income of $1.5 billion per year, and strong opposition in the Congress to raising premium levels substantially, it is questionable whether the PBGC will be able to meet its obligations without government support.

In this chapter, we model a generic plan to help analyze the extent to which these problems are inherent to a fund to protect DB pensions. Recognizing that corporate pensions are similar to corporate debt obligations, we show that the PPF is likely to face many years of low claims interspersed irregularly with periods of very large claims when prolonged weakness in equity markets coincide with widespread corporate insolvencies. We argue that it will not be possible to build up sufficient surpluses in the PPF in the good years to pay for the bad years. It will also be difficult to raise premiums sufficiently after a run of bad years to bring the PPF back to solvency. The government will not be able to let the PPF default, so it will be underwritten by the government whether the guarantee is recognized formally or not.

We consider, and reject, the argument that the problem can be mitigated by levying 'risk-based' premia.[2] They will have a limited impact on moral hazard. What they will do, however, is ensure that the burden of making good any deficit in the PPF will fall particularly on those schemes least able to bear it, making it more difficult to keep the PPF solvent, and increasing the likelihood of recourse to government. We also investigate the relation between the PPF and solvency requirements. The issue of pension default was the major focus of the Goode Report in 1994 set up by the British government following the theft by Robert Maxwell, Chairman of Mirror Group Newspapers, of the assets of its pension fund. The Goode Report considered, and rejected, the idea of a PPF. Instead, it recommended the introduction of a funding requirement to help ensure that there would be adequate assets in the pension fund to meet liabilities if the employer became insolvent or closed the fund for other reasons. This was subsequently introduced by the Pensions Act 1995 as the minimum funding requirement (MFR). Following criticism of its inflexibility and its distorting effect on pension fund investment, the government decided to withdraw the MFR. We argue that the need to protect the finances of the PPF will require constraints on scheme funding that are very similar to those imposed by a strong solvency-based MFR.

To address these issues, we develop a simple model of a pension plan. In its simplest form, company insolvency is a random (Poisson) event with a constant hazard rate. If the firm becomes insolvent, any deficit in the pension plan is picked up by the PPF. The contribution of the firm to the pension plan follows a simple smoothing rule that ensures that any deficits and surpluses are amortized over a number of years. Plan solvency varies because of the mismatch between the assets and liabilities; the assets are partly invested in equities, while the liabilities are bondlike. The investment policy and the contribution policy are exogenous. The model shows how the premium the PPF needs to charge to remain solvent depends on key parameters such as the investment policy of the pension plan, the contribution policy, the equity risk premium, and so on. The model is also used to dynamically simulate the behavior of claims over time.

We also develop a more sophisticated model in which the default rate is stochastic. Since a downturn in equity markets will not only increase pension fund deficits, but will also tend to be accompanied by an increase in insolvencies, the stochastic default model shows much greater volatility in the claims on the PPF. To model the default rate, we treat the PPF insurance as a guarantee of a corporate debt obligation, the firm's pension promise to its employees. We use a structural model of the firm, based on Collin-Dufresne and Goldstein (2001), where the firm's assets follow a stochastic process, and the firm defaults when its leverage ratio reaches a critical level. With defaults being correlated across firms (because of the positive correlation in asset values across firms), the claims process is much more volatile than with Poisson default. With default being correlated with deficits in pension plans (because the assets of the firm are positively correlated with the assets of the pension plan), the claims level also becomes much larger.

The original paper on the topic of pension guarantees was by Marcus (1987), who also used an options framework to value pension insurance; in many respects, our model builds on his work. While he computes the value of insurance on a fixed portfolio of risks, which evolve with time in a nonstationary way, we compute the value of insurance for a steady-state population of firms. We choose to model firm funding policy in a way which ensures that firm assumptions about the equity risk premium enter into the steady-state risk-neutral density of firm solvency ratios. In common with other more recent work by Pennacchi and Lewis (1994) and Lewis and Cooperstein (1993), we assume that the pension protection fund does not receive the pension surplus if a firm declares bankruptcy and does not have any claim on the assets of a bankrupt firm.

The models we use take the firm's policy as exogenous. We also discuss how the existence of the PPF provides incentives may affect behavior—the moral hazard issue. We examine the consequences of varying premia according to the solvency of the pension fund, and the credit standing of the employer. For risk-based premia to have any significant impact on the future solvency of the PPF, they need to create a strong financial incentive on weak sponsors to fully fund their plans and to reduce the mismatch between assets and liabilities.

The Nature of Pension Liabilities and Claims on the PPF

In this section, we discuss the nature of the claims on the PPF in order to explain and motivate the model we will be using. Our main concern is with the factors determining the level of the premium to be charged and the pattern of claims over time. We model a representative firm and its pension plan. The investment policy of the plan and the contribution policy of the firm are exogenous; later, we consider how they may be affected by the existence of the PPF.

Firms offering DB pensions to their employees are obliged to fund their obligations. The adequacy of the pension fund is reviewed every three years by an independent actuary who recommends to the trustees the level of future contributions required to ensure that the fund is able to meet its liabilities on a continuing basis. The actuarial valuation of the fund is not related to solvency—ensuring that the assets of the plan exceed its liabilities—but rather to funding—setting a smooth path for contributions that will over the long term allow the plan to pay the promised pensions. In deciding whether a DB plan is adequately funded, the actuary must make judgments about future investment returns, though they are irrelevant to solvency. So a DB scheme that is technically fully funded may actually be in substantial deficit.[3] That does not mean it will not meet its obligations, but it will need ongoing support from the employer to be sure of doing so.

If the plan is underfunded, the actuary will recommend an increased level of contributions that will, assuming reasonable investment performance, allow it to become fully funded in a number of years. The relation between the sponsoring firm's financial state and its contribution policy is complex. On the one hand, a firm facing financial distress may be particularly inclined to defer contributions; on the other hand, it is precisely in these cases where a rapid return to fund solvency is of greatest importance to pensioners. Recent evidence on the relationship between pension fund solvency and the financial status of sponsoring firms is difficult to find. In the USA, Bodie et al. (1985) reported a negative relationship between the credit rating of a firm and the solvency of its pension plan in weaker firms. Orszag (2004), however, found little evidence that weaker UK firms systematically underfund their pension plans.

The distribution of pension liabilities and underfunding in the UK can be seen in Table 7-1. It shows the median funding ratio, the total pension

TABLE 7-1 Total UK DB Pension Liabilities for FTSE-350 Companies

S&P credit rating	Number of companies	UK pension liability (FRS17, £mil)	Unfunded UK pension liability (FRS17, £mil)	Median plan funding ratio
AA+	2	11,816	523	0.91
AA	5	21,184	3,349	0.87
AA−	5	14,743	3,267	0.76
A+	12	32,225	5,801	0.74
A	10	21,145	4,187	0.82
A−	12	55,230	14,539	0.78
BBB+	13	13,228	3,325	0.74
BBB	14	18,977	2,427	0.81
BBB−	7	12,760	1,730	0.84
BB+	2	3,784	453	0.85
BB	3	8,711	503	0.79
Not rated	163	63,886	14,180	0.70
Total	*248*	*277,689*	*54,285*	*0.73*

Source: Authors' calculations using Watson Wyatt Pension Risk Database on published accounts for the company financial year ending between June 2002 and May 2003.

Notes: Liability figures are in millions of pounds, calculated on the FRS17 basis reported in the accounts and include only UK liabilities. Figures include only those companies in the FTSE 350 which have DB plan liabilities. The credit rating is as reported by Standard and Poor's at the date of the accounts.

liability, and the total unfunded pension liability for all FTSE-350 companies with DB pensions. It is derived from the FRS17 disclosures in their accounts for fiscal year 2002/3.[4] Several patterns can be noted. First, the majority of pension liabilities (67 percent) and pension underfunding (69 percent) is with companies rated BBB or above, even making the conservative assumption that all nonrated companies have true credit ratings below BBB. The third column shows the median funding ratio in each rating category. There is no clear trend in funding as the credit strength of the sponsoring firm declines.

In the light of this, and to keep the model simple, we take the contribution policy to be independent of the firm's financial state, and to depend only on the plan's solvency level so that, over the long term, the assets equal the liabilities, although we later make allowance for the fact that pension plans may fund to a different standard.

The potential for a large deficit when an employer becomes insolvent depends on the investment policy of the pension plan. The plan's liabilities resemble a long-dated inflation-indexed bond. The assets of UK pension plans are typically at least 50 percent invested in equities. One might expect trustees of plans that are more precarious (larger deficits, weaker employers) to be more cautious about protecting their solvency, but the evidence does not bear this out. Table 7-2 shows the average equity proportion of a variety of types of fund and finds no strong relationship, except that plans that are less well funded appear to invest slightly more heavily in equities. In our model, we assume that the asset mix of the pension fund is constant.

It is clear that the level of claims on the PPF is heavily dependent on the mismatch between the assets and liabilities of pension plans, and the speed with which any over- or underfunding is corrected. The time profile of claims on the Fund will closely reflect the performance of the equity market, with a prolonged downturn leading to widespread underfunding, and large claims when firms become insolvent.

TABLE 7-2 Average Equity Proportion in Pension Fund Asset Portfolio for Different Pension Plan Types

	Below median	Above median
Pension plan assets/Pension plan FRS17 liabilities	0.72	0.58
Pension plan FRS17 liabilities/Company market capitalization	0.68	0.62
Book value of company debt/Company market capitalization	0.66	0.63
Company market capitalization/Book value of firm assets	0.65	0.65

Source: Authors' calculations using Watson Wyatt Pension Risk Database.

Notes: Each cell shows the proportion of the plans assets invested in equities for plans below and above the median value of each plan variable. Means differ as not all data are available for every company.

Modeling the Guarantee

In what follows we describe the model in outline; a detailed description appears in the Appendix. The PPF we model guarantees the pension liabilities of a set of firms. In this section, we assume that there is an infinite number of small, identical firms, and focus on one representative firm. The insolvency of a firm is modeled as a Poisson process, so a constant fraction of the firms becomes insolvent in each period. The present value of the accrued liabilities of a scheme but we assume that it is nonstochastic.

The assets of the pension plan comprise a riskless bond with constant interest rate, and an equity portfolio. We assume that each plan invests in the same market index fund. Equity returns are risky and attract a risk premium. The pension scheme receives contributions and pays out pensions. We assume a simple rule for determining the level of contributions that increases the level of contributions the greater the degree of underfunding in the scheme. If the firm becomes insolvent, and if the guaranteed liabilities of the plan at that time exceed the assets, the PPF pays the difference. The expenditure of the PPF in a period in the model is the equal to the sum of the deficits of the schemes whose sponsors become insolvent in the period.

So far as the income of the PPF is concerned, there are many possible ways of levying the premium. The PBGC uses a combination of a charge per member covered and a charge proportional to the dollar size of any deficit in the scheme. In the UK, the PPF is required to take account of other matters including the solvency of the scheme sponsor. We do not address the question of the optimum premium schedule directly. For the present, we assume that the premium is a constant proportion of the scheme's liabilities.

We wish to equate the present value of future claims on the PPF with the present value of its premium income in steady state. The simple market we model is complete—the only stochastic component in the revenue and expenditure of the PPF is the return on the equity market—so both assets and liabilities can be valued using standard contingent pricing arguments. We show in the Appendix that the fair premium level, measured in dollars per dollar of insured liabilities is a function of seven parameters:

- $\hat{\alpha}$, the market risk premium assumed by the scheme in determining contributions
- σ_m, the volatility of the market
- δ, the bankruptcy hazard rate of the sponsor company
- a^*, the maximum permitted funding ratio
- x, the equity proportion in the fund
- T, the time over which fund deficits are amortized
- λ, the proportion of liabilities that are guaranteed

Estimating the Model. For the purposes of our analysis we take $\hat{\alpha} = 6\%$ and $\sigma = 18\%$. The probability of the firm becoming insolvent, δ, is difficult to estimate. Using Moody's global database on long-term default rates by rating category for 1983–2003 (Hamilton et al. 2004, Exhibit 31), we apply it to the observed credit-rate distribution of UK pension liabilities. Table 7-1 implies a 10-year cumulative default rate of 2.95 percent, corresponding to an annual rate of 0.30 percent. This may be too high as a long-term estimate since it takes as its base ratings in 2002/3 when the corporate sector was in a financially weak state. Also, a firm that defaults on its debt may refinance and continue without defaulting on its pension obligations. On the other hand, the Moody's data apply only to rated companies; by contrast, the PPF insures plans of companies that are not rated, and the latter are likely to have, on average, higher probability of default. In the light of this, we take δ to be 0.25 percent per year. Consistent with the observed behavior of pension schemes, we take as our central case a maximum funding ratio a^* of 120 percent, an equity proportion of 2/3, a 10-year amortization period (T), and we assume that the PPF liabilities are 90 percent of liabilities assumed for funding purposes (so $\lambda = 0.9$). Since these parameters will vary between pension schemes, we also conduct sensitivity analysis.

Table 7-3 explores the effects of varying the investment strategy (as measured by x) and the funding strategy (as measured by T) on the size of the premium. In the base case, the premium level is £0.50/£1,000 of liability.[5] The difficulty of estimating the mean default rate means that the absolute level of premium that we obtain from our model should be treated with great caution. But since the premium is directly proportional to the

TABLE 7-3 Premium with Poisson Default (£/year per £1,000 of liabilities)

	Equity proportion		
	1/3	2/3	100%
Base case	0.206	0.497	0.726
Higher solvency cap: $a^* = 200\%$ (120%)	0.206	0.494	0.716
Stricter solvency: $T = 4$ yrs (10)	0.044	0.191	0.339
No assumed risk premium: $\hat{\alpha} = 0\%$ (6%)	0.039	0.171	0.314
Partial guarantee: $\lambda = 80\%$ (90%)	0.062	0.297	0.510

Source: Authors' calculations.

Notes: The base case shows the unconditional fair value premium for guaranteeing a pension fund against default when the risk of default is 0.25% per annum, equities have an expected return of 6% in excess of the risk-free rate, deficits in the fund are made up over 10 years, and the fund value is not permitted to exceed 120% of liabilities. The premium is shown as a percentage of liabilities for different investment strategies. The other lines of the table show how the cost varies as each of the input parameters is varied. Base-case values are shown in parentheses.

default rate, the sensitivity of the premium to varying assumptions should be not be affected by the uncertainty in the default rate

The direction of the sensitivities is as one would expect: the higher the equity proportion, the larger the premium. Having a higher solvency cap does reduce the premium because the fund is allowed to build up large surpluses when the market does well. But the effect is small; raising the cap on assets from 120 to 200 percent of liabilities, even assuming 100 percent equity funding, reduces the premium by less than 2 percent.[6] Stricter solvency requirements, as modeled by amortizing deficits over 4 rather than 10 years, have a very substantial effect, cutting the premium by over 50 percent.

The assumed risk premium has a substantial impact, with a zero-risk premium cutting the insurance premium by nearly two-thirds in the central case. This can be interpreted in two ways. The first is as a measure of the importance of funding policy: if companies, in computing their contribution rate, assume that all their assets would just earn the risk-free interest rate, they would pay higher contributions for any given level of the solvency ratio, and so would on average achieve a higher solvency ratio. The burden on the Protection Fund would be lower because of the more conservative contribution policy, just as it would be with a more rapid amortization policy. A second interpretation is to see it as a measure of the importance of the price of risk in setting a fair insurance premium. The premium computed using a zero-risk premium is the same as the expected rate of claims (under the objective measure) when the true and assumed risk premium coincide. Taking the base case with 2/3 equity, the table shows that while the fair premium is 0.050 percent of liabilities each year, the (objective) expected rate of claims is about one-third of that level, at only 0.017 percent of liabilities each year. The difference between the two arises because claims on the Fund are most likely to occur when the market declines, and the cost of insuring against bad states of the world is higher than the objective probability of those states occurring.

The bottom line of Table 7-3 shows that restricting the guarantee to 80 rather than 90 percent of liabilities, while retaining the PPF's senior claim on all a pension plan's assets, also reduces the premium significantly. This is not only because the sum guaranteed is smaller, but because the first part of any deficit in the pension plan falls fully on the beneficiaries. With 2/3 equity, the effect of restricting the guarantee to 80 percent of liabilities reduces the premium per dollar of pension liabilities by 40 percent.

A Structural Model of Default Rates

Next, we extend the model to include a stochastic default rate. Allowing for variable default rates is important for pension plan guarantees, since the risk of default varies substantially over time and is correlated across firms.

It is also negatively correlated with the equity market. These facts have three important implications:

(1) A falling equity market increases both the probability of sponsor firms becoming insolvent and also the size of pension plan deficits. So stochastic default induces a positive correlation between the probability of a claim on the PPF and the size of the claim. This increases the fair premium.

(2) The correlation between default risk and equity returns means that default risk is priced. This will further increase the difference between the (objective) expected rate of claims on the Fund and the fair premium.

(3) The correlation of default risk across firms increases the skewness of the claims process.

To explore the practical significance of these issues, we need a model of default that captures correlations across firms and correlations with the equity market—phenomena not well-captured in the Poisson default model. We explore three strategies for modeling default: fitting the empirical evidence on default directly, fitting the behavior of corporate debt spreads, and structural models of the firm. Next, we explain why we prefer the structural model approach and why we choose mean reverting leverage à la Collin-Dufresne and Goldstein (2001). We then present premium calculations and claim simulations implied by this model.

Choice of Default Model. The simplest strategy for modeling default is to take historic default rates, postulate some functional form for their time series behavior, and estimate a relationship. The problem with this is the paucity of data. Defaults are rare—fewer than 1500 defaulted issuers are included in Moody's database between 1970 and 2003. As shown in Figure 7-1, default rates are highly autocorrelated over time. This is obviously important for modeling the PPF. But basing a model purely on the limited empirical data would be hard to do with any reliability. The peaks in 1990–91 and 2000–02 would drive results.

An alternative approach is to use information from the behavior of credit spreads. The empirical evidence does strongly support correlations in changes in credit spread across firms and strong negative correlation between credit spreads and the equity market. Pedrosa and Roll (1998) document the existence of strong common factors in credit spreads for portfolios of credits, where the sixty portfolios in question are characterized by broad industry group, credit rating category, and maturity. A more detailed analysis of the spreads on individual US industrial bonds is provided by Collin-Dufresne, Goldstein, and Martin (2001). They look at weekly changes in spreads against comparable Treasury bonds on a universe of 688 straight (not callable or convertible) bonds from 261 different issuers

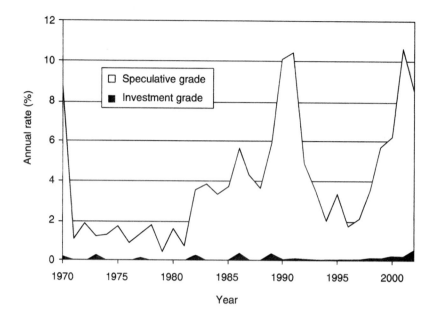

Figure 7-1. Global issuer-weighted default rates, 1970–2003.
Source: Hamilton et al. (2004).

over the period 1988–97. They regress the changes in a number of factors suggested by theory, including the firm leverage ratio, the level and slope of the government yield curve, the level and slope of implied volatility on the equity market, and the level of the equity market. They find that a 1 percent increase in the S&P500 index is associated with a credit-spread decrease of about 1.6 basis points. Their regressions explain about 25 percent of spread changes; by examining the residuals from the regression, they show that 75 percent of the unexplained change can be ascribed to a common factor that they fail to identify with any other macroeconomic variable. These results are based on US data, but similar results in the sterling Eurobond market are obtained by Manzoni (2002) where daily changes in the spread of the yield on the market index to UK Treasury yields are negatively correlated with returns on the UK stock market. Over the period 1991–99, a 1 percent increase in the FTSE 100 index is associated with a credit spread decrease of 2.1 to 3.5 basis points depending on the specification.

Building a model of default that is calibrated to bond prices is attractive because of the large amount of high quality data on the behavior of bond yield spreads. But it faces a serious obstacle. There is mounting evidence (Elton et al. 2001; Huang and Huang 2003) that credit risk accounts for only a part—according to Huang and Huang, in the case of investment grade bonds, less than a quarter—of the yield spread. In the absence of any generally accepted explanation of why the risk-adjusted expected return on corporate bonds is higher than on default free bonds, the credibility of a model would be in doubt if it incorporates the whole yield spread in valuing the pension fund guarantee.

Accordingly, we model the default process from fundamentals, using a structural model of the firm. Structural models originate with Merton (1974) who describes a risky bond as a portfolio consisting of riskless bond and a short position in a put option on the assets of the firm. This simple idea has been developed by many other authors (Duffie and Singleton 2003 offer an overview). Structural models are widely used as a basis for pricing credit sensitive instruments though they do not appear to capture yield spreads on corporate bonds with great accuracy. Nevertheless, Huang and Huang (2003) show that structural models, when suitably calibrated, do fit the empirical data on default rather well. For our specific purpose, structural models have three other advantages: the correlation between corporate default and the behavior of the equity market arises naturally within the model; the correlation in default rates across firms arises naturally in the model from the correlation in firms' asset values; and, unlike models based on the yield spread, the price of default risk can be computed within the model, without the need to make any assumptions about the behavior of recovery rates.

Previously we had a stationary process for pension plan deficits that allowed us to compute an unconditionally fair insurance premium that is a constant proportion of the value of insured liabilities. To retain this feature, we need a structural model of default that is also stationary. The natural candidate is Collin-Dufresne and Goldstein (2001, hereafter CDG) who have a model with mean-reverting leverage ratios. As in other structural Merton-type models, debt is a claim on the firm's assets V. The assets follow a diffusion process with constant volatility σ_v, and the firm's leverage varies accordingly. But CDG argue that firms tend to adjust their leverage over time through their financing strategy. This causes the leverage ratio to revert to some target level. The key variable is the log leverage ratio of the firm, l. The leverage ratio is defined as the ratio of the critical asset level at which default will occur to the current asset level. CDG model the dynamics of l as a first-order autoregressive process where l reverts to some long run mean level $\bar{l}$ with speed κ and volatility σ_v. The correlation between changes in l and equity market returns is a constant, ρ.

The log leverage ratio l is strictly negative so long as the firm is solvent; if it hits zero, the firm defaults. Two additional elements complete the specification of the model. First, we need to specify the correlation structure of firm asset returns. We assume that each firm's return is the market return plus a noise term that is identically and independently distributed across firms. Second, we assume that idiosyncratic risk is unpriced. Starting with a portfolio of firms with the same leverage and the same pension funding, the pension funding level varies over time with the equity market but remains the same across firms, while leverage ratios disperse because of firm idiosyncratic risk. We have now fully specified the processes governing the claims on the PPF; a more formal presentation appears in the Appendix.

With no new firms being born, the steady-state joint probability function of the scheme solvency level a and the firm leverage level l is $g(a,l)e^{-\delta t}$, where δ is now the steady-state default rate driven by the condition that $l = 0$ is an absorbing barrier. The results would be unaltered if there is a steady entry of new firms into the portfolio provided that their distribution in (a, l) space is the same as the steady-state distribution.

Estimating the Model. To estimate the model, we generally follow Huang and Huang (2003); their estimates are broadly consistent with CDG. Since those estimates vary slightly according to the credit rating of the bond in question, we take their results for an A-rated issuer (Moody's or S & P's). In particular, we take the mean reversion parameter κ to be 0.2, the asset volatility σ_v to be 24.5 percent and the asset risk premium 4.89 percent. Huang and Huang show this is consistent with an equity premium for the firm of 5.99 percent. Taking the equity β to be one, the market risk premium is also 5.99 percent, and the asset β is 0.82. Using an equity market volatility σ_m of 18 percent, the correlation between the change in firm asset value and the equity market return is $\rho = \beta \frac{\sigma_m}{\sigma_v} = 0.60$.

Using Huang and Huang's estimate of the long-term average leverage ratio of 38 percent gives a long-run average default rate of 0.75 percent per year. For the reasons already discussed, this looks very high, so we use an average leverage ratio of 31.7 percent; this gives a long-run default rate of 0.25 percent per year. We compute the steady-state joint density of the solvency ratio a and the leverage ratio l using a two-dimensional binomial tree with births and deaths, and iterate forward in time until the default rate and rate of claims on the fund converge to their limiting values. In all the iterations, we use a time step of 0.1 year.

Table 7-4 shows the premium and expected claims rate for a variety of parameter values. Using the same base-case parameters as before (2/3 of the pension fund invested in equity, 120 percent ceiling on overfunding, 10-year deficit amortization period, 90 percent of liabilities guaranteed), the average rate of claims is calculated to be £0.68/£1,000 of liabilities per year. This compares with a claims rate of £0.17/£1,000 in Table 7-3 with a Poisson default process. This fourfold increase in claims is entirely attributable to adding a correlation between corporate defaults and pension underfunding in the structural model.

The impact of the structural default model on the premium is still greater. With Poisson default, the fair premium in Table 7-3 was £0.50/£1,000. In the structural default model, it is more than seven times as high, at £3.90/£1,000. The other two rows of the table show that the level of

TABLE 7-4 Premium and Average Claims with Structural Default (£/year per
£1,000 of liabilities)

Equity proportion (x):	2/3		100%	
	Premium	Claim	Premium	Claim
Poisson default	0.50	0.17	0.73	0.31
Structural default:				
Base case	3.90	0.68	5.23	1.01
λ = 80% (90%)	2.86	0.45	4.19	0.77
T = 4 (10)	2.34	0.43	3.50	0.70

Source: Authors' calculations.

Notes: The Poisson default case is from Table 7-3. The Structural Default model base case
has the same dynamics for the solvency ratio as the Poisson model; the two also have the
same expected default rate (0.245%). The first variant on the base case has only 80% of
liabilities guaranteed by the PPF, and the second has an amortization period for pension
fund deficits of 4 years rather than 10. The other parameters of the models are: $a^* = 120\%$,
$\sigma_m = 18\%$, $\sigma_v = 24.5\%$, $\bar{l} = -1.15$, $\kappa = 0.2$, and $\rho = 0.6$.

premiums, and the average rate of claim, can be reduced significantly by
limiting the proportion of liabilities guaranteed (with the PPF retaining
first claim on all the assets of the pension fund), and by stricter pension
fund solvency requirements.

Evidently, fair premium levels are substantially higher than those envis-
aged for the PPF. It is difficult to compare our calculated premia with
actual premia charged by the US PBGC, as the latter depend on actual
pension underfunding while our calculations assume a steady-state distribution of funding and firm leverage. In any event, in fiscal 2004, the PBGC
collected $1,481 million in premia on its single-employer program. Guar-
anteed liabilities amounted to $1.35 trillion in 2001 (the latest date for
which figures are available; PBGC 2003) and the premium amounted to
$1.10 per $1,000 of liability. Our calculated premium is thus more than
three times greater than the PBGC premium, yet our expected claims are
roughly half. We caution that it would be wrong to attach too much
importance to the absolute numbers, as they are sensitive to model parameters, in particular to the assumptions concerning the long-run average
leverage ratio. Using Huang and Huang's estimate of 38 percent, rather
than the value we have used of 31.65 percent, would imply fair premia that
are more than twice as high.

Claims Distribution. Thus far we have established the average level of
claims in the long run, reflecting the average long-run claims experience
of the PPF. Of course the variation in the claims level is also a matter of
considerable concern. To investigate the variation in the claims level, we

simulate the claims process, and ask: how high a claims rate can one reasonably expect over a period of say thirty years? To address this point, simulations are carried out with the same base case as Table 7-4, using the structural default model, and an equity proportion of 2/3. As in Table 7-4, the fair premium is £3.90/£1,000 of liabilities, while the expected level of claims is £0.68/£1,000.

Table 7-5 shows the distribution of the thirty-year worst case, using objective probabilities; it is based on 1,000 simulations, with a time step of one-tenth of a year. The simulations start with the steady-state distribution of firm leverage and pension fund solvency. A path for the equity market is then simulated. The liabilities of schemes grow at a constant rate equal to the average rate of insolvency, so ensuring that the level of insured liabilities is stationary. Since the pension assets of all firms are perfectly correlated, and deficits are corrected by adjusting contribution policy, the initial dispersion in pension funding levels across firms quickly narrows. Firm asset value is subject to idiosyncratic risk, so while there is comovement, there is also substantial dispersion. In running the simulations, the first seventy years are used as a conditioning period, and the following thirty years are then used as the sample period. The conditioning period is needed to ensure that the start of the sample period is suitably randomized. For comparison, we also show comparable figures for the Poisson default case. The claims are expressed as a percentage of the average size of liabilities over the thirty-year period.

The table shows how the structural model of default not only increases the magnitude of average claims, but also greatly increases their skewness. In the Poisson model, the level of claims in the worst year in thirty was just over three times the average claim level in the median case. By contrast, the

TABLE 7-5 Claims/£1,000 in Worst Period in 30 Years (simulation)

	Structural default		Poisson default	
Fair premium	3.90		0.50	
Average claim	0.68		0.17	
	1 year	*5 years*	*1 year*	*5 years*
Median	4.1	6.9	0.59	2.1
Top quartile	11.5	19.2	0.74	2.9
Top decile	24.1	42.8	0.87	3.6

Source: Authors' calculations.

Notes: The table is based on 1,000 simulations of the evolution of the distribution of firm leverage and solvency level for the population of insured firms, and shows the average and peak annual claim level over each 30-year period. The parameter values for the base case are: $a^* = 120\%$, $T = 10$, $\lambda = 90\%$, $\beta = 1$, $\sigma_m = 18\%$, $\sigma_v = 24.5\%$, $l = -1.15$, $\kappa = 0.2$, and $\rho = 0.6$. The Poisson default case is identical except that $\rho = 0$.

structural default model has a ratio in excess of six. In the worst decile of 30-year period, the contrast is even starker: with Poisson default, the ratio is about 5, while with structural default the ratio is well over 30. The effect is strongly visible even looking at five-year periods, with the worst five-year period being comparable to twice the worst single-year experience.

While it would be wrong to attach much precision to the numbers—these are rare and extreme events—the results of the simulation do illustrate the extent to which correlated defaults across firms, and the correlation between the mean default rate and the equity market, may create considerable skewness in claims experience. This has important implications for the setting of premia. If the PPF seeks to build up reserves sufficient to meet claims in the worst year in 30 years with 90 percent probability, Table 7-5 suggests it would need to have reserves in excess of 24 years of average claims, or roughly 2.5 percent of insured liabilities. It is difficult to believe that agreement could be reached on setting the level of premiums necessary to build up such a high level of reserves.

In the absence of such reserves and of any support from government, the PPF would need to borrow to pay claims, using its future premium income as collateral. But this alternative looks barely more palatable, since it would require premia to be raised very substantially. If, for example, there were claims equal to 2.5 percent of liabilities in 1 year, and they were met by borrowing that had to be repaid over 10 years, then additional premia equal to nearly four times the normal average claims level would need to be charged to repay the debt, ignoring any real interest due on the debt. This high premium would have to be charged at a time when, by assumption, the solvent firms that remain are heavily leveraged, and themselves have pension funds in substantial deficit.

If the PPF cannot weather extreme events either by way of reserves or by way of borrowing backed by increased premia, then that leaves two alternatives: default or some form of government involvement. The PPF will have powers to reduce the amount guaranteed under extreme circumstances, but this is a route that is fraught with problems. The very name of the fund, and the fact that the government has frequently stated that it has acted to restore confidence in the pensions promise[7] means that it will be very difficult politically for a government to allow the PPF to significantly reduce its commitment. It is hard to avoid the conclusion that the government will be left as the final guarantor of DB pensions.

Cross Subsidy and Moral Hazard

In our base case, the fair insurance premium is £3.90/£1,000 of insured liabilities per year, and the expected claim level is £0.68 per year. This is not a deadweight loss to pension plans. The total cost of the premia to all pension plans is exactly matched by the gains to pensioners in failed pension plans. But for individual firms, the benefits and costs will not match. For pensioners of firms with high credit ratings, the probability of default is very small, and for them (or their employers), the PPF represents, in effect, a significant tax from which they derive little benefit. Since it is a tax just on DB pensions, it will tend to discourage the provision of such pensions.

As yet, we have assumed that the existence of the PPF and the way that its premiums are set has no effect on pension fund investment strategy and plan sponsors' contribution/benefit policy. But there is reason to doubt these assumptions. The difference between the costs and the benefits of the PPF insurance at the fund level creates incentives for firms to maximize the net value of their own PPF cover, with potential consequences for the solvency of the PPF as a whole. For instance, members and firms receive the benefits of a risky investment strategy, but the costs may be paid by the PPF. Therefore, trustees have an incentive to follow a riskier investment strategy than they would otherwise. Weaker firms might find that an underfunded pension plan—effectively a loan from employees guaranteed by the PPF— is cheaper than a loan from the markets and has no consequence for pension fund members because it is guaranteed by the PPF. The PPF could thus become a source of subsidized financing for unscrupulous firms. Firms may also collude with employees to increase pension benefits— guaranteed by the PPF—in lieu of current wages, effectively a joint raid on the PPF. Firms may also alter the relative funding of their pension plans to take into account benefit limits on the PPF. The list of opportunities for dishonest behavior is limited only by the imagination of firms and their advisors, as pointed out by two ex-PBGC Executive Directors (Kandarian 2003; Utgoff 1993).

Our model can be used to assess the size of incentives for bad behavior if we assume that the PPF charges our constant base-case premium of £3.90/ £1,000 of liability to all firms. In our model, a firm that invested its pension assets entirely in bonds would never be underfunded and so would derive no value from the PPF insurance. It would therefore suffer a loss of £3.90/ £1,000 of liability per year. A firm which invested its assets entirely in equities, on the other hand, would receive pension insurance with a value of £5.23/£1,000 per year, but would pay only £3.90, hence receiving an annual windfall of £1.33/£1,000 of liability. Similarly, a firm which main- tained full pension funding at all times would derive no value from pension insurance but would pay £3.90/£1,000 of liability. A firm which amortized any surpluses and deficits over four instead of ten years—a stricter funding standard than the base case—would value the PPF insurance at only £2.34/ £1,000 per year, but would pay £3.90/£1,000—a loss of £1.44/£1,000 of liability per year. Similarly, firms with an average leverage ratio of 38 percent (these firms would be financially weaker than our base-case firms, which have an average leverage ratio of 31.6 percent), would value insurance at £8.20/£1,000 per year and pay £3.90—and hence would pay less than half the fair premium.

One way of reducing these transfers would be to set premia for guaranteeing pensions that more closely reflect their risk level. The PPF is required by law to ensure that 80 percent of the premium is 'risk-rated', related to factors such as the degree of pension underfunding, pension investment policy, and the strength of the corporate sponsor. Although risk-rating with these factors would remove some of the moral hazards associated with the PPF, it would probably do little to control the extreme lumpiness of the claims process pointed out in the previous section. We have already seen that, in the absence of the PPF, schemes are heavily invested in equities and are often seriously underfunded. As Table 7-4 shows, the value of the PPF to a sponsor and the beneficiaries are greater, the more the equity investment and the less strict the funding. Consequently, considerable risk-rating in setting the premium would be necessary just to offset these benefits.

The lumpiness of the claims process can only be mitigated by forcing financially weak sponsors to ensure their schemes are fully funded. The premiums required to do this are large. In the absence of premium penalties, underfunding a pension scheme is similar to borrowing from the scheme at the riskless rate to fund the business. To induce a sponsor to put additional money into a scheme, the penalty on maintaining a deficit needs to be of the same order as the borrowing spread the sponsor would pay. Similarly, in order to induce firms to switch from equities into bonds, the penalty on equity investment would need to be of the same order as the equity risk premium—up to 6 percent per annum of the amount invested in equities.

So risk-related premiums may improve fairness by ensuring that those schemes benefiting most from the PPF pay more toward its cost, but they will do little to reduce the probability of very high claims unless they lead to radical changes in the level of contributions and investment policy. Indeed, risk-related premia may make it more likely that a run of bad years could force government intervention. For if, as we have argued, the PPF will be unable to build up large reserves, and if it is unlikely in practice to cut back benefits, then the only way it can react to a run of bad years is to raise premiums. But the constraint on raising premiums is the damage it does to companies and to employment. The pressure to raise premiums will be particularly acute if premia bear more heavily on the highest risk sponsors, since these are precisely the companies where raising premiums is most likely to cause financial distress.

In order for the PPF to work effectively, something other than risk-rating may well be required. A strong MFR on a transparent basis will effectively control underfunding, and hence claims on the PPF. The PPF itself will have to lay down precise rules for computing the solvency ratio, and could not allow pension funds leeway in making their own assumptions. Further, the PPF could cut back on the level of guaranteed benefits without changing the funding process. Under current legislation, the PPF guarantees only 90 percent of deferred pensions, there is a cap on the amount of each pension that is protected, and some pension increases are not covered by the PPF. Lowering the level of guaranteed benefits will have a significant effect on the cost of insurance to pension funds and, eventually, to the taxpayer but will not reduce the volatility of claims.

Conclusions

Our analysis illustrates some of the problems that may be faced by PPF, and we offer way to adapt the design of such a guarantee fund to rectify these problems. Although failure of pension plans to pay people their entitlements have been unusual in the UK, it would be dangerous and wrong to conclude that failures will be rare and small in the future. The way that pension schemes are funded, and the way that funds are invested, imply that a deep and prolonged decline in financial markets could readily lead to widespread failure. An inherent feature of the claims process facing the PPF is likely to be that many years of small claims will be interspersed with rare and unpredictable periods of exceedingly large claims. These periods will coincide with periods when the stability of the whole of the financial sector is under maximum strain.

Though we do not claim to have a very accurate or even a practical method of determining fair premiums, our models imply that the magnitude of the claims in these unstable periods will be so large that it will not be politically feasible or economically sensible to build up reserves to meet them. When such a crisis does occur, it may well be impossible to meet claims by a steep increase in the levy on employers since they will simultaneously be facing heavy financial demands to rebuild their own depleted pension funds. There may be little alternative to having the government step in, even though in the UK case, the government has repeatedly made clear that it will not guarantee the PPF. Consequently, a substantial part of the cost of the scheme will actually fall to the taxpayer. Further, the PPF will necessarily involve large transfers from companies that are unlikely to default to companies that may well default. These transfers are inefficient, and create opportunities for moral hazard.

To minimize the cost of the insurance and to keep down the level of cross-subsidy, the government has argued that the PPF must risk-rate its premiums. We argue that risk-rated premia will need to be sufficiently steep to alter the current investment and funding policy of UK pension plans if they are to have a significant impact. Premium risk-rating may need to be implemented in tandem with a strong minimum funding ratio, to reduce the potential cost of the PPF to future UK taxpayers.

Our model is necessarily simplistic, but we note that the assumptions we make tend to underplay the nature of the problem. That is, we model the liabilities as a continuum of small plans, which therefore ignores the lumpiness in claims that comes from a large plan failing. We also assume zero correlation in the idiosyncratic risk of companies, and so we take no account of whole industries facing financial distress. We have set aside the problems that might arise if the PPF fails to match the assets and liabilities of the defaulted plans it is managing. If the fund were to invest in equities, the volatility in the PPF's net worth would be further increased. Finally, we assume that the only systemic risk affecting the sector is equity market risk; other risks, such as unpredicted changes in interest rates and longevity, could further increase volatility of claims on the PPF. Integrating these elements is a task for future research.

Appendix: Modeling the Pension Guarantee

Our model assumes that the PPF guarantees the pension liabilities of a continuum of small, identical firms, and focuses on one representative firm.

The Poisson Case

The insolvency of a firm is first taken to follow a Poisson process with hazard rate δ. With δ being constant and default risk uncorrelated across firms, each firm faces a constant and equal probability of default in each time period. With an infinite number of firms, a constant fraction δdt of the firms become insolvent in each period dt. The present value of the accrued liabilities of the firm's pension plan at time t, denoted by L_t, may vary over time, but is assumed to be nonstochastic. The assets of the plan have value A_t. If the firm becomes insolvent at time t, and if the guaranteed liabilities of the plan exceed the assets, the PPF pays $L_t - A_t$.

In practice, pension plan liabilities are measured in several different ways. For the purpose of this model, L_t should be interpreted as the cost at time t of buying out the guaranteed liabilities of the pension plan at that time, and A_t is the market value of the assets of the plan, after allowing for any costs of winding up. Implicitly, we are assuming that if the firm becomes insolvent, the PPF has full access to the assets of the pension plan, at least so far as they do not exceed the guaranteed liabilities, but no access to the assets of the firm itself. By topping up the pension plan's assets to equal its liabilities, the PPF can ensure that there is no further claim on the PPF from that pension plan.

The assets of the pension plan comprise a riskless bond with constant interest rate r, and an equity portfolio. We assume that each plan invests in the same market index fund, which may be assumed to be the portfolio of all available equities, weighted in proportion to their market capitalization. We assume that the instantaneous return on the market portfolio, dS/S, follows an Ito process:

$$\frac{dS}{S} = (r + \alpha)\, dt + \sigma_m dz_m, \tag{1}$$

where z_m is a standard Brownian process, α the market risk premium, and σ_m the volatility of the market.

We wish to compute the present value of future claims on the PPF. The claims are stochastic, and depend on future stock market performance. Rather than compute the expected level of future claims, and taking their present value by discounting back to the present at a suitably chosen discount rate that reflects the riskiness of the cash flows, we use the risk-neutral methodology that is standard in the finance literature. Where, as in our model, all risks are hedgeable,[8] present values can be obtained by projecting future outcomes using a pricing or risk-neutral pricing measure Q in place of the objective probability measure, and discounting the expected claims using the risk-free interest rate. The risk-neutral probability measure is that measure under which all the assets have an expected return equal to the risk-free rate. Hence, Equation (1) can be rewritten as

$$\frac{dS}{S} = rdt + \sigma_m dz_m^Q, \tag{2}$$

where dz_m^Q is a standard Brownian motion process under measure Q. Setting the right-hand sides of Equations (1) and (2) equal, we can derive an expression for dz_m^Q in terms of dz_m:

$$dz_m^Q = \frac{\alpha}{\sigma_m} dt + dz_m. \tag{3}$$

The expected value of dz_m^Q under measure Q is 0, so taking expectations of both sides under the risk-neutral measure Q gives

$$E^Q[dz_m] = -\frac{\alpha}{\sigma_m} dt \tag{4}$$

I_t is an indicator function that takes the value 1 if the firm is still solvent at time t, and 0 otherwise. If the firm becomes insolvent, the pension plan is closed. If the firm becomes insolvent at time t (so $dI_t = -1$) and if the pension fund is in surplus at that time ($L_t \leq A_t$) then the pension plan is able to pay pensions due in full, and no liability falls on the Protection Fund.[9] If there is a deficit in the pension plan when the firm becomes insolvent, the Protection Fund takes over both the assets and the liabilities. The cost to the Fund at the time the firm becomes insolvent is thus:

$$- \int_t^\infty [L_u - A_u]^+ \mathrm{d}I_u \quad \text{where } [x]^+ \equiv Max\ (x,0). \tag{5}$$

Determining the Premium. The firm pays an insurance premium P_t to the PPF. From the Fund's perspective, insuring the plan has a present value equal to the expected value of the premiums paid by the firm when it is solvent, less the expected value of the payments that the PPF will have to make if a firm defaults, both discounted at the risk-free rate. We take expectations using the risk-neutral measure Q to ensure that the value obtained takes proper account of the risk in the Fund's premiums and its liabilities:

$$E^Q\left[\int_t^\infty P_u I_u e^{-r(u-t)}\ \mathrm{d}u + \int_t^\infty [L_u - A_u]^+ e^{-r(u-t)}\ \mathrm{d}I_u\right]. \tag{6}$$

If the PPF is to be able to cover the cost of claims from its premium income then, ignoring administrative costs, the present value of premium income less claims must be 0. Hence, any premium must satisfy the condition:

$$E^Q\left[\int_t^\infty P_u I_u e^{-r(u-t)}\ \mathrm{d}u + \int_t^\infty [L_u - A_u]^+ e^{-r(u-t)}\ \mathrm{d}I_u\right] = 0 \tag{7}$$

In principle, there are many ways of levying the premium. We do not address the question of the optimum premium schedule directly. For the present, we assume that the premium is a constant proportion of the scheme's liabilities.

If the premium is levied at rate p:

$$P_t = pL_t. \tag{8}$$

From (7), using the Poisson default rate process and the nonstochastic nature of the liabilities, the rate p is given by:

$$p = \frac{\int_t^\infty E_t^Q[\delta(1 - A_u/L_u)]^+ L_u e^{-(r+\delta)(u-t)}\ \mathrm{d}u}{\int_t^\infty L_u e^{-(r+\delta)(u-t)}\ \mathrm{d}u}. \tag{9}$$

Modeling default as a Poisson event among a continuum of atomistic schemes with uncorrelated default rates ensures that a constant proportion δdu of plans become insolvent in each time period du. This gives rise to the δ inside the expectation term. The δ in the discount factor reflects the fact that the number of plans is declining at rate δ because of insolvencies. The premium rate is a weighted average of the expected claim rate into the future. It depends on the current solvency level of the scheme. The main focus of this chapter is on the impact of different contribution schedules, investment policies, and guarantee arrangements on the level of the premium. To abstract from variations caused by initial conditions, we look at processes that generate stationary distributions of insolvency rates and deficit levels, and take unconditional expectations.

With unconditional expectations, Equation (9) simplifies to:

$$p = E^Q [\delta(1 - \frac{A_u}{L_u})]^+. \tag{10}$$

The Dynamics of Scheme Solvency. In order to evaluate the expectation in Equation (10), we need to specify the dynamics of the scheme solvency ratio A_u/L_u under the risk-neutral measure Q. The dynamics of A depend on the return on the portfolio, outflows to pensioners, and inflows from contributions. Again, written as an Ito process, we have:

$$dA = [(r + x\alpha)A + (\kappa_t - \pi_t)]dt + x\sigma_m A dz_m, \tag{11}$$

where x is the (fixed) proportion of the assets held as equity, κ the contribution rate, and π the rate of pay out to pensioners. The first component of the dt term states that the expected rate of return on the assets is the risk-free rate plus the equity risk premium on the equities held by the plan. The second component shows that the assets increase at rate κ because of contributions to the fund and decrease at rate π because of payments to pensioners. As before, the dz term has zero expected value and models how the value of the assets changes as a result of random fluctuations in the value of the equities held by the fund.

The firm's contribution to the pension plan has two components: the first maintains the current solvency level after allowing for payments to pensioners, any change in net liabilities, and the expected return on the assets of the plan. The second component is designed to eliminate any surplus or deficit in the plan over a specified period of T years. The lower the level of T, the faster any deficit is eliminated and the lower the potential claim on the PPF. The simplest formulation that achieves this is:

$$\kappa_t = \left(\pi_t + \frac{dL_t}{dt}\frac{A_t}{L_t} - (r + x\hat{\alpha})A_t\right) + \left(\frac{L_t - A_t}{T}\right). \tag{12}$$

$\hat{\alpha}$ is the excess return on equities assumed by the firm in setting its contribution rate; it may be identical with the true α, but is not necessarily so. Define the solvency ratio of the fund a as:

$$a_t = \frac{A_t}{L_t}. \tag{13}$$

Then, using Ito's lemma, we can calculate the stochastic differential equation governing the evolution of the solvency ratio as follows:

$$da = dA/L - \frac{adL}{L}$$

$$= \left[\left(r + x\alpha - \frac{dL}{Ldt} \right) a + (\kappa_t - \pi_t)/L \right] dt + x\sigma_m a dz_m \qquad (14)$$

$$= \left(\frac{1 - a}{T} + x(\alpha - \hat{\alpha})a \right) dt + x\sigma_m a dz_m.$$

We can express this equation in terms of the risk-neutral probability measure Q by substituting Equation (3) to give:

$$da = \left(\frac{1 - a}{T} - \hat{\alpha}ax \right) dt + x\sigma_m a dz_m^Q \qquad (15)$$

Given the investment policy and the contribution policy, the solvency ratio follows a stationary stochastic process that is independent of the behavior of liabilities. We can derive the unconditional distribution of a at time t under the risk-neutral measure by stating the condition that the distribution is stationary using Equation (15) to derive a differential equation. Formula (10) then gives the fair premium rate p (expressed as a proportion of the liabilities of the pension plan) as:

$$p = \delta \int_0^1 (1 - a)g^Q(a) \, da. \qquad (16)$$

Note that the true equity risk premium, α, does not enter into Equation (14), and hence will not affect the risk neutral density function g^Q or the premium rate p. A higher equity premium raises the expected future solvency level of pension schemes, but this is offset by the increase in discount rates used for valuing the PPFs. However the equity premium assumed by the scheme $(\hat{\alpha})$ does enter into the premium; the higher the assumed premium, the lower the contribution rate and the greater the expected claim on the Fund.

The premium can be compared with the unconditional objective expectation of the rate of claims as a proportion of liabilities, c, which we calculate in a similar way, using Equation (14) instead of Equation (15). The resulting expected cost of claims is:

$$c = \delta \int_0^1 (1 - a)g^P(a) \, da \quad \text{where } g^P \text{satisfies:}$$

$$\frac{1}{2} \frac{d^2}{da^2} (x^2 \sigma_m^2 a^2 g^P(a)) - \frac{d}{da} \left(\left(\frac{1 - a}{T} + x(\alpha - \hat{\alpha})a \right) g^P(a) \right) = 0.$$

The differential equation expresses the condition that the distribution of the solvency ratio is stationary.

Extending the Model. One element of unrealism in our model is that the solvency ratio of the pension fund is not bounded above. There are limits on the degree to which the pension fund can hold assets in excess of its liabilities, imposed largely to prevent the sponsor company using the pension fund as a tax avoidance device. We can readily impose the condition in our model that a is not permitted to exceed some limit a^*. Whenever a does exceed the limit, the contribution rate is constrained to force a below the limit. a^* acts as a reflecting barrier.

We assume that firms are able to reclaim investment surpluses from their pension plans over the same time horizon over which deficits are amortized. In practice, firms may struggle to reclaim investment surpluses because they face pressure to improve benefits or because they do not wish to be seen 'raiding' the pension plan of their employees.

We have also assumed that the liabilities that are guaranteed by the PPF are *the* same as those used to determine the firm's pension contribution. In practice these two measures of liability may well differ substantially, and in either direction. Not all accrued liabilities are guaranteed; there is a cap on the level of wages on which the pension is guaranteed; the PPF only guarantees 90 percent of deferred pensions, and certain pension increases are not guaranteed. In addition, the definition of liabilities used by actuaries in computing funding levels generally takes account of future wage growth in computing the pension liability arriving from past service. Finally, the actuarial valuation may also use a higher discount rate in valuing liabilities than the rate at which the liabilities can be bought out in the market.

The model can readily be adapted to distinguish between the liabilities used for funding requirements and those that are guaranteed by the PPF if we assume that the ratio of guaranteed liabilities to the actuary's measure of liabilities is constant. Denote the ratio by λ. Assume also that the PPF retains a prior claim on all the assets of the fund if the firm becomes insolvent. Maintain the definition of a as the ratio of plan assets to the cost of meeting the liabilities guaranteed by the PPF. Then a mean reverts to $1/\lambda$ rather than to 1. The adjustments to the model are obvious. For example Equation (14) becomes:

$$da = \left(\frac{1/\lambda - a}{T} + x(\alpha - \hat{\alpha})a\right)dt + x\sigma_m a\,dz_m. \tag{17}$$

The Stochastic Default Approach

With stochastic default, the log-leverage ratio l^i of firm i follows the stochastic process:

$$dl^i = \kappa(\bar{l} - l^i)\,dt + \sigma_v dz_v^i \tag{18}$$

and the firm defaults when the leverage ratio hits an absorbing barrier at 0. The correlation between innovations in the log-leverage ratio and innovations in the market index is constant, and the idiosyncratic risk is uncorrelated across firms so:

$$E[dz_v^i \cdot dz_m] = \rho dt;$$
$$E[dz_v^i \cdot dz_v^j] = \rho^2 dt \ (i \neq j).$$

(19)

Endnotes

1. For brevity, this chapter uses the word 'pension' to mean a private-sector DB occupational pension.

2. Legislation provides that at least 80 percent of the premium should be risk-based, tied to scheme solvency, sponsor credit rating, investment policy, and other factors relevant to the likelihood of a claim.

3. We use the term 'deficit' to mean the difference between the market value of assets and the cost of buying out accrued liabilities. According to a forthcoming report by an Institute and Faculty of Actuaries working party, of 685 actuarial valuations surveyed in 2001 and 2002, the average valuation discount rate was approximately 140 b.p's above gilt rates (Institute and Faculty of Actuaries 2004).

4. These figures should be treated with caution inasmuch as the valuations for each firm are at the balance sheet date which varies across firms.

5. This figure appears comparable with the premium rates initially proposed for the PPF, which is expected to raise £300 m per year in revenues. While it is not easy to give a precise estimate of the insured liabilities, it is worth noting that the DB liabilities of FTSE-350 companies in Table 7-1 amount to nearly £300 billion, and the pension liabilities of non UK-based companies, including UK subsidiaries of overseas companies may be of the same order.

6. The reason that raising the cap has such a small effect is that the risk-adjusted probability of reaching 120 percent solvency is rather small, so the cap does not greatly affect contribution levels.

7. For example: 'We will make sure that in future individuals in final salary schemes will never again face the injustice of saving throughout their lives only to have their hard-earned pension slashed just before they retire. The Pension Protection Fund will allow individuals to save with confidence.' (Smith 2004)

8. The level of liabilities faced by the PPF is perfectly correlated with the level of the equity market. This means that the PPF could, in principle, reduce or even eliminate credit risk by selling equities. While this hedging might not be desirable or even practicable, it does provide a price for the risks to which the PPF is exposed.

9. We are implicitly assuming that the investment policy of a closed fund precludes the trustees from investing in risky assets and putting the solvency of the fund at risk.

References

Bodie, Zvi, Jay O. Light, Randall Morck, and Robert A. Taggart, Jr. (1985, reprinted 2000). 'Corporate Pension Policy: An Empirical Investigation', in Zvi Bodie and Philip Davis (eds.), *The Foundations of Pension Finance* 2. Cheltenham, UK: Elgar Reference Collection, pp. 265–71.

Collin-Dufresne, Pierre and Robert S. Goldstein (2001). 'Do Credit Spreads Reflect Stationary Leverage Ratios?' *Journal of Finance*, 56(5) Oct.: 1929–57.

—— and Spencer J. Martin (2001). 'The Determinants of Credit Spread Changes', *Journal of Finance*, 56(6) Dec: 2177–207.

Duffie, Darrell and Kenneth J. Singleton (2003). *Credit Risk: Pricing, Measurement and Management.* Princeton, NJ: Princeton University Press.

Elton, Edwin, Martin Gruber, Deepak Agrawal, and Christopher Mann (2001). 'Explaining the Rate Spread on Corporate Bonds', *Journal of Finance*, 56(1) Feb.: 247–77.

Hamilton, David T., Praveen Varma, Sharon Ou, and Richard Cantor (2004). *Default and Recovery Rates of Corporate Bond Issuers.* New York: Moody's Investors Service Special Comment, January.

Huang, Jing-Zhi and Huang, Ming (2003). 'How Much of the Corporate-Treasury Yield Spread is Due to Credit Risk?' Working Paper, Penn State University, *pages.stern.nyu.edu/~jhuang*

Institute and Faculty of Actuaries (2004). 'Report of the Valuation Discount Rates Working Party', Institute and Faculty of Actuaries, London and Edinburgh: Institute of Actuaries.

Kandarian, Steven (2003). Statement before the Committee on Finance, United States Senate, March 11th 2003, *http://www.pbgc.gov/news/speeches/Testimony 031103.pdf*

Lewis, Christopher M. and Richard L. Cooperstein (1993). 'Estimating the Current Exposure of the Pension Benefit Guaranty Corporation to Single-Employer Pension Plan Terminations', in Ray Schmitt (ed.), *The Future of Pensions in the United States.* Philadelphia, PA: University of Pennsylvania Press, pp. 247–76.

Marcus, Alan J. (1987). 'Corporate Pension Policy and the Value of PBGC Insurance', in Zvi Bodie, John Shoven, and David Wise (eds.), *Issues in Pension Economics.* Chicago, IL: University of Chicago Press, pp. 49–76.

Manzoni, Katiusca (2002). 'Modelling Credit Spreads: An Application to the Sterling Eurobond Market', *International Review of Financial Analysis*, 11(2): 183–218.

Merton, Robert C. (1974). 'On the Pricing of Corporate Debt: The Risk Structure of Interest Rates', *Journal of Finance*, 29(2) May: 449–70.

Orszag, Michael J. (2004). 'The Relationship Between Pension Funding and Firm Strength and Size in the UK', Working Paper, Watson Wyatt.

Pennacchi, George G. and Christopher M. Lewis (1994). 'The Value of Pension Benefit Guaranty Corporation Insurance', *Journal of Money, Credit and Banking*, 26(3): 735–53.

Pension Benefit Guaranty Corporation (2003). *Pension Insurance Data Book 2003.* Washington, DC, *http://www.pbgc.gov/publications/databook/databook03.pdf*

—— (2004). '2004 Annual Report', Washington, DC, *http://www.pbgc.gov/publications/ annrpt/default.htm*

Pedrosa, Monica and Richard Roll (1998). 'Systematic Risk in Corporate Bond Credit Spreads', *Journal of Fixed Income*, 8(3) Dec.: 7–26.

Smith, Andrew, Secretary of State for Work and Pensions, 12 February 2004, quoted at *www.dwp.gov.uk/publications/dwp/2004/pensions_bill/ppf_factsheet.pdf* Department of Work and Pensions website.

Utgoff, Kathleen P. (1993). 'The PBGC: A Costly Lesson in the Economics of Federal Insurance', in Mark Sniderman (ed.), *Government Risk-Bearing: Proceedings of a Conference Held at the Federal Reserve Bank of Cleveland*. Norwell, MA: Kluwer Academic, pp. 145–60.

Watson Wyatt Pension Risk Database (2005). Research Department, Watson Wyatt Partners, London Road, Reigate, Surrey RH2 9PQ.

Chapter 8

Risk-Sharing in Retiree Medical Benefits

George Wagoner, Anna Rappaport, Brian Fuller, and Frank Yeager

This chapter discusses the changing dynamics and risks of employer-provided retiree health benefits. In the USA, more of the risk of health care in retirement is being shifting to retirees, often without their having access to adequate and affordable health care solutions until becoming eligible for Medicare (generally available at age 65). Employer coverage for health care insurance is therefore very important to those retiring before Medicare eligibility age.

In what follows, we first review US health care expenditures and discuss the impact of demographic changes such as the aging of baby boomers. Next we analyze government-provided retiree health benefits and some of the potential challenges and risks related to this coverage. Against this backdrop we assess the pressures on employer-provided health care benefits,[1] by tracking total health care costs for employees and retirees; this is followed by a summary of employer responses. The discussion also examines the risks facing retirees and indicates what they can do to mitigate those risks. Finally, we review the interactions between government risk, employer risk, and retiree risk, as they relate to public policy. The discussion concludes with an evaluation of the impact of public policy on access to affordable retiree health care coverage, along with some systemwide health care solutions. We conclude that in the USA, health care costs will continue to rise and more risk will be shifted to retirees, posing a major threat to the affordability of a good retirement for many Americans.

The Setting

US health care expenditures have grown more rapidly than the economy for many years. Figure 8-1 shows that the medical care component of the consumer price index (CPI) increased 5.5 percent from 1990 to 2004, compared to 3.1 percent for all CPI items (USBLS 2005). A national survey of employer-sponsored health plans (Mercer 2004) found that employer health care cost increases in the same period averaged 8.2 percent.[2] These costs can be particularly burdensome for companies who offer health care benefits to both employees and retirees.

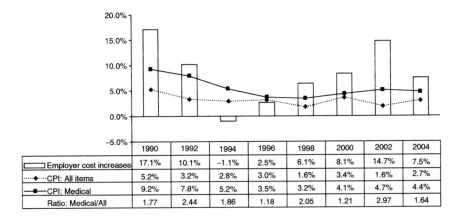

	1990	1992	1994	1996	1998	2000	2002	2004
Employer cost increases	17.1%	10.1%	−1.1%	2.5%	6.1%	8.1%	14.7%	7.5%
CPI: All items	5.2%	3.2%	2.8%	3.0%	1.6%	3.4%	1.6%	2.7%
CPI: Medical	9.2%	7.8%	5.2%	3.5%	3.2%	4.1%	4.7%	4.4%
Ratio: Medical/All	1.77	2.44	1.86	1.18	2.05	1.21	2.97	1.64

Average annual increase	1990–2004
CPI: all items	3.1 percent
CPI: medical	5.5 percent
Employer cost increases	8.2 percent

Figure 8-1. CPI and active employee health care cost: annual percentage increase. *Source*. Authors' calculations using USBLS (2005) and Mercer (2004).

As a percentage of gross domestic product (GDP), health care spending rose from 5.1 percent in 1960 to almost three times that level by 2000, and the percentages are expected to continue increasing (CMS 2001). The increasingly expensive nature of health care makes it more difficult for companies located in the USA to compete globally. In 2002, Switzerland (at 11.2 percent of GDP) and Germany (at 10.9 percent) were the only industrialized nations other than the USA (at 14.6 percent) where health care costs accounted for more than 10 percent of the GDP (OECD 2004). The public sector in the USA picked up 46 percent of this ever-increasing component of GDP, with Medicare, a federal program mainly for those age 65+, picking up the majority of the costs. Medicaid, for low-income people of all ages, is jointly funded by federal and state governments. Forty percent is paid by the private sector, which includes employers, unions, insurance companies, and others. Individuals pay the balance of the health care bill, 14 percent, through premiums, deductibles, and other payments.

The percentage borne by individuals has been decreasing steadily for over forty years, as shown in Figure 8-2. Many say that consumers are so insulated from the cost of health care that they 'overutilize' health care services (often to their detriment) or fail to consider all treatment options. Increasingly, private- and public-sector experts support more consumerism in the health care marketplace—through increased education and higher

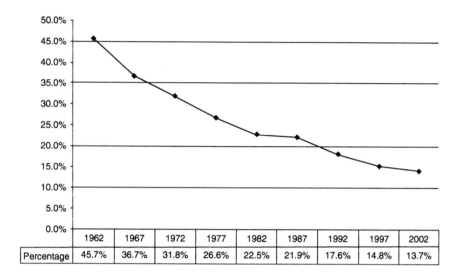

	1962	1967	1972	1977	1982	1987	1992	1997	2002
Percentage	45.7%	36.7%	31.8%	26.6%	22.5%	21.9%	17.6%	14.8%	13.7%

Figure 8-2. Consumer share of health care expenditures.
Source. Authors' calculations using USBLS (2005) and CMS (2004).

out-of-pocket costs—to encourage people to think more carefully about what is needed and what treatment option would be most beneficial. These costs can be particularly burdensome for companies who offer health care benefits to both employees and retirees.

Part of the reason for this trend in the USA is population aging. People born between 1946 and 1964, called Baby Boomers, were age 41–59 in 2005; this group made up 44 percent of the USA prime age population (20–64) and 26 percent of the total population (US Census 2005). As shown in Figure 8-3, substantially more people will attain age 65 and become eligible for Medicare by 2010, a process that fuels the overall upward trend in health care costs.

Health care costs increase with age and vary by gender, as shown in Figure 8-4. Women tend to use more health care services at younger ages, primarily because of maternity-related costs, while men have greater expenses at older ages.

Government-Provided Retiree Health Care Benefits

The cost of employer-provided retiree health benefits in the USA is strongly influenced by government programs. This is because the government pays for well over half of all health care costs for people covered by Medicare, and significantly more for people with both Medicare and Medicaid coverage. As the Medicare Part D prescription drug coverage takes effect, the

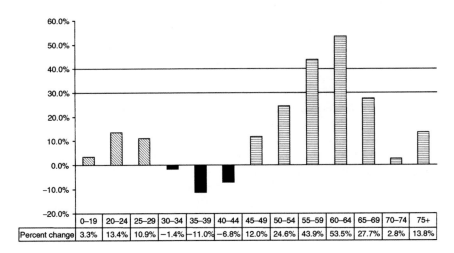

Percent change	0–19	20–24	25–29	30–34	35–39	40–44	45–49	50–54	55–59	60–64	65–69	70–74	75+
	3.3%	13.4%	10.9%	−1.4%	−11.0%	−6.8%	12.0%	24.6%	43.9%	53.5%	27.7%	2.8%	13.8%

Figure 8-3. Percent change in population by age group, 2000–2010.
Source: Authors' calculations from US Census Bureau (2005)

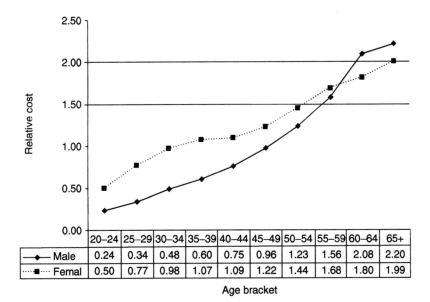

	20–24	25–29	30–34	35–39	40–44	45–49	50–54	55–59	60–64	65+
Male	0.24	0.34	0.48	0.60	0.75	0.96	1.23	1.56	2.08	2.20
Femal	0.50	0.77	0.98	1.07	1.09	1.22	1.44	1.68	1.80	1.99

Age bracket

Figure 8-4. Relative health care costs by age and gender for employer-sponsored health plans.
Source: Authors' calculations using Mercer proprietary data.

government will take on an even larger portion of the costs. For retirees not yet eligible for Medicare (pre-Medicare retirees), government programs provide very little health care coverage with the exception of Medicaid programs for lower-income people and Medicare for those disabled for more than twenty-four months.

Because of the significant impact of Medicare on employer-provided retiree health benefits, we will briefly review that program, including the recently enacted Medicare reform law (known as the Medicare Prescription Drug, Improvement, and Modernization Act of 2003).[3] In 1965 when Medicare started, it had two parts known as Part A, providing hospital insurance and Part B, providing supplementary medical insurance. This nomenclature is still in effect: Part A covers inpatient hospital, skilled nursing facility, hospice, and home health care; and as Part A is financed by a payroll tax collected from employees and employers, enrollees do not pay a Part A premium. Part B covers physician care, outpatient hospital care, lab tests, medical supplies, and some home health care not covered in Part A. Part B coverage is voluntary, and people opting for it must pay a premium that covers one quarter of the cost of Part B (DHHS 2005). The remainder of Part B is financed through general revenues. Neither Part A nor Part B has traditionally covered outpatient prescription drugs, except in a few narrowly defined circumstances (such as pain medications for people qualifying for hospice benefits and certain cancer and immunosuppressive drugs).

Over the years, many Medicare enrollees have purchased supplemental health care coverage from employers, unions, or private companies; Medigap coverage can be purchased from private companies in all fifty states. Federal law requires a six-month initial enrollment period that begins when a person is first eligible for Part B coverage. During this time, a person cannot be denied Medigap coverage or charged a higher price because of current or past health problems. Under the Medicare reform law, beginning in 2006, these Medigap plans may continue to supplement Parts A and B of Medicare, but they may not supplement Part D. Also, Medigap carriers will be able to offer two new lower-priced products (called Medigap plans K and L).

In 1982, Congress created what was then called Medicare Risk Plans; subsequent legislation in the Balanced Budget Act then expanded the concept and changed the name to 'Medicare + Choice' or Medicare Part C, and the 2005 Medicare reform law further expanded the concept. Today these plans are called Medicare Advantage (MA) plans. These are offered by insurance companies and others who receive a payment per member per month in return for assuming the risk. Medicare Advantage plans must agree to cover all services covered by original Medicare, and most cover additional services as well; they are permitted to charge enrollees a premium if their costs are higher than what Medicare pays them. The most common type of MA plan is a health maintenance organization (HMO) in which networks of doctors and hospitals, and their members, may use only network or other approved providers except for medical emergencies. Two other MA plans that use networks are point-of-service (POS) and preferred provider organization (PPO) plans. The POS and PPO plans allow members to use out-of-network providers, but members then pay more out-of-pocket costs. From 2006, the Medicare reform law requires that these three types of MA vendors must offer at least one plan that includes prescription drug benefits at least as rich as those under Medicare Part D.

An additional MA option is the private fee-for-service (PFFS) plan. Private insurance companies and vendors offer these plans, and they receive a predetermined amount of money each month from Medicare to provide benefits that are at least as rich as Parts A and B. These plans are not required to have a provider network, and they are often offered in more rural areas than the other MA plans. The PFFS plans can charge additional premiums over what people pay under Medicare Part B, just like other MA plans. The PFFS plans, however, are not required to offer prescription drug benefits equivalent to those of Medicare Part D.

The concept behind the MA plan is that, by aggressively managing care, private companies can control costs more effectively than the 'non-managed' original Medicare, bringing about lower premiums for members, benefit packages that cover more services than original Medicare, and/or lower costs for the federal government. These advantages have been realized in many instances. As Table 8-1 shows, 56 percent of people eligible for Medicare lived in counties where they could purchase an MA plan at a 'zero premium' in 2005, that is, at no additional payment above the Part B

TABLE 8-1   Retirees Eligible for Medicare Summarized by the Lowest Premium for Available MA Plans

Lowest premium available	Retirees eligible for Medicare	Percent of eligible retirees (%)	Cumulative (%)
$0	23,917,775	56	56
$0.01–$35.00	4,905,508	12	68
$35.01–$70.00	5,572,282	13	81
$70.01–$100.00	848,816	2	83
$100.01–$160.00	489,114	1	84
Subtotal	35,733,495	84	84
No MA plan	6,888,486	16	100
Grand total	42,621,981	100	100

Source: CMS (2005*a*, 2005*b*, 2005*c*) and authors' calculations.

payment (which all Medicare and MA enrollees must pay). In total, using proprietary data we compute that 84 percent of people eligible for Medicare lived in counties where they could purchase an MA plan. Both health care costs and Medicare reimbursement to MA plans can vary by county, so the premiums and coverage also vary by county, sometimes significantly.

The Medicare reform law of 2005 brought about the most fundamental change in the program since it was launched in 1965, mainly through the addition of Medicare Part D, a benefit for outpatient prescription drugs. The Part D benefit is delivered by prescription drug plans (PDPs) or as Medicare Advantage prescription drug plans (MA-PDPs). While this new drug benefit does offer some additional protection, many people will still have significant out-of-pocket costs. With Part D coverage, people must pay an initial $250 deductible, then 25 percent coinsurance for the next $2,000 in costs, then 100 percent of costs until they reach a $3,600 out-of-pocket level. (These values are indexed in future years.) Amounts paid by employers or insurance companies do not count toward the retirees' out-of-pocket cost requirement. Part D pays roughly 95 percent of remaining costs after a person's expenses reach the out-of-pocket requirement. Enrollees are intended to pay about one quarter of the cost of Part D coverage, which has been estimated at under $500 per year in 2006, with the remainder paid from general revenues.

Employer-Provided Retiree Health Care Benefits

In the USA, employers expend substantial amounts on employee and retiree health care costs. As Figure 8-1 shows, employer health care cost increases have tended to track increases in the medical component of the CPS, but cost swings for employer coverage have been greater. During the 1990s, cost increases moderated because of the increased popularity of managed care plans; cost increases then again accelerated in the late 1990s and early 2000s mainly due to some mis-estimation of the incremental impact of managed care on costs.

These patterns also drive employer-provided retiree medical care costs. Indeed, retiree health care costs in 2004 rose 8 percent faster than in 2003 for pre-Medicare retirees, and 7.8 percent higher for Medicare enrollees; Figure 8-5 shows that the pre-Medicare group's cost per retiree was greater than the cost per employee, while the Medicare group's cost was less than for employees. The cost differential between pre- and post-Medicare retirees is partly reflective of rising costs with age; it can also vary depending on retirees' age and sex mix, the level of dependent coverage, and whether disabled people, who have higher claims, are included with the early retirees or employees.[4] Lower costs for the Medicare group are also attributable to the significant amount of retiree expenses paid by Medicare.

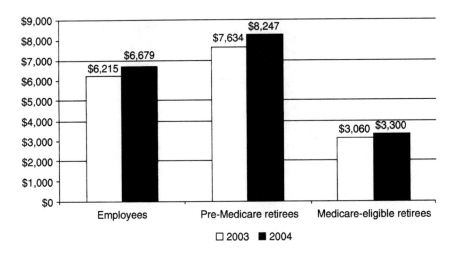

Figure 8-5. Employer costs for employees and retirees: 2003 and 2004.
Source: Authors' calculations using Mercer (2004).
*Includes covered dependants.

When considering costs for both employees and retirees, another important factor is 'adverse selection', sometimes called 'intelligent employee choice'. As employers increase the premium that employees or retirees have to pay, some healthier people will tend to drop health care coverage. Consequently, the average cost for the remaining covered group will tend to go up faster than the underlying cost increase. In turn, even more people might leave the program, putting still more pressure on the price. As this adverse selection cycle continues, the program can quickly move into a 'death spiral' unless an employer takes corrective action. This adverse selection phenomenon is fueled by the fact that a very small number of people can account for the majority of the cost. As shown in Figure 8-6, the most expensive 5 percent of the claimants can account for over 50 percent of the total cost, while the healthiest 50 percent accounted for less than 5 percent of the total cost.[5,6]

As the number of retirees with health care coverage began to rise after World War II in the USA, the Financial Accounting Standards Board (FASB) became concerned that employers were not appropriately recognizing that expense. (Unlike pension costs that were accrued over a working person's lifetime, retiree health care costs were not.) Accordingly FASB (1990) issued its Statement of Financial Accounting Standards Number 106 (FAS 106), requiring corporations to begin accounting for retiree health care costs on an accrual cost instead of on a cash basis. Expenses using the accrued liability, based on the present value of

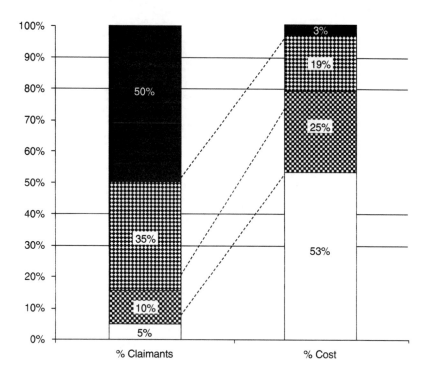

Figure 8-6. Few claimants incur the majority of cost.
Source: Authors' calculations using Mercer (2004).

future retiree health care costs, proved to be substantially higher than cash costs; indeed estimated FAS 106 liabilities often rivaled firms' pension liabilities, but, unlike pension plans, typically had no offsetting assets.

In response to the increased awareness of the cost of these plans, many private-sector employers began tying decisions about future coverage more closely to their overall business plan. Some continued offering retiree coverage because they wanted to attract mid-career employees, wanted employees to retire before age 65 to improve productivity, or had collective bargaining pressure. Others, however, decided to reduce or eliminate the coverage entirely. Figure 8-7 shows the consequent and steady decrease in retiree health care coverage from over time.

In 2004, the Governmental Accounting Standards Board (GASB) issued new accounting standards for governmental retiree benefits other than pensions. This statement (GASB 43) will require public-sector employers to follow accounting guidelines similar to those of FAS 106, generally beginning in 2007.[7]

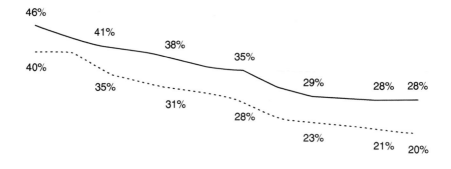

Figure 8-7. Percentage of US employers offering medical coverage to retirees[*].
Source: Authors' calculations using Mercer (2004) for employers with 500 or more employees.
[*]Represents employers planning to offer coverage to current employees and new employees when they retire.

Controlling Retiree Health Care Costs. Employer efforts to control retiree medical costs have been varied, including (*a*) tightening eligibility requirements; (*b*) increasing deductibles, copays, and other retiree out-of-pocket costs and thereby reducing amounts paid by the employer's plan (in keeping with the movement to consumerism in employee health care plans); (*c*) increasing the percentage of premium paid by retirees; (*d*) increasing the management of care; and (*e*) prefunding the employer's liability (through vehicles such as a 501(c)(9) trust [known as a VEBA], 401(h) sub-accounts in pension plans, and trust-owned health insurance). Another tack has been to take a 'defined contribution' approach to health care (DC Health), which defines the employer's obligation as a fixed dollar amount. In addition to 'defining' their contribution, employers must also decide on the types of health insurance benefits that retirees will be able to purchase.

The choice between self-funded or insured approaches determines how precisely an employer has defined the cost of coverage and what level of future involvement will be required. The impact of three approaches can be summarized as follows:

- If an employer offers self-funded coverage, the firm first projects plan costs and then sets the retiree premium to pay what is not covered by the employer's DC premium. When actual experience varies from what was assumed when setting the retiree's contribution, the employer's actual per capita contribution will vary from the 'defined' amount.

- If the employer sponsors an insured plan, the employer's per capita contribution is defined because the insured cost (the premium) is guaranteed at least for a term. Insuring coverage does not relieve employers of long-term involvement because they must renew coverage annually, with significant premium increase or terminated coverage a possibility. Also, there is often pressure for greater subsidy of the employer plan.

- If an employer does not sponsor a plan, individual coverage must be purchased in the marketplace. This approach, like the prior one, may define the employer's contribution; it also may get the employer out of the retiree health care coverage business, eliminating even the requirement to negotiate with carriers. The retiree bears the risk that coverage may be inadequate, very expensive, or not available at all.

Employers adopting the DC health approach have a great deal of flexibility in defining their commitment to retirees through the use of various account-based approaches. Accounts can be defined on a periodic basis (such as monthly, annually) or an aggregate basis; they can provide amounts on a retiree-only basis or include additional payments for dependants; and the accounts can be funded or unfunded.[8] For both the periodic and aggregate amounts, the tax code contains opportunities for the contribution to be tax deductible to the employer and not taxable to the retiree. For example, the contribution amount could be provided through a Health Reimbursement Arrangement (HRA) or under other plans satisfying Sections 105 or 106 of the Internal Revenue Code. If the DC approach were to be used for pre-Medicare retirees, it would typically be in conjunction with an employer's self-funded medical plan because of the dearth of insured products in the pre-Medicare market. For retirees eligible for Medicare, however, the situation is quite different. As previously mentioned, MA products are available to over 80 percent of those eligible for Medicare. Medigap supplement plans are available to virtually 100 percent upon initial eligibility for Medicare. It is quite feasible to arrange either an employer-sponsored insured product or to let retirees purchase coverage in the open market. With the addition of Part D prescription drug coverage to Medicare, even those who do not buy coverage other than Medicare may still be able to cover a large portion of their expenses.

As employers move to DC options, many will make a number of changes in their underlying retiree health care benefit strategy. Employers often offer more choices in plan design (such as a 'high option plan' that is very similar to the employee plan as well as some more affordable options). They may also provide opportunities for employees to save for future retiree health care expenses; or increase communication with employees and retirees on general health issues, the need to save for future health care expenses, and the business rationale for the change.

Challenges and Risks for Employers Offering Retiree Health Plans.   As noted, rising retiree health care costs present significant challenges for employers. The level of increase has varied over the years, as shown in Figure 8-8, but the trend has been relentless. Typically, employers require retirees to pay a portion of the cost for health care coverage. The Mercer 2004 Survey showed that 38 percent of employers offering retiree health care plans required enrollees to pay the entire premium as well as out-of-pocket benefit costs: such plans offer coverage, but not necessarily affordable coverage. Only 13 percent of employers provided coverage at no cost to retirees. For the 49 percent that shared the cost with retirees, the average retiree portion was 34 percent of the plan cost. The results for Medicare-eligible plan coverage were similar: 37 percent require the retirees to bear the full cost; 15 percent provide coverage at no cost to retirees; and 47 percent share the cost, requiring retirees to pay 35 percent of it.

Another major challenge facing employers is the growing ratio of retirees to active workers, combined with the possibility that the federal government might increase cost-shifting as the Medicare program approaches insolvency. Larger-than-anticipated Medicare premium increases or benefit reductions could seriously challenge both employers and retirees. An additional employer risk is adverse selection, particularly with DC health approaches. For example, relatively healthier Medicare-eligible retirees may drop employer coverage and purchase lower cost insured coverage (via an MA or a Medigap plan), or rely fully on Medicare as the gap widens between the premium charged and the employer's DC. Remaining less-healthy retirees will have higher health care costs, forcing still higher premiums. If only the sicker retirees remain covered in employer plans, these plans may go into a death spiral where cost increases cannot be appropriately reflected in the premium.

Retiree Options and Challenges

Retirees confront substantial risk regarding both health care expenditures and employer-provided health insurance benefits. In the case where the employer offers coverage, retirees below age 65 face higher premiums for coverage in the open market; and in some areas, it is virtually impossible for someone in poor health to purchase needed coverage. Even for retirees enrolled in Medicare, premiums plus out-of-pocket costs can still be quite high, even unaffordable for some. Furthermore, Medicare Parts B and D premiums (set to cover one quarter of program costs) will clearly rise with total Medicare spending, likely to grow faster social security benefits. Private insurance premiums, premiums for employer coverage, and direct payments to providers are also likely to increase in a similar manner. If

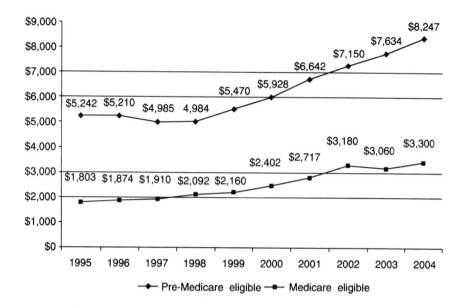

	Average increases in annual health plan costs	
Year	Pre-Medicare retirees	Medicare-eligible retirees
1999–2004	8.6 percent	8.8 percent
1995–2004	5.2 percent	6.9 percent

Figure 8-8. Average employer health plan cost per retiree.
Source: Authors' calculations using Mercer (2004).

employer contributions are capped or otherwise limited, retiree premium increases will be even higher.

Other than through employer programs, retired workers not yet eligible for Medicare can be rather limited: low-income people may qualify for Medicaid or other governmental programs, and those eligible for social security disability benefits for twenty-four months are eligible for Medicare. But anyone who is healthy and meets insurance underwriting rules might have to pay the full cost of coverage, which will seem quite high compared to the subsidized cost paid before retirement. Retirees often pay more because of premium caps or other limits on employer contributions, and because employers may boost out-of-pocket benefit costs (deductibles, copays, and out-of-pocket maximums) as they seek to control retiree coverage costs and maintain consistency with the move to consumerism and higher cost sharing for those still working and enrolled in employee plans. The other problem is that early retirees often receive lower pension and social security payments, compared to those retiring later. The dual problems of accessibility and affordability of coverage mean that employees will have to save more money for retiree health care expenses, allocate more financial resources to health care, work longer, rely on help from family, or use a combination of these approaches. Unless people are healthy, or government regulations support guaranteed access, many people might find it advisable or necessary to work until they become eligible for Medicare even if they have enough funds to pay for coverage.

For those retirees covered by Medicare, the picture is brighter. Accessibility has not been a problem, as they can participate in Medicare Parts A, B, and D, and Part C coverage is available to many. During the first six months of eligibility for Medicare, anyone in original Medicare is guaranteed the right to purchase a Medigap policy to supplement Parts A and B of Medicare at 'standard' rates. Yet even with Medicare coverage, many older Americans will face affordability problems: premiums for Medicare coverage are expensive, as are premiums for Medigap insurance and employer-sponsored insurance, or private insurance. In addition, direct payment to providers of service for deductibles, copays, and coinsurance are costly, as are other expenses not covered by Medicare. And even with the new Part D coverage, prescription drugs will remain a large expense for many people. In addition to health care expenses, some retirees will also have significant long-term care (LTC) expenses, primarily custodial in nature. For those who qualify, Medicaid covers a significant percentage of LTC services. Because Medicare provides only limited LTC coverage, people who are not eligible for Medicaid must rely on LTC insurance they purchase, on their own funds, or on financial assistance from family members and others.

Possible Roles for Tax-Favored Saving Opportunities.   Several challenges face future retiree expenses and opportunities to save for retiree medical costs. To these we turn next.

Potential Retiree Expenses.   According to Fronstin and Salisbury (2003), a person age 65 with employer-paid benefits might need between $37,000 and $750,000 to pay future claims that Medicare does not cover; a retiree lacking employment-based benefits who purchases Medigap coverage could need from $47,000 to $1,458,000. Using Mercer Survey data, we modeled average future expenses using five sets of assumptions. First, we assumed that cost trends over the most recent five years of the Mercer Survey would be repeated in future years, and second we hypothesized that the historical trends from the most recent decade years would be repeated. Third, we averaged findings from the two previous sets. Last, we assumed that health care cost trends would be consistent with FAS 106 assumptions for large employer plans and that the trend would have shown 10 percent increase per year. These variants were used to project costs to 2006 and adjust the projection for the impact of Medicare reform on Medicare enrollees. Next we projected these costs to 2031 using the five sets of trend assumptions, shown in Table 8-2.[9]

Table 8-2 Hypothetical Average Cost for Individual Retirees in 2031

	Estimated 2006 cost	Trend assumption for projection to 2031				
	Mercer Survey projected[1]	1999–2004 Experience repeated[6]	1995–2004 Experience repeated[7]	Average of two experience periods	Representative FAS 106 trend	10 percent trend
Pre-Medicare						
Employer plan cost (ErPC)[1,2]	$5,712	$44,928	$20,284	$32,606	$25,099	$61,885
Retiree benefit out-of-pocket[3] (OOP)	$1,008	$7,928	$3,580	$5,754	$4,429	$10,921
OOP + 50 percent ErPC	$3,864	$30,392	$13,722	$22,057	$16,978	$41,863
OOP + 100 percent ErPC	$6,720	$52,856	$23,864	$38,360	$29,528	$72,806
Medicare-eligible						
Employer plan cost[1,2]	$1,423	$11,720	$7,545	$9,633	$6,253	$15,418
Retiree benefit OOP[4]	$1,290	$10,627	$6,841	$8,734	$5,670	$13,980
Medicare premiums[5]	$1,459	$12,018	$7,737	$9,877	$6,412	$15,810
Total retiree OOP	$2,749	$22,645	$14,578	$18,611	$12,082	$29,790
OOP + 50 percent ErPC	$3,461	$28,505	$18,350	$23,428	$15,208	$37,499
OOP + 100 percent ErPC	$4,172	$34,365	$22,123	$28,244	$18,335	$45,208

Source: Authors' calculations.

Notes:

[1] Employer plan cost does not include retiree out-of-pocket costs. The individual pre-Medicare cost is derived from an amount that includes covered dependents, assuming 1.65 risk units per covered retiree (individual cost = total cost ÷ 1.65). Medicare-eligible cost was derived from an amount that includes covered dependents, assuming 1.60 risk units per covered retiree.

[2] Based on 2004 Mercer Survey data for individual retiree cost in 2004, projected to 2006 using the average 'starting costs' of two historical periods; the Medicare groups' cost adjusted for impact of Medicare reform law assuming employer plan is secondary to Medicare Parts B and D with nonduplication of benefits integration. (Assumed Part D offset of $976 to employer cost or 55.6 percent of the $1,755 estimated part D cost.)

[3] Assumes an employer plan that covers 85 percent of total cost.

[4] Based on pre-Medicare benefits integrated with Medicare A, B, and D using the nonduplication of benefits approach ('carveout') and 2.5 percent aging factor for 10 years.

[5] Assumes Medicare-eligible retiree pays Part B premium (assumed to be $85 per month in 2006) and Part D premium ($36.60 per month) out-of-pocket. In addition, the retiree pays benefit expenses out-of-pocket.

[6] Based on Mercer Survey data from 1999 through 2004, the pre-Medicare annual trend is 8.6 percent, and the Medicare-eligible annual trend is 8.8 percent.

[7] Based on Mercer Survey data from 1995 through 2004, the pre-Medicare annual trend is 5.2 percent, and the Medicare-eligible annual trend is 6.9 percent.

To obtain a better understanding of the funds needed at the time of retirement for future health care expenses, we considered people who were age 35 in 2006 and retiring in 20, 25, 30, or 35 years. Using these scenarios, we calculated the present value of future costs at retirement for each age, using the five alternative trend assumptions and a discount rate of 5 percent along with mortality, termination of coverage, and other assumptions from representative FAS 106 valuations. The present value of future costs at retirement can be thought of as the amount of money needed in a bank account at retirement so that expected future payments can be made using principal and interest earned at an assumed rate, with the bank account running out when the expected period ends. Table 8-3 shows the present values at retirement for an age 35 worker in 2006, assuming he or she retires in 25 years at age 60. Present values are shown where the retiree pays out-of-pocket benefit costs (for copays, coinsurance, and deductibles) plus a range of costs for premiums.

Even under these simple assumptions and using the same average starting cost, we see a wide range of potential results: these start at a low of $76,000 for a typical FAS 106 trend (if the employer pays 100 percent of cost—probably unlikely in 2031) to a high of $2.26 million with a 10 percent trend and the retiree paying full cost. Note that the values vary importantly with changes in trend, discount rate, mortality, and other assumptions. While these hypothetical examples illustrate potential outcomes, results for individuals can vary significantly. Values for retirement at ages 55, 60, 65, and 70 are shown in Figure 8-9.

Tax-Favored/Saving Opportunities.   Using these estimates of what future retirees will need for health care costs, we next examine what options they might have to start boosting their saving rates. In the US case, there is an increasing number of tax-advantaged savings options to employees: Table 8-4 outlines six of these. For example, a health savings account (HSA), authorized under the Medicare reform law, provides outstanding saving opportunities for employees who can meet the requirements and have the financial resources and discipline to save. Both employees and employers can contribute to an HSA before employee entitlement to Medicare, as long as the employees participate in a qualifying high deductible health plan (HDHP). These plans must have a minimum deductible (of at least $1,000 in 2004 for an individual and $2,000 for family, both values indexed thereafter), and they must meet other requirements (the least attractive of which is the prohibition on having almost any other health coverage during the periods that HSA contributions are made by or for an individual). The maximum contribution, from employee and employer, is the lesser of the deductible in the HDHP and $2,600 ($5,150 for a family, both values indexed from 2004). The range of possible contributions for an individual in 2004 was

TABLE 8-3 Hypothetical Present Value of Future Benefits at Retirement Age for an Employee Age 35 in 2006, Retiring at Age 60 in 2031[1] (Thousands)

Retiree cost basis	Trend assumption for projection to 2031				
	1999–2004 Experience repeated[4]	1995–2004 Experience repeated[5]	Average of two experience periods	Representative FAS 106 trend	10 Percent trend
Out-of-pocket (OOP)[2]	$214.1	$98.1	$156.1	$76.0	$339.4
OOP + 33 percent ErPC[3]	$614.6	$281.6	$448.1	$218.0	$974.1
OOP + 50 percent ErPC	$820.9	$376.1	$598.5	$291.2	$1,301.0
OOP + 67 percent ErPC	$1,027.1	$470.6	$748.9	$364.3	$1,628.0
OOP +100 percent ErPC	$1,427.6	$654.1	$1,040.8	$506.4	$2,262.6

Source: Authors' calculations.

Notes:

[1] Assuming a 5 percent discount rate.

[2] Benefit OOP, plus premium OOP for Medicare Part B and Part D after Medicare eligibility.

[3] Employer plan cost.

[4] Based on Mercer Survey data from 1999 through 2004, the pre-Medicare annual trend is 8.6 percent, and the Medicare annual trend is 8.8 percent.

[5] Based on Mercer Survey data from 1995 through 2004, the pre-Medicare annual trend is 5.2 percent, and the Medicare-eligible annual trend is 6.9 percent.

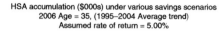

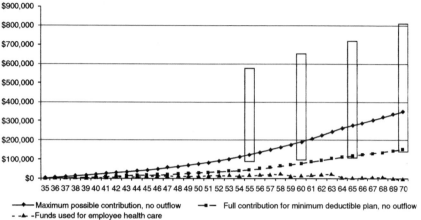

Figure 8-9. HSA accumulations assuming 5 percent return investment compared to expenses assuming repeat of historical Mercer Survey experience from 1995 to 2004.

Source. Authors' calculations using Mercer (2004). Range of cost will vary depending on retiree's health, employer plan, etc.

Costs and accumulations at retirement age for people 35 years of age in 2006, assuming average trend from 1995–2004 Mercer Surveys, and 5 percent HSA investment return

Retirement		PVFC-R[1] for out-of-pocket benefit cost plus percentage of premium for employer plan			HSA funds, No out-flow		HSA with out-flow[4]
Age	Year	0 Percent contribution	33 percent contribution	100 percent contribution	Maximum contribution[2]	Minimum contribution[3]	
55	2026	$86,602	$248,548	$577,347	$122,337	$47,989	$14,856
60	2031	$98,119	$281,601	$654,126	$191,741	$80,500	$14,828
65	2036	$108,101	$310,249	$720,672	$277,325	$120,373	$6,319
70	2041	$143,186	$363,693	$811,389	$353,945	$153,630	$0

Notes:

[1]Present value of future costs at retirement, based on a 5 percent discount rate. Trends for 1995–2004 are 5.2 percent pre-Medicare and 6.9 percent for people eligible for Medicare.
[2]Maximum contribution allowed ($2,600 in 2004, indexed); no outflow.
[3]Maximum contribution allowed with minimum deductible ($1,000 in 2004, indexed); no outflow.
[4]Maximum contribution of $1,000 with minimum deductible of $1,000 in 2004, indexed; experience of four times average out-of-pocket benefit costs once every four years.

TABLE 8-4 Comparison of Tax-Advantaged Savings Vehicles

Savings vehicle	Contribution	Investment earnings	Disbursements for health care	Limitations on contributions
HSA	Pretax	Tax-free	Not taxable	Maximum contribution, HDHP[2]
401(k)	Pretax	Tax-deferred	Taxable	Employer must offer plan; pretax and total contribution limits; minimum required distributions after specified age
Traditional IRA	Pretax	Tax-deferred	Taxable	Maximum contribution; tax-deduction limit for active retirement plan participant based on income; minimum required distributions after specified age
Roth IRA	Posttax	Tax-free	Not taxable[1]	Contribution limits based on income
VEBA	Posttax	Tax-free	Not taxable	Employer must offer plan
Roth 401(k)	Posttax	Tax-free	Not taxable[1]	Not available until 2006; can designate portion of 401(k) contributions as after-tax; contribution limits unclear; additional regulations expected

Source: Authors' calculations.

Notes:

[1]Distributions are not taxable after age 59½ and 5 years of participation.

[2]High deductible health plan; minimum deductible of $1,000 in 2004; indexed; maximum contribution of $2,600 in 2004 (indexed).

$1,000–$2,600 (indexed thereafter), depending on the level of the deductible. The contributions are before taxes, investment earnings are not taxable, and withdrawals from the account for health care—either while an employee or a retiree—are not taxable. The funds in an HSA are portable, nonforfeitable, and can be carried over into retirement.

As an example of what an individual employee could save, we assess the HSA in three situations: (*a*) saving the maximum each year ($2,600 in 2004, indexed thereafter) and spending no HSA funds for current health care costs (Scenario A); (*b*) saving the largest amount possible while in a plan with the lowest deductible level allowed ($1,000 in 2004, indexed) and spending nothing on current health care costs (Scenario B); and (*c*) saving the largest amount allowable while in the plan with the lowest deductible but using the HSA for current health care costs (Scenario C). The first two situations are unlikely and not possible unless the employee had virtually no health care expenses while still employed, or had enough income and discipline to pay those health care costs from non-HSA sources. We find that accumulations after 25 years (in 2031 for someone starting to save in 2006) are approximately \$192,000 under Scenario A, \$80,000 under Scenario B, and \$15,000 under Scenario C.

Comparison of Expenses to Savings. Figure 8-9 also shows the annual accumulation for all three scenarios and compares them to the present value of future health care costs at retirement for four ages at retirement: 55, 60, 65, and 70 (the amount that should be 'in the bank' at retirement so that projected future retiree costs could be paid from principal and interest). For each age at retirement, we show the range of out-of-pocket costs (copays, coinsurance, and deductibles plus premiums for Parts B and D), and premium payments for the employer-sponsored retiree coverage from 0 to 100 percent, based on cost increase trends that duplicate experience in the Mercer Survey data from 1995 to 2004 (average annual trends of 5.2 percent for pre-Medicare and 6.9 percent for Medicare-eligible retirees).

Even retirees who have enough financial resources and discipline to save in an HSA and not use the funds before retirement would need to use other savings, work longer, or work for an employer who provides a very generous retiree health care plan if they want to retire before becoming eligible for Medicare. Many may face the same challenges even when eligible for Medicare. Given the substantial fluctuation in health care costs over the last ten years, any estimate should be viewed only as a hypothetical projection of what future experience could be. Funds actually needed for retiree health care coverage will vary depending on retiree health status, employer coverage, and other factors that will be different for each individual. Even if actual investment earnings are higher and retiree costs are lower than the range projected in Figure 8-9, older adults may still have to devote significant portions of their income to health care in retirement. Many baby boomers' situations may not prepare them for retirement as well as they have hoped. The financial challenges and burdens of health care costs will be particularly painful for lower-income adults who do not have employer coverage and who do not qualify for Medicaid.

Outstanding Policy Issues

The US health care system faces serious challenges. Solutions to the problems, or lack thereof, will be a major force behind changes in retiree health care coverage. While a full outline of all the challenges and solutions is beyond the scope of this chapter, we briefly discuss these and then focus on issues specific to retiree health care coverage.

US health care delivery and financing is the result of a hybrid system of employer coverage, government-sponsored programs, individual insurance, and individual payments, with many people uninsured. Solutions to cover all US citizens have been discussed and rejected in the past, although Medicare is essentially universal coverage for the age 65 and older population. Going forward, some believe incremental changes will be sufficient to meet the challenges; reforms to adapt current programs have been suggested to help early retirees, including reducing Medicare's eligibility age, allowing some early retirees to purchase Medicare, and mandating COBRA[10] coverage for early retirees.[11] Others believe that reform of the individual insurance market will provide solutions. A major obstacle is the current practice of underwriting individual risk to determine whether to offer coverage and how much to charge for the coverage. This underwriting, which adds to the challenge of covering sicker people, reduces the insurance companies' problem of adverse selection. Fundamental change would be needed in the individual insurance market before providers can offer a solution to the unhealthy uninsured.

Some policy experts believe small, incremental changes will be insufficient to effect systemic reform, favoring instead comprehensive, system-wide solutions such as employer mandates supplemented with individual mandates as necessary; expansion of current public programs; creation of new programs that target subsets of the uninsured; and establishment of a universal, publicly financed program (Simmons 2005). The debate continues as to how—and whether—employers provide health care coverage to retirees. If health care reform relies on incremental changes, employer programs are not likely to change much. If employer mandates occur, there will be a significantly greater role for employers in providing retiree health care coverage. But a single-payer national program could mean no direct employer role in providing health care to retirees.

Retiree Health Care Policy Issues. Retirees, employers, and the government—the three sources of funds to finance health care cost in retirement—face challenges and should have a seat at the retiree health care policy table. In evaluating their challenges and roles, we first consider issues of accessibility and affordability of coverage for retirees' eligible for Medicare and those not eligible for Medicare; then we turn to challenges for Medicare; and finish with an assessment of the impact of federal policy on employer-provided health care coverage.

Access and Affordability of Retiree Health Care Coverage. Historically, retirees have faced the dual challenges of access to coverage and affordability of coverage. The addition of Part D prescription drug coverage makes access less of a concern for retirees able to access Medicare, though affordability will still be a problem. Projections by Johnson and Penner (2004) indicate that health care spending for older married couples will rise increasing from 16 percent of net after-tax income in 2000 to 35 percent in 2030; they further estimate that unmarried older adults will face an increase from 17 to 30 percent. The problems will be most severe for lower-income people, and for unhealthy individuals.

Retirees ineligible for Medicare will face even more obstacles. Some with low income or employer-provided coverage, and those disabled under social security for twenty-four months, will have access to benefits. Others may obtain coverage if they are healthy enough to pass underwriting or because they qualify through HIPAA,[12] COBRA, high-risk pools, or insurers of last resort. Yet a significant number is still unable to purchase adequate coverage, while others choose not to purchase coverage. The National Academy of Social Insurance (NASI 2001) found that 15 percent of people age 55–64 were uninsured in 1999.[13] As to affordability of coverage, people ineligible for Medicare face even greater challenges than those eligible: coverage is more expensive for them because there is no government benefit to pay some of the costs, and they have additional years when they need coverage. They also have fewer years as an employee to save for future health care expenses.

The Future of Medicare. Medicare faces serious long-term financing challenges because the population eligible for Medicare is growing more rapidly than the number of active workers, and health care costs are increasing at a higher rate than the economy as a whole. A related risk is the reaction of employers to similar problems; as economic pressures cause employers to cut back on retiree health care coverage, there will be growing pressure to increase Medicare benefits. Direct cost pressure will also come to Part D of Medicare if employers end the coverage for which they get a tax-free subsidy. Medicare's cost per retiree for those in Part D will be greater on average than its cost for the employer subsidy, and therefore Medicare's total cost will increase when retirees move from the employers' plans to Part D (US CBO 2004). Regarding long-term financing challenges, the American Academy of Actuaries has defined four major areas for addressing future Medicare policy: these include long-term access to care, maintaining access to care while avoiding unnecessary utilization, meeting the insurance needs of Americans age 55–64, and private-sector competition strategies (American Academy of Actuaries 2005).

Clearly much uncertainty surrounds Medicare in the future. Some want Medicare to remain a government-run program, while advocates of competition want to see much more participation by the private sector, with vendors assuming risk such as allowed under the MA and prescription drug provisions of the Medicare reform law.[14] There is also uncertainty about how private providers will respond to increased market opportunities. Experience with prior legislation may offer some guidance. The 1997 Balanced Budget Act encouraged a substantial shift of risk to private-sector Medicare + Choice plans, predecessors of MA plans. After some initial success, these plans faltered and declined; many employers strongly promoted Medicare + Choice plans in the 1990s, but they then became skeptical as plans closed and physicians dropped out. Insurers and other potential sponsors of MA plans may still be skeptical of their future. While there has been recent growth in the number of plans and enrollees, it remains to be seen how many plans will be available in future years and whether they will be stable. Similar issues may affect market participation in the new Medicare Part D. Uncertainty about Medicare is a backdrop for uncertainty about the future distribution of risk-sharing of retiree health care costs among the government, employers, and retirees.

Federal Policy and the Role of the Employer. In the USA, there has long been a strong connection between receiving health care benefits and one's employment, yet some health policy experts are now challenging that nexus. That is, there is a sense in which employers might not be the best option for providing health benefits for employees or retirees. The tax system has also been an important force encouraging and supporting the current system. Employers can deduct expenses for health benefits, and employees and retirees do not pay taxes on their value. From a federal budget point of view, employee benefits constitute a large tax expenditure. Of course, though employer programs do decrease tax revenue, they still benefit a large number of people. One of the strengths of employer-provided coverage is that it automatically spreads risk and enables coverage of sicker as well as healthier people. This is not true for individual coverage or retiree-pay-all employer plans where selection becomes a huge issue.

Employer health care plans in the USA are voluntary; nevertheless, they are still subject to extensive regulation such as employee benefits law, requirements that employer health plans must be offered for a limited period after termination of employment, and requirements that individual insurance plans must accept people who had previously been covered by employer plans.[15] While employer sponsorship of both pensions and retiree health benefits is voluntary, regulations are more specific and extensive for DB pension plans than health benefits. Pension law generally requires vesting, includes minimum coverage rules, and outlines benefit accrual requirements. There are no similar requirements for retiree health plans. Pensions are subject to mandatory funding, but retiree health benefits are generally not prefunded. (Even if an employer wants to prefund voluntarily, it is difficult to do so on a tax-favored basis.) The application of age discrimination law creates uncertainly for both types of benefits. Legal requirements and uncertainty about them interact with cost and financial risk to discourage employers from offering both retiree health and conventional pension benefits.

Conclusions

The dynamics and risks of employer-provided retiree health care benefits are changing. The combination of health care costs increasing at a faster rate than the overall economy and the increasing ratio of retirees to employees is challenging both government and employer programs. Employers continue to reduce benefits or terminate retiree health benefits plans entirely. The projected insolvency of the Medicare Part A Trust Fund by 2020 could force Congress to raise premiums and/or cut benefits.

Of all those who pay for health care, retirees face the greatest uncertainty and potential risk. Finding affordable coverage is a major challenge today, one likely to become more difficult in the future. Even when coverage is available, it is often expensive. Tax-favored savings vehicles, such as HSAs, can help some people save for retiree health care expenses. However, many will not be able to save enough to pay for future health care coverage without diverting other funds to health care coverage needs and/or working longer.

Retiree needs for affordable health coverage and adequate retirement income will greatly affect retirement security in the future, and their problems will likely grow more severe. It seems likely that solutions must be part of a broader national approach to health care reform. Nevertheless, agreement on a specific approach does not appear likely in the near term.

Endnotes

1. In this chapter we do not cover long-term care benefits which are custodial in nature.
2. The Mercer Survey has been conducted annually since 1993, and it is based on a statistically valid random sample of all US employers with ten or more employees; it is projectable to the US labor force. (For private firms in the survey, a random sample is drawn from the Dun & Bradstreet database. All state governments are included; a random sample of county and local governments comes from the Census of Governments.) The survey includes only employers who sponsor insurance. For each plan type that they sponsor, respondents provide information about the plan with the largest enrollment. In 2004, the total number of participants was 3,020.
3. Further information on benefits and program details are available in DHSS (2005).
4. The Mercer Survey data on cost per person include costs for covered dependents.
5. Authors' calculations based on unpublished Mercer proprietary data.

6. Figure 8-6 shows that in any year, 15 percent of the population can account for roughly 75 percent of health care spending. In this group are chronically ill people who account for substantial costs year after year. In most areas, individual insurance regulations allow private health insurers to underwrite and insure only the better risks. In such markets, people in poorer health are either unable to purchase coverage, or if they can, they do so at a very high price. Healthier people, on the other hand, are sometimes reluctant to share in the cost of care for the sicker population in a system of voluntary purchase. The combination of the risk distribution and use of underwriting has been a barrier to the development of a working private individual insurance market that serves the entire population well. An alternative to permitting underwriting is risk adjustment or mandatory risk-sharing so that payments to health care plans are redistributed on the basis of anticipated health care utilization and status of the covered population. Risk adjustment is used by Medicare and in some states for individual coverage, but experience is currently limited.

7. The Governmental Accounting Standards Board (GASB) has issued similar accounting standards (GASB Statement 45) for governmental employers that offer retiree health and other nonpension postemployment benefits (OPEB). The GASB 45 establishes accrual accounting and financial reporting requirements for OPEB, including a requirement to disclose unfunded OPEB obligations, that could lead to lower debt ratings for some governmental employers. The GASB 45 was phased in for large employers beginning December 2006; one year later for medium-sized employers; and two years later for small employers. A related standard (GASB 43) on financial reporting funded by OPEB plans takes effect one year earlier.

8. As an example of a monthly account, the plan could give each retiree $600 per month before Medicare eligibility and $200 per month after Medicare coverage begins. This amount could vary by years of service or be the same regardless of service. The amount could increase annually at a specific index (such as the CPI or a flat percentage); it could remain at the initial level; or it could be increased on an ad hoc basis. The amount not used could be carried over to future years, or the funds not used could be forfeited. An example of an aggregate or 'lump sum' approach is the commitment of an aggregate amount such as $20,000 (based, e.g. on $1,000 per year for 20 years of service or a flat $20,000 for all retirees) to be used over the life of the retiree to pay for health care premiums and/or expenses. A retiree would not receive funds from this account until health care expenses are actually incurred or premiums are paid. Prefunding would not be required, although the employer could prefund through some of the methods mentioned previously. Accounts could be credited with interest or not; the funds could be used on a draw-down basis as expenses are incurred, or the aggregate amount could be converted to a monthly payment amount similar to an annuity.

9. More detail on the calculation methods is available from the authors.

10. The Consolidated Omnibus Budget Reconciliation Act (COBRA) was passed in 1986, requiring employers with 20+ employees to allow those leaving service to continue medical coverage (if offered) by paying 102 percent of the cost for employee coverage (150 percent for those disabled).

11. The American Academy of Actuaries recently examined future policy issues for Medicare and they outlined some conditions needed to make buy-ins and focused on adequate participation and getting a reasonable spread of lives including healthy lives (American Academy of Actuaries 2005).

12. The Health Insurance Portability and Accountability Act (HIPAA) law passed in 1996 increases availability of health insurance to people with preexisting conditions if they have maintained continuous health care coverage.

13. In 1999, 66 percent of people aged 55–64 had employer-sponsored health coverage; 11 percent had public program coverage; 8 percent had individually purchased coverage; and 15 percent were uninsured; 77 percent of those employed and 48 percent of those not employed had employer coverage. Of those in the labor force, 13 percent were uninsured while 18 percent of those not in the labor force were uninsured. Three percent of those in the labor force and 24 percent of those not in the labor force were covered by public programs. Seven percent of those in the labor force and 10 percent of those not in the labor force had individually purchased coverage (NASI 2001).

14. The Medicare reform law shifts the majority of risk for MA plans and prescription drug plans to private-sector programs. The new law also encourages employers to share in the risk of offering prescription drug coverage in return for a tax-free subsidy. However, the details of risk shifting sometimes do not make it attractive to the private sector.

15. State regulations also shape benefit mandates, though self-insured employee benefit plans are exempt from state law under the federal Employee Retirement Income Security Act.

References

American Academy of Actuaries (2005). *Medicare: Next Steps*. American Academy of Actuaries. Issue Brief. Washington, DC: AAoA. February: 1–8.

Centers for Medicare and Medicaid Services (CMS) (2001). *An Overview of the United States Health Care System: Two Decades of Change, 1980–2000*. Washington, DC: CMS, p. 2. *http://www.cms.hhs.gov/charts/healthcaresystem/chapter1.pdf*

—— (2004). *Medicare and Medicaid Expenditures as Share of GDP*. Office of the Actuary, National Health Statistics Group *www.cms.hhs.gov/charts/series/sec1.ppt*

—— (2005*a*). *The 2005 Annual Report of the Boards of Trustees of the Federal Hospital Insurance and Federal Supplementary Medical Insurance Trust Funds*. Washington, DC: CMS: 3, 23, 115–116. *http://www.cms.hhs.gov/publications/trusteesreport/tr2005.pdf*

—— (2005*b*). *Medicare Managed Care Contract (MMCC) Plans—Monthly Summary Report*. Washington, DC. *http://www.cms.hhs.gov/healthplans/statistics/mmcc/default.asp*

—— (2005*c*). *National Health Accounts*. Washington, DC. http://*www.cms.hhs.gov/ statistics/nhe/default.asp#download*

Department of Health and Human Services (DHHS) (2005). *Medicare and You*. Washington, DC: USGPO. *www.medicare.gov/publications/pubs/pdf/10050.pdf*

Financial Accounting Standards Board (FASB) (1990). *Employers' Accounting for Post-Retirement Benefits Other Than Pensions*. Statement of Financial Accounting Standards Number 106 (FAS 106), Hartford, CT: FASB.

Fronstin, Paul and Dallas Salisbury (2003). *Retiree Benefits: Savings Needed to Fund Health Care in Retirement.* Washington, DC: *EBRI Issue Brief*, 254: 1–28.

Governmental Accounting Standards Board (GASB) (2004). *Accounting and Financial Reporting by Employers for Postemployment Benefits Other Than Pensions.* June 2004, Norwalk, CT.

Johnson, Richard W. and Rudolph G. Penner (2004). *Will Health Care Costs Erode Retirement Security?* Washington, DC: CRR Issues in Brief, 23: 1–10.

Mercer Human Resource Consulting (Mercer) (2004). *Mercer National Survey of Employer-Sponsored Health Plans.* Chicago, IL: Mercer.

National Academy of Social Insurance (NASI) (2001). *Health Insurance Coverage of People in the Ten Years Before Medicare Eligibility.* Washington, DC: NASI.

Organization for Economic Co-operation and Development (OECD) (2004). *Total expenditures on health, percent GDP. http://www.oecd.org/dataoecd/13/13/31963469.xls*

Simmons, Henry F. (2005). *Our Nation's Health Care Crisis: Solutions for Reform.* Washington, DC: National Coalition on Health Care. *http://www.nchc.org/materials/speeches/NCCMP.pdf*

United States Census Bureau (US Census) (2004). *Statistical Abstract of the United States: 2004–2005,* 124th edn. Washington, DC: USGPO, Table 139, p. 103.

—— (2005). *Interim Projections Consistent with Census 2000.* Washington, DC: USGPO. *http://www.census.gov/ipc/www/usinterimproj/natprojtab02a.xls*

United States Congressional Budget Office (USCBO) (2004). *A Detailed Description of CBO's Cost Estimate for the Medicare Prescription Drug Benefit.* Washington, DC: USGPO.

United States Department of Health and Human Services (USDHHS) (2005). 'Medicare & You', *http://www.medicare.gov/publications/pubs/pdf/10050.pdf*

United States Department of Labor, Bureau of Labor Statistics (USBLS) (2005). *Bureau of Labor Statistics Data.* Washington, DC: USGPO *http://www.bls.gov/data/home.htm*

Part III

New Strategies for Managing Retirement Risk

Chapter 9

Restructuring the Defined Benefit Pension

P. Brett Hammond and Douglas Fore

Funded defined benefit (DB) pension plans were a foundational pillar of US private and public retirement security in the twentieth century. Their appeal stemmed, in part, from the perspective that retirement promises should rely on pooling saving, risk, uncertainty, and costs, with assets and liabilities managed at the plan sponsor level. The appeal of company-sponsored DB plans also flowed from the belief that any problems associated with a pooled, centralized approach could be managed and controlled through sufficient regulation. Yet developments in the early twenty-first century have precipitated the traditional DB model into serious decline. Observers cite several reasons for this sea change, including higher worker mobility, the maturing of DB plans in older and highly competitive manufacturing sectors with few new entrants, workers' desire to control their own saving, high rates of labor mobility,[1] and the high costs of DB plan management, along with unexpectedly poor stock market performance and low interest rates (Borzi, this volume).

In our view, the root cause of the decline of the DB model is broader, since we argue that it is the unintended consequence of the risk-management mechanisms adopted to reduce risk, correct agency problems, and address pension administrative concerns. In this chapter, we offer a brief overview of the problems that are tying DB plans into knots, including principal–agent issues, regulation, accounting, and economic fallacies. Next, we outline steps that could be taken to help employers meet the goals and promises originally offered to workers in these plans. These include consideration of economics-based approaches to analyzing funding adequacies, changes in accounting rules, curtailing option and interest-rate arbitrage features, and strengthening the DB system insurer, among other measures. Finally, we turn to the task of creating a new DB structure attractive to employers, workers, and regulators alike—one that might offer a resilient model for the twenty-first century.

The DB Challenge: A Principal–Agent Problem

At the heart of the DB issue is a simple but seemingly intractable conflict arising from the so-called 'agency problem' in economics. This refers to the fact that multiple actors involved in providing, regulating, supervising, and paying out DB plans may come into conflict, such that their motivations and distinctions may become muddled, driving a wedge between pension participants and those acting on their behalf. This lack of transparency can lead to conflict, introduce new uncertainty, increase risk, and raise costs, even though the intent was quite the opposite. Such problems arise from conflicts between different sets of well-meaning controllers adopted by multiple agents who seek to protect the principals.

This conflict stems from a conflict of interest between the plan sponsor and the employees in a firm offering pension. The economic model of deferred compensation posits that workers will forgo current earnings if they are offered a future pension from the employer. In turn, the employer is responsible for making good on this promise, long into the future. A key problem is that once workers retire, they are of little use to the firm (except in convincing current workers that they will be 'taken care of' when they are old); this raises enforceability questions. Moreover, no one knows how current employer actions might affect the financial security of the sponsoring company and its retirees into the long-distant future. The result is that employers face mixed incentives to protect retirees.

This conundrum gives rise to a justification for pension regulation. Ostensibly, regulation is adopted to protect the covered employee; US examples include the Employee Retirement Income Security Act (ERISA), the establishment of the Pension Benefit Guaranty Corporation (PBGC), and related pension laws (Sass 1997). Nevertheless, the impact of regulation has at times undermined that protection. In particular, regulatory confusion and dysfunction has driven up pension costs due to fragmented and competing regulatory responsibilities, and prompted some plan termination. Many analysts agree that ERISA-compliance costs have had the unintended effect of causing employers to shift away from DB plans; in fact, Perun and Steuerle (2000) point out that one new and far-reaching legal requirement has been added to the Internal Revenue Service (IRS) code regulating pension plans each year since 1974, greatly raising compliance costs.[2]

The sudden increase in DB plan terminations for reversion in the early 1980s also had a major impact on the way DB plan risk was perceived and managed. Initially, DB plans terminated only when their parent firm filed for bankruptcy; in the early 1980s, however, a new tax policy permitted plan sponsors to terminate the plans under circumstances other than financial distress of the plan sponsor. This change introduced substantial new uncertainty into the long-term pension arrangement. Indeed, a wave of terminations was initiated by corporate takeovers, where the acquirer interested in an overfunded DB plan would unilaterally terminate the plan and run the surplus assets through the income statement. Often the acquirer would immediately create a new DB plan, making the process appear to be a straightforward violation of tax law, since plan sponsors are not permitted to appropriate assets from the plan. Nevertheless, the IRS allowed the transaction (Ippolito 2003). Not long thereafter, the Congress reacted by imposing a reversion tax which eventually reached a confiscatory 50 percent, sharply reducing corporate incentives to maintain excess assets in the plan. This episode also led to sponsors' efforts to substitute cash balance or DC plans in place of traditional DB plans.

These trends would logically have prompted workers still covered by a DB plan to lose faith that their remaining plans would survive. That is, it would be rational for workers to become leery of deferring further compensation unless it appeared to offer an extraordinary rate of return, particularly young workers likely to discount heavily the probability of accruing full pension rights in an unchanged plan. This would have also been true for longer-tenured workers caught up in the waves of downsizing and plan conversions of the past twenty years.

The cumulative effect of reversions, defunding, and conversions has eroded the trust that is the basis for deferred compensation—the basis for the DB pension contract. As a result, a kind of 'lemons market' has developed: many of the agents charged with protecting pension participants have faced increasingly conflictive incentives and mixed mandates. While this problem crept into the system over time, it took on much greater salience recently, given the coincidence of historically low interest rates and negative equity returns. These were compounded by problems in the government's pension insurance system, and changes in accounting rules. To these we turn next.

Problems in Pension Insurance

Regulatory efforts to control the most important risks faced by individuals and employers in the DB environment have often had counterproductive impacts, which ignore the underlying economics and further undermine the system. One striking manifestation of this problem concerns the national DB plan insurance program, the PBGC.

The PBGC was initially established under ERISA to protect workers with DB plans against employer pension defaults. Nonetheless, it is widely perceived today that the agency itself has become part of the problem: the aggregate funding deficit for private sector DB plans has been in the hundreds of billions of dollars for several years and it is expected to grow further (Credit Suisse First Boston 2005; Morgan Stanley 2003). As an involuntary unsecured creditor, the PBGC has swung from an asset–liability surplus of $7 billion in 2001 to a deficit of $23 billion in its reported 2004 results—a swing of $30 billion in just three years (PBGC 2004). In addition, the insurer reports exposure of $100 billion to firms rated below investment grade (BIG) by the rating agencies; the latter estimate total underfunding in the DB system to be $450 billion. Finally, the PBGC's deficit is expected to grow in the near term as a number of large plans concentrated in troubled legacy industries experiencing global competition are expected to have further plan terminations.

Many observers of the system do not believe that, under current law, the PBGC can return to surplus (CFFI 2004). Even the US Government Accountability Office (USGAO 2005) has concluded that current funding rules create a potentially large financial risk to the PBGC and consequently to retirement income security. Interestingly, the PBGC is not subject to the reserve and capital standards of the privately regulated insurance industry, which allows it to continue operating under conditions that would result in insolvency if the agency were a private insurer.

Several factors make it administratively difficult for the PBGC to oversee individual DB plans. One is that funding rules permitting plan sponsors to follow the 'letter of the law' while avoiding fully funding their plans. Another is the use of a current liability minimum funding standard that ignores significant changes in payout assumptions that are triggered if a plan terminates. Other factors include credits from past overfunding, waivers from required contributions, and the inability to enforce funding rules (see Chapter 11) leading to poor funding when plans are taken over by the PBGC.

Also important is the role of outdated information. By the time an underfunded terminated plan arrives at the PBGC, the plan's informational report filed with the government (the 5500 Form) is approximately two years old. In other words, firms can often report their plans as financially healthy on the Form 5500, but at termination shortly, they can be in much worse shape. For instance, Bethlehem Steel and United Airlines reported their plans as over 80 percent funded on an ongoing basis, but when they handed the terminated plans over to the PBGC, the plans has less than 50 percent of the assets required to cover promised benefits.

Another structural problem is that pension insurance premiums have been insufficient to pay for past losses and expected future claims; indeed, many have argued there should be closer links between premiums charged and the actuarially fair value of the insurance. Traditionally, premiums have not varied across firms despite widely varying expected risk of sponsor failure. A recent examination of the credit history of 27 of the largest PBGC claims found that none had been rated investment grade within 3 years of plan termination, and nearly 90 percent were rated below investment grade up to 10 years prior to plan termination. Recent proposals suggest raising premiums and adjusting future premiums according to the sponsor's credit rating (Warshawsky et al., this volume). Whether these are actuarially fair prices for PBGC insurance remains to be determined.

Accounting Regulation and Pension Valuation

Another manifestation of principal–agent problems in the DB pension arena is due to the complicated nexus of accounting rules. Appropriately, the theoretical goal in this area is to limit discretion, enhance transparency, and engender consistency for the benefit of shareholders, workers, managers, and regulators. In the DB context, the reality is that plans have very long time horizons, both with regard to the accumulation and to the payout phases. Employers sponsoring DB plans are responsible not only for providing sufficient cash flows to meet current service and interest contributions, but also obligations at far distant points in time. As a consequence, actuarial projections for funding purposes must be made over long time horizons involving such factors as future mortality experience and assumptions regarding asset returns.

The reality of pension accounting, however, is that the accounting rules themselves have been a source of DB dysfunction; both alone and in combination with other forms of regulation. Specifically, problems arise in conjunction with accounting rules that call for the use of single summary numbers for liabilities, assets, returns, and discount rates. This issue goes a long way to explaining why the equity share in pension portfolios has remained high over several decades, despite changes that should arguably have encouraged a shift to fixed income investment to better match changes in the liability structure (particularly demographic aging). These rules produced a situation where pension returns were decoupled from pension risks.

Liability Accounting. From 1986 through 2005, the prevailing US standard for pension accounting was the Financial Accounting Standards Board (FASB) rule known as SFAS 87, which embodied a smoothing methodology to dampen fluctuations in pension assets and liabilities from one year to the next. Under this rule, pension liabilities were treated as fixed-income instruments and discounted at a specified long-term interest rate. Many rules govern permissible actuarial assumptions when measuring a plan's accumulated liabilities; however, the discount rate used to measure plan liabilities never depended on the plan's actual demographic structure. Thus the rules insisted that the proper discount rate was invariant to expected cash flows actually payable by DB plan sponsors. For example, in the case of an old-line industrial firm with many workers nearing retirement age, the DB plan would face the prospect of having to pay out large sums to these workers as they began to retire in large numbers. Finance experts would have recommended that plan liabilities in this case be discounted with a yield curve of interest rates matching the timing of required cash flows (US Treasury Department 2005). Nevertheless, SFAS 87 required a single interest rate unrelated to the place on the yield curve that a plan sponsor might need to discount benefit payments using finance methodology.

When assessing changes in liabilities, SFAS 87 also required the use of a standardized measurement approach including the projected unit credit method (PUC), the accumulated benefit obligation (ABO), and the projected benefit obligation (PBO).[3] The main problem with this approach is that it produces deterministic values to set the pension obligation, depending on the regulatory goal. However, in addition to the many technical choices that can limit measurement reliability, none of these measures envisions variability of liabilities. In other words, choosing any of these numbers is like buying a bond without knowing its duration. Just as a bond's duration affects its behavior (and hence its price), so too can the duration of the liabilities affect behavior and valuation.

In 2003, the FASB released Exposure Draft Statement 132, which included draft requirements helpful in formulating duration-like assessments of a firm's liability structure and the magnitude of cash flows payable over time. These and other duration-related disclosures could help those seeking to conduct sensitivity analysis and test key assumptions about the firm's asset management strategies and stress-test the firm's liability immunization strategy. Unfortunately, FASB rejected these potentially helpful requirements.

Asset Accounting. Similar concerns may be raised regarding asset accounting: thus under previous versions of SFAS 87 and 132 (in effect from 1986 to 2003), a single rate of return assumption was used for accounting for plan assets, and returns were smoothed over a period of years. This had the very powerful effect of making actual volatility virtually unrelated to the rate of return assumption selected by the plan sponsor. Further, during that period, plan sponsors were not required to disclose volatility assumptions for asset returns. As a result, the accounting rules embedded a strong proequity bias; some argue that pension assets were managed with such a 'tilt' that it appeared as if they had a beta of zero in financial terms (Gold 2001).

Instead of requiring disclosure of the expected rate of return by individual asset category, the revised SFAS 132 requires only a narrative description of the investment strategies employed by the DB plans and the basis used to determine the overall expected rate of return. The FASB did require that the disclosure explain the general approach taken, which data were used in forming the long-term rate of return assumption, or whether or not adjustments were made to historical data. These disclosures still allow assumptions to vary significantly from one plan sponsor to the next. Also, anticipated returns can be booked on the income statement today, but the risks can be smoothed on the balance sheet over a period of several years (Gold 2001). This has led some plans to raise anticipated return assumptions and further boost the share of the portfolio devoted to equities. Such behavior may be reinforced by internal company dynamics that provide incentives for a CFO to avoid reallocating out of equities (Fore 2005). In the post-2000 period, as the equity bubble burst and analysts undertook more detailed examinations of balance sheets (Coronado and Sharpe 2003), this smoothing strategy was recognized as problematic. In particular, the smoothing strategy was found to have a built-in negative reinforcement mechanism, so that DB plans which appeared comfortably overfunded in 1999, became dramatically underfunded by 2002. These continue to be underfunded in 2005, and they now face the prospect of many years of deficit-reduction contributions.

The principal–agent problem for DB pensions has resulted in a less-than-full embrace of some key economic and statistical lessons that, when ignored, can lead to some of the pathologies outlined earlier. The most important of these is the inability of pension regulation to promote or even acknowledge the benefit of dynamic, stochastic, and shortfall analysis rather than deterministic and point estimates. The effect is to create incentives for companies and regulators alike to ignore factors that can severely undermine the DB pension and have led to the tenuous situation it is in today.

Prospects for Reform

Next we evaluate whether some relatively simple regulatory and legislative changes could enhance the DB plan regulatory environment, so as to prevent further erosion of DB plans to improve future funding. Our analysis of potential remedies appears in Table 9-1, which arrays these along two

TABLE 9-1 Opportunities for Pension Reform

	Easy	*Difficult*
Incremental	Credits	Discount rates
		Remove pension call option
Reform	Exp. rate of return on plan assets	Reversion tax reform
	Form 5500 timing/ transparency	
Fundamental reform	Interest rate arbitrage	Smoothing new income statement
		Fair market valuation of assets and liabilities
		Agree on transition period to new paradigm

Source. Authors' elaboration.

dimensions: the degree of reform proposed (from incremental to fundamental) and the ease of realizing the reform (from 'easy' to 'difficult').
Many of these reforms would be true improvements, in our view.

The DB pension problem has attracted comparisons to the US savings
and loan debacle of the late 1980s, although the scale of pension write-
downs is unlikely to be as large in real terms. Under the *status quo*, the
reality is that DB pension beneficiaries will suffer in the form of reduced
benefit checks. Going forward, different options would address the pension funding gap through regulatory reorientation; for instance, measures
might involve adopting economic and statistical methods to valuing pension funding, boosting PBGC premiums, restricting lump-sum payments,
better capitalizing the PBGC, and reforming its premium structure. As we
shall show, some of these measures would have long-term impacts, while
others would have more immediate effects. Whether these would be sufficient to save the DB pension system is not clear.

Insights from Financial Economics. To better understand the pension
funding problem, the first step would be to properly value a DB plan's
liabilities, by treating them as future cash flows. That is, the financial view of
a DB plan's liability is the expected present value of all cash flows the plan
commits to pay, inclusive of benefits associated with past and future service
of current and future employees, accrued to their expected retirement
dates. Furthermore, these cash flows would be discounted using a rate
consistent with the market-related risk of the liabilities, rather than the
more traditional expected return on the assets used to defease them.

A financial assessment of actual DB plan liabilities would view the liabilities as representing a bundle of exposures to various market risk factors,
plus an idiosyncratic stochastic risk term unrelated to market factors (Scott
2002). Accordingly, the appropriate discount rates would be based on a
permanent set of standard 'benchmark' securities matched to the date on
the yield curve of the cash flows payable.[4] A financial economics perspective would also propose more transparency in measuring DB plan assets.
Currently, DB plan assets must be (mostly) marked to market as of the
plan's reporting date, but Form 5500 documents still allow substantial time
lags.[5] Further, DB plans are permitted to 'smooth' the value of their assets
over several years. The financial economics approach would prefer frequent market-updating of asset values, and little or no smoothing.

Adopting a financial economics perspective would likely prompt the
adoption of many new tools in the DB environment. These could include
dynamic asset allocation, shortfall risk, stochastic valuation, and the use of
nontraditional financial instruments (such as inflation bonds and options).
Dynamic asset allocation involves a class of models introduced to alleviate
the funding and opacity problems traditionally associated with DB pensions
(Guillen et al. 2004). The approach has been used in Denmark, where

returns-smoothing functions solely as an accounting device, and the pension contract, in finance terms, is modeled as a path-dependent contingent claim combining elements of both DB plans and DC plans. Recently, dynamic portfolio optimization models of asset–liability management have been proposed which incorporate options to minimize the probability of funding shortfalls. Results by Boender et al. (1997) suggest that pension funds can achieve significant risk-neutral reductions in contribution rates by implementing a liability-driven path-dependent put strategy. Nevertheless, few US DB plan sponsors or consultants have used this tactic as yet.

The use of shortfall risk (cf. Leibowitz et al. 1994) and stochastic models (Boulier et al. 1995; Haberman and Owadally 2001) for analyzing and managing DB pensions are well known but not particularly widely adopted. One interesting fact is that stochastic control models imply nonlinear contribution rates and asset allocation patterns. Thus when a plan's funding ratio is low, contributions should be maximized and the asset allocation tilted in favor of riskier assets. As the funding ratio improves, the models predict that contribution rates and the allocation to risky assets be dialed back. Finally, if the plan's funding ratio exceeds 100 percent, contributions can be suspended and gains locked in.

Perhaps the central insight offered by stochastic control models is that spreading volatile gains and losses over shorter periods and recognizing them faster leads to better funding (Dufresne 1989; Haberman and Owadally 2001). Contribution rate stability and fund security cannot be traded off over longer spreading periods. Further, these models imply that there may be a minimum funding level (higher than some may suspect), below which the plans cannot return to stable equilibrium.[6] One limitation to implementing stochastic models has to do with 'transition effects'—that is, a sponsor adopting this approach might face substantial up-front costs. For example, the expected present value of benefits using the stochastic framework can rise by one-third, as compared to traditional valuation methods (Sherris 1995).[7]

Along with better statistical tools for pension valuation, moving to a financial economics-based perspective on DB pensions could also spur investments in new assets. Most retirees default into joint and survivor annuities, so that plan sponsors and asset managers must begin thinking about how to design an immunization strategy matched against both nominal wage growth and beneficiary demographics.[8] Currently, no sovereign or high-grade private entity issues securities that match expected wage trajectories of employees in a corporate or public sector DB plan. Accordingly, Bodie (1995) has championed inflation-indexed treasury bonds, arguing that these can be an essential component of the DB plan portfolio. Of course if this asset were to constitute the entire DB plan portfolio, it would imply high contribution rates and lower earnings for the plan sponsor.

Improving Accounting Rules. Earlier we have argued that the fundamental principal–agent problem facing DB plans has been exacerbated by accounting rules. Accordingly, several specific accounting changes could help promote fairer valuation and immunization, while helping US and international accounting standards converge. They would also curtail sponsors' opportunities to smooth/arbitrage pension assets and liabilities, and take advantage of the pension 'call option'.

The ultimate arbiter of accounting practice in the USA is the Securities and Exchange Commission (SEC). This entity could, for instance, announce that it would not allow the filing of financial statements with pension assumptions that allow for arbitraging of assets and liabilities. This would put a stop to cases such as at General Motors, where debt was issued to the DB plan, but simultaneously a higher rate of return was reported on plan assets.

Accounting standards could also be revised to prohibit credits from past asset returns as a means of cutting current contributions, unless the plan sponsor could demonstrate to a fiduciary that the credits represented real assets. Indeed, the use of such credits is not currently seen with favor by regulators (US Department of Treasury 2005). In addition, plan funding could be treated in a more symmetrical fashion so that asset gains would not automatically reduce the need for contributions, nor would asset losses produce reversions or terminations. This would remove the firm's pension plan 'call option' while reconsidering the IRS rule on reversion taxes. The intended consequence would be to place full responsibility for the current plan firmly on the firm's shoulders.[9] In addition, if the call option could be removed and the reversion tax problem solved, convergence could perhaps lead to the Dutch approach to plan funding. In the Netherlands, DB plans typically target funding levels between 115 and 135 percent of full funding; as a consequence, there is no widespread DB funding problem in that country. In our view, the most urgent change in accounting rules would be to move to fair valuation of pensions. This trend is well under way in Europe, launched by the UK Accounting Standards Board (ASB) issuance of Financial Reporting Standard (FRS) 17 in the year 2000. In a nutshell, this approach moves toward the use of market prices to value assets and liabilities, in lieu of smoothing techniques. It should be noted that adopting of fair value accounting forced sponsors to recognize the stochastic nature of asset returns; that is, plan sponsors could no longer act as if returns and risks were unrelated. To put it another way, plan sponsors could no longer assume that equities had a financial beta of zero, and pension gains and losses had to be immediately recognized. (By contrast, in the USA, plan asset values can still be smoothed over a period of up to five years.)[10] Some argue that this introduces excessive volatility into sponsors' financial statements, and that it has made accounting regulations drive economic and financial decision-making. In response, the UK ASB noted that recognizing year-to-year fluctuations in asset values in the financial statements was similar to recognizing revaluation gains and losses on fixed corporate assets (ASB 2000: 71).

In addition to fair valuation, convergence of other pension accounting rules in the international context would also be beneficial. For instance, the US FASB has promised to the International Accounting Standards Board (IASB) that it will work on convergence for retirement plan benefit accounting. This project has proposed that actuarial gains and losses must be recognized immediately, outside the income statement, in a statement of total recognized income and expenses, and also included immediately in retained earnings. In addition, indexation agreements and future salary increases must now be taken into account when valuing liabilities (IAS 2004); plan sponsors and fund managers must also describe the assumptions and logic used to determine the overall expected rate of return on assets as well as the expected rate of return for each major asset class.

Proponents of these new standards believe that moving to the more transparent world of fair value accounting, and away from actuarial smoothing of gains and losses, will prevent periodic funding crises by highlighting small problems before they can grow into large problems. Opponents of the new standards argue, conversely, that introducing fair value accounting into a system of long-dated commitments introduces excessive volatility for too little gain. Clearly an immediate move to fair value accounting standards in the USA would have serious consequences, given the large number of underfunded plans. On the other hand, having the data to obtain a clear reading of troubled firms' financial situation would make clear that many intend to terminate their plans in the near future.

Closing the Funding Gap.   Restoring solvency to the DB system requires closing the PBGC's funding gap. One approach would boost premiums paid by insured firms. One proposal would raise premiums by more than half, index them to the growth in nominal earnings, and charge an additional premium to firms rated BIG (McCall et al., this volume). This approach would also give the PBGC's Board, composed of the cabinet secretaries from the departments of Commerce, Labor and Treasury, the authority to adjust premiums in the future so that the PBGC could charge actuarially fair prices for its insurance. This would be a revolutionary development for the PBGC because it would significantly improve the odds that future premium revenue could cover future expected losses.

Yet even if this occurs, it would not solve the so-called 'legacy costs' driving a wedge between PBGC assets and liabilities. These are attributable, in part, to the fact that Bethlehem Steel, United Airlines, and many other plan sponsors never paid for the full value of the pension insurance they received and 'put' to the PBGC. Of course boosting premiums on healthy

plan sponsors to cover past losses would likely produce more plan terminations and, in the extreme, a collapse of the DB system. The reality, of
course, is that the PBGC is an undercapitalized insurance company with a
single line of business; its revenues consist of writing naked put options.
Reforms that would raise revenues in the same manner as previously does
not change the business model. Rather, the PBGC needs a new approach to
raising capital and bringing in new revenue. Another option might be to
'socialize' the PBGC's past losses, by raising taxes on the current taxpayers,
or passing costs onto future generations by selling bonds. These choices
may not appeal to taxpayers who view with alarm increasing federal deficits
and social security shortfalls.

Reinventing the DB Plan

Up to this point, we have argued that critiques of the DB pension fall prey
to two problems. One is conceptual: well-meaning policymakers have too
often proposed piecemeal changes in the DB system, without taking the big
picture into account. The second problem is practical: while solutions may
be available, they are often expensive. For instance, financial economics
suggests that employers hold more fixed income in their DB portfolios and
contribute more. Reforms might also decouple the pension from the
income statement and balance sheet, which regulators might find difficult.
And reform might require an infusion of cash to capitalize the PBGC,
which again will be expensive. The odds against a comeback of traditional
DB plans are very long indeed.

Accordingly, in this section, we ask whether individuals, households and
employers might find appealing a new class of DB plan, one which would
hold onto the essential elements of DB retirement programs, while moving
away from other aspects. To make headway, we posit that the main goal of a
DB pension is to be a consumption-smoothing device,[11] and we turn to the
consumption-based asset pricing literature (Cochrane 2005) to show that
forward-thinking individuals will seek assets that pay off well when times are
bad and hence most needed.[12]

Let us next consider the position of an individual DB plan participant.
The younger employee, recently vested in the plan, has accrued only a
small future benefit; as he is likely to exit the firm and the plan for
employment elsewhere, the DB promise is akin to BIG bonds in default.
In other words, the young employee will eventually receive, at retirement, a
small benefit comparable to a defaulted bond paying in recovery settlement cents on the dollar. By contrast, the older and longer-tenured employee intending to remain with the firm until retirement has a DB promise
akin to an investment-grade corporate bond; he is likely to receive the full
face value of the bond in retirement, but there remains some chance of a
default (due either to employee or employer actions). Only at retirement

will the full-career employee value the DB promise as akin to Treasury bonds, as long as the plan is fully funded (and abstracting from PBGC insurance ceilings and other problems).

The question, then, is how one might replicate the DB pension from the point of view of the participant. One way would be to replicate the 'pseudo portfolio' held by the participant with fixed-income instruments having the same characteristics as the plan accrual pattern, embodying its separation rates and eventual benefit levels. Rather than doing this with bonds directly, we propose treating the promises as a series of credit option derivatives, one for each year of potential employment. In the worker's first year, the probability of leaving employment would set the option value or price, other elements of the design being equal. The second year's pension option value would be similar, except that it would be conditional on remaining employed after the first year and the probability of leaving employment might change. Each succeeding year would follow in like fashion. This would be akin to a life insurance product where the payout is unknown (the convexity of the benefit structure over time would also be a factor).

A related approach would be consistent with Valdés-Prieto's proposal (this volume) to have companies (or governments) offer securitized Covered Wage Bill (CWB) bonds. He argues that in particular CWB bonds would be good inflation hedges, as the wage bill should be highly correlated with inflation at least in the medium term. He further argues for the place of CWB bonds in a pension portfolio as a means to match the participants' human capital. Another technique would replicate the portfolio by investing in a riskless asset and then in a second portfolio consisting of risky assets; portfolio shares would vary within specified bands.

Toward a Portable DB Pension. One commonly cited drawback to DB plans is the fact that workers lack portability. In most cases DB plans evolved as distinct entities because sponsoring firms offered benefit features suited to their business and to their workforces; sometimes sponsors negotiated benefits with unions; and early retirement subsidies were used to influence the age distribution of the staff at some firms. Plans differ in their retirement ages, generosity factors, special disability rules, and funding, all of which tend to make DB promises nonportable.

Yet lack of portability is not a necessary element of DB plans: for instance, Blake (2000) notes that in the Netherlands DB plans are portable because all plans share critical common features, including the use of the same actuarial assumptions to value liabilities and accrued benefits. This means that workers can transfer service credits when changing jobs and pension plans. In our view, several plan design features would benefit from standardization, which would in turn foster portability, lower regulatory needs, and cut compliance costs. Specifically, actuarial assumptions would be made uniform across plans, as well as a common benefit accrual formula. Of course any particular benefit accrual rate could be set, though a relatively low accrual rate could be more attractive since the plan becomes more expensive to fund as the accrual rate rises. At the same time a plan design where participants could purchase additional years of service credits would presumably be a desirable feature. This is a not-uncommon feature of state and local government DB plans, and is reportedly popular with plan participants. Of course, as the accrual rate is ratcheted up, it would become progressively more difficult for individuals to buy service credits. Conversely, if the accrual rate were set too low, plan participants would only receive adequate incomes in retirement if they purchased additional credits. From a practical viewpoint, the only early retirement feature of the plan would be to permit purchase of additional service credits, to maintain actuarial and labor market neutrality.

In this type of portable DB plan, two workers having similar earnings trajectories over their careers but different numbers of jobs would arrive at retirement with identical retirement benefits. By contrast, in a traditional DB plan, at retirement, job changers have much reduced benefits. A portable DB plan therefore resembles the US social security system (abstracting from social security's spousal benefit and disability features; disability insurance could be covered under separate insurance arrangements and the plan could be neutral with regard to family status).

Standardizing assumptions generates a standardized DB plan, portable across firms, industries, and occupations. If assumptions were suitably standardized, different workers earning similar annual amounts participating in this plan with different employers (plan sponsors) would originate similar liabilities in the plan and accrue the right to similar benefits from the plan. If they were to terminate employment for whatever reason, their accrued benefits would stay the same, as would the flow of liabilities their participation in the plan had caused. It would also be necessary to standardize mortality assumptions. A standard population table with cohort adjustments for expected improvements in longevity would likely be the appropriate choice. Standardization of actuarial assumptions might not necessarily extend to the full annuitization period, if some plan sponsors wanted to offer pure life annuities while others would offer participating provisions. One option would be to target a standard floor or base benefit which could then be enhanced by plan sponsors as they saw fit.

While asset allocation patterns could be standardized via regulation, a better approach might be to anticipate that reformed accounting rules would produce certain common practice along with a healthy respect for duration with regard to plan liabilities. An asset allocation approach we find interesting would have an accumulation structure with two pillars. One pillar would provide a guaranteed rate of return to participants plus the possibility of additional accumulations, and while the second pillar would offer risky returns with no guarantee. The portion of the portfolio containing the riskless asset would have a variety of restrictions concerning the investments that could be held, ensuring that the guaranteed rate of return could be met or surpassed, and that other desirable features such as immunization could be followed as investment strategy. The portfolio share containing the risky asset would function as a percentage of the overall DB plan and would be invested in equities. Each year, the plan sponsor would be expected to contribute an amount equal to the plan service cost in a predetermined ratio to the guaranteed asset percentage of the plan and the risky asset percentage of the plan. These ratios could change over time as a result of market performance, as could plan contributions.

Possible Critiques. A potential criticism of the portable DB idea is that benefit portability implies much higher eventual benefit payouts and consequently much higher total plan liabilities. This, in turn, could imply an unacceptably high plan sponsor contribution rate. There are several ways to respond to such a criticism. First, benefit levels and plan liabilities can be adjusted by offering a lower accrual rate. Second, young workers who turn over subsidize higher-paid longer-tenure employees in the traditional DB plan. It is difficult to justify this if policymakers are concerned about security for all retirees. Third, it may be possible to reduce costs by using better asset-management and asset–liability matching models.[13] Finally, this portable DB plan would be expected to have much lower regulatory and compliance costs compared to traditional DB plans. Separate portable DB plans for different groups could be sponsored by professional associations, unions, insurance companies, or other financial services companies.[14]

Conclusion

The traditional DB plan suffers from many problems, including well-intended but misguided disciplinary and regulatory regimes. Here we argue that a stochastic, more financially based approach to asset/liability matching would enable DB plan sponsors to improve their ability to consider expected risks in both liabilities and asset returns. Incentives can be instituted to make plan funding more robust to changes in asset returns and other vital economic and financial variables. With this, governments will be asked to provide increased support for the needs of the pension community. That is why we propose a new approach to the DB plan, an approach preferable to piecemeal reform. It is a portable DB pension plan, most likely to appeal to firms seeking to attract younger and more mobile workers concerned with lifelong retirement security. It combines the best of what DB and DC plans have to offer and in so doing, incorporates the key roles of pensions in retirement security. We anticipate that this model can prove practical and attractive to interest a wide range of sponsors.

Endnotes

1. The decline of job tenure and the apparent changing nature of the employee–employer relationship partly explains the shift away from DB pensions, since securing long job tenure is less valuable than previously. There is little evidence that employers offering DC plans value long-tenured employees (Friedberg and Owyang 2004).
2. Of course, an additional consequence of ERISA and related regulations might be a loss of innovation potential by the various actors involved in DB plan design and management, as they have become increasingly bound in a regulatory and compliance straitjacket.
3. Details and uses of these measures are widely known, as are specific issues with each; see McGill et al. (2004).
4. Financially appropriate yield curve discounting raises plan liabilities for mature plans with a large fraction of annuitants, as compared to current actuarial practice. Yield curve discounting could also improve incentives for pension immunization.
5. Along these lines it should be noted that private equity poses a particular valuation problem, as it typically has a 7–10-year time horizon over which it is not marked to market. Private equity is a rising share of pension plan portfolios.
6. Other uses of stochastic control include modeling the option value of early retirement benefits (Chen 2002), and a spread method of funding assuming changes in plan liabilities are random (Josa-Fombellida and Rincon-Zapatero 2004).
7. A stochastic differential equation seems to improve the accuracy of such accruals, but at a current cost for the sponsor (Bacinello 2000). Similarly, using a partial differential equation, Taylor (2002) shows that a funding or solvency level below 80 percent represented an unstable equilibrium, and funding tends to fall even further.
8. At the individual level, workers who invest their annual retirement contributions in a series of five-year insured products, perhaps based on inflation bonds, could have a higher probability of meeting their retirement income targets than if they were to invest the same amount in the S&P 500 index (Bodie and Crane 1999). A participant would buy a series of these during the accumulation phase, and these retirement income contracts could guarantee a monthly income for life in retirement. In theory, these contracts could be designed to provide the best features of both DC and DB plans, but in practice their transaction costs might make them less attractive.
9. To avoid unintended consequences, however, such policies might require FASB movement and action on a statement of comprehensive income so that firms also face incentives to preserve pension over funding when asset totals are larger than anticipated (i.e. so there will be assets held in a kind of reserve for when returns are lower than anticipated). We are aware that FASB action on a new income statement is a major reform and no simple task.

10. Fair valuation of liabilities represents a challenge because of the pattern of salary increases and recognition that the 'true' liability horizon is a worker's life expectancy. Acknowledging the lack of an active market in long pension liabilities, the UK ASB considered alternative actuarial methods to unlink the discount rate on liabilities from the expected return on plan assets. These included the use of inflation bonds as the liability benchmark or a weighted portfolio of equities and bonds. In the end, the ASB settled on a single discount rate, the AA corporate bond, noting that part of the rationale for this decision was to bring about convergence in standards.

11. The traditional DB pension also fulfilled labor market objectives such as encouraging employee loyalty in firms where the development and retention of firm-specific human capital was a valuable management objective; these are usually thought of as secondary objectives in the USA.

12. Most 401(k) plans do not do a good job of smoothing lifetime consumption for their participants. For instance, 401(k) plans tend not to provide financial planning guidance nor payout annuities, though most offer a wide menu of investment fund choices, especially in the equity area.

13. Alternative asset allocation models could be constructed using contingent-claims pricing techniques to replicate the benefit accrual paths of a standardized, portable DB plan. The plan could be modeled using contingent-claims techniques where the payoff function is a discrete event with a known maturity date. For a large enough pool of participants, path-dependence in the contingent claim can be handled via a sufficiently conservative investment strategy. Termination from the plan can be expressed as a surrender option. In practice, individuals will exit the plan due to death, disability, and withdrawal. Practical actuarial work realizes this and constructs what are called multiple decrement tables to model survival rates. Decrement models exist to handle mortality rates at various ages, disability rates, and turnover; they also vary according to how they model key variables.

14. Alternatively, such plans could be organized along loose lines of affiliation, such as wage earners versus salary earners; the main supplemental public pension schemes in France are structured in this way.

References

Bacinello, Anna Rita (2000). 'Valuation of Contingent-Claims Characterising Particular Pension Schemes', *Insurance: Mathematics and Economics*, 27: 177–88.

Bader, Lawrence N. and Jeremy Gold (2003). 'Reinventing Pension Actuarial Science', Society of Actuaries, *The Pension Forum*, 14(2): 1–13.

Blake, David (2000). 'Two Decades of Pension Reform in the UK: What Are the Implications for Occupational Pension Schemes', *The Pensions Institute: Discussion Paper PI-0004*.

Bodie, Zvi (1995). 'On the Risks of Stocks in the Long Run', *Financial Analysts Journal*, 51(3): 18–22.

—— and Dwight B. Crane (1999). 'The Design and Production of New Retirement Savings Products', *Journal of Portfolio Management*, 25(2): 77–82.

Boender, Guss, Bart Oldenkamp, and Martijn Vos (1997). 'Solvency Insurance with Optioned Portfolios: An Empirical Investigation', in W. T. Ziemba and

J. M. Mulvey (eds.), *World Wide Asset and Liability Modeling*. Cambridge: Cambridge University Press, pp. 167–77.

Borzi, Phyllis C. (2006). 'Changing Risks Confronting Pension Participants', this volume.

Boulier, Jean Francois, Etienne Florens, and Daniele Trussant (1995). 'A Dynamic Model for Pension Funds Management', *Proceedings of the 5th AFIR International Colloquium*, 1: 361–84.

—— Stephane Michel, and Vanessa Wisnia (1996). 'Optimizing Investment and Contribution Policies of a Defined Benefit Pension Fund', *Proceedings of the 6th AFIR International Colloquium*, 1: 593–607.

Cairns, Andrew J. G. (1997). 'A Comparison of Optimal and Dynamic Control Strategies for Continuous-Time Pension Fund Models', *Proceedings of the 7th AFIR International Colloquium*, 1: 309–26.

Center on Federal Financial Institutions (CFFI) (2004). *PBGC: When Will the Cash Run Out?* Washington, DC: CFFI, September 13.

Chen, Hui (2002). 'Valuation of Defined Benefit Plans Using a Two-Factor Stochastic Term Structure Model', University of Michigan Working Paper.

Cochrane, John H. (2005). 'Financial Markets and the Real Economy', NBER Working Paper No. 11193, March.

Coronado, Julia Lynn, and Steven A. Sharpe (2003). 'Did Pension Plan Accounting Contribute to a Stock Market Bubble?' *Brookings Papers on Economic Activity*, 1: 323–71.

Credit Suisse First Boston (2005). *The Magic of Pension Accounting, Part III*. Credit Suisse Americas/United States Accounting & Tax Group, February 4.

Dufresne, D. (1989). 'Stability of Pension Systems when Rates of Return are Random', *Insurance: Mathematics and Economics*, 8: 71–6.

Fore, Douglas (2005). 'Changes in Accounting Practices Will Drive Pension Paradigm Shift', in Robert L. Clark and Olivia S. Mitchell (eds.), *Reinventing the Retirement Paradigm*. Oxford: Oxford University Press, pp. 173–87.

Friedberg, Leora and Michael Owyang (2004). 'Explaining the Evolution of Pension Structure and Job Tenure', NBER Working Paper 10714, August.

Gold, Jeremy (2001). 'Accounting/Actuarial Bias Enables Equity Investment by Defined Benefit Pension Plans', Pension Research Council Working Paper 2001–5, The Wharton School.

Guillen, Monsterrat, Peter Lochte Jorgensen, and Jens Perch Nielsen (2004). 'Return Smoothing Mechanisms in Life and Pension Insurance: Path-Dependent Contingent Claims', Autonomous University of Barcelona Working Paper, September.

Haberman, Steven and Iqbal Owadally (2001). 'Modelling Defined Benefit Pension Schemes: Funding and Asset Valuation', Paper presented at the International Actuarial Association, International Pensions Seminar, June.

Ippolito, Richard (2003). 'Tenuous Property Rights: The Unraveling of Defined Benefit Pension Contracts in the United States', in Onorato Castellino and Elsa Fornero (eds.), *Pension Policy in an Integrated Europe*. Cheltenham, UK: Edward Elgar, pp. 175–97.

Jennings, William W. and William Reichenstein (2003). 'Valuing Defined-Benefit Plans', *Financial Services Review*, 12(3): 179–99.

Josa-Fombellida, Ricardo and JuanPablo Rincon-Zapatero (2004). 'Optimal Risk Management in Defined Benefit Stochastic Pension Funds', *Insurance: Mathematics and Economics*, 34: 489–503.

Leibowitz, Martin L., Stanley Kogelman, and Lawrence N. Bader (1994). 'Funding Ratio Return', *Journal of Portfolio Management*, 21(1): 39–47.

McGill, Dan M., Kyle N. Brown, John J. Haley, and Sylvester J. Schieber (2004). *Fundamentals of Private Pensions*, 8th edn. The Pension Research Council of the Wharton School of the University of Pennsylvania. Philadelphia, PA: University of Pennsylvania Press.

Morgan Stanley (2003). *Yawn or Yell on Pensions: An Update*. Morgan Stanley Global Valuation and Accounting Group, July 8.

Neuberger, Anthony and David McCarthy (2006). 'The UK Approach to Insuring Defined Benefit Pension Plans', this volume.

Panis, Constantijn (2004). 'Annuities and Retirement Well-Being', in Olivia S. Mitchell and Stephen P. Utkus (eds.), *Pension Design and Structure*. Oxford: Oxford University Press, pp. 259–74.

Perold, Andre F. and Jay O. Light (1985). 'Risk Sharing and Corporate Pension Policy', Paper presented at the Meeting of the American Finance Associates, December.

Perun, Pamela and C. Eugene Steuerle (2000). 'ERISA at 50: A New Model for the Private Pension System', Urban Institute, Occasional Paper, 4: 1–21.

Rauh, Joshua (2005). 'Investment and Financing Constraints: Evidence from the Funding of Corporate Pension Plans', Paper presented at the 2005 AFA Meetings in Philadelphia.

Ryan, Ronald J. and Frank J. Fabozzi (2002). 'Rethinking Pension Liabilities and Asset Allocation', *Journal of Portfolio Management*, Summer: 1–9.

Sass, Steven A. (1997). *The Promise of Private Pensions: The First Hundred Years*. Cambridge: Harvard University Press.

Scott, Jason (2002). 'Outcomes-Based Investing with Efficient Monte Carlo Simulation', in Olivia S. Mitchell, Zvi Bodie, P. Brett Hammond and Stephen Zeldes (eds.), *Innovations in Retirement Financing*. Philadelphia, PA: University of Pennsylvania Press, pp. 132–45.

Sherris, Michael (1995). 'The Valuation of Option Features in Retirement Benefits', *The Journal of Risk and Insurance*, 62(3): 509–35.

Taylor, Greg (2002). 'Stochastic Control of Funding Systems', *Insurance: Mathematics and Economics*, 30(3): 323–50.

US Department of the Treasury (2005). *Testimony of Assistant Secretary Mark Warshawsky before Congress*, March.

US Government Accountability Office (USGAO) (2005). *Private Pensions: Recent Experiences of Large Defined Benefit Plans Illustrate Weaknesses in Funding Rules*. Final Report. Washington, DC: US GAO, May.

Valdés-Prieto, Salvador (2006). 'Market-Based Social Security as a Better Means of Risk-Sharing', this volume.

Warshawsky, Mark, Neal McCall, and John D. Worth (2006). 'Regulating Single Employer Defined Benefit Pension Plans: A Modern Approach', this volume.

Chapter 10

Dimensions of 401(k) Plan Design

Olivia S. Mitchell, Stephen P. Utkus, and Tongxuan (Stella) Yang

Defined contribution (DC) plans today are at the core of the US retirement system, with over 60 million employees holding $2.4 trillion in DC plan assets.[1] The number of DC plan participants has also grown rapidly in the past two decades, at almost double the rate of labor force increase. Today it is estimated that employer-sponsored DC plans will provide larger retirement benefits than social security for the Baby Boom generation (Poterba et al. 2004). Prior research has explored how DC plan features shape employee saving behavior, particularly in the case of the popular 401(k) plan.[2] By contrast, in the present chapter, we focus on the question of how and why employers select their plan design features.

Our analysis seeks to evaluate various rationales provided to explain 401(k) plan design features. Some contend that employers utilize such plans to shape workforce characteristics—such as age, tenure, or even the male–female mix. Others argue that 401(k) plans are mainly a way to tax-defer compensation, albeit under complex rules. To highlight the relevant issues, we examine a rich new data-set of several hundred 401(k) plans covering more than 740,000 employees, containing unique detail on plan design features, workforce characteristics, and industry sectors. We are able to model employer matching contributions with exceptional precision, and we also incorporate important nonmonetary design features including the plan investment menu and the presence of loans which we argue reflect liquidity and investment constraints inherent in 401(k) plans.

We show that promised 401(k) matches vary from 0 to more than 6 percent of pay, and that the median employer *promises* a match equivalent to 3 percent of pay. We evaluate the factors which explain the wide variation in promised matches, acknowledging that this variation may be driven in part by the value assigned to compensation paid in the form of matching contributions, presumably influenced by workers' marginal propensity to save and marginal tax rates. As well, employers may intentionally direct a portion of their compensation budgets toward (or away from) workers with particular age, tenure, or other characteristics. The latter view has found support in prior research which shows that employee utilization of 401(k) plans is linked to workers' age, tenure, sex, and income levels. Our evidence shows that these plans appear to mainly be tax motivated, constrained by federal nondiscrimination rules. In other words, to appeal to better-paid workers, employers offer more generous monetary and nonmonetary plan design features. At the same time, complex federal tax rules restrict pay discrimination in favor of the highly paid employees.

In what follows, we first briefly describe our methodology and data. Next we report our analysis of the determinants of employer plan design decisions. A final section offers conclusions and implications.

Hypothesis and Method

Prior studies have mainly focused on how the employees respond to 401(k) plan designs. Typically these analyses relate worker participation and contribution levels in 401(k) plans to employees' age, income, tenure, and other characteristics. A serious drawback of these studies is that they all treat employer matching contributions as exogenous, without asking why firms might offer matching contributions—and indeed, other plan features—in the first place. One explanation for the observed heterogeneity in 401(k) design could be that plan design represents a form of compensation motivated predominantly or exclusively by the tax deferral incentives offered under the federal tax code, about which we say more in the next section. Another possibility is that 401(k) plans, like other benefit programs, are used by employers to attract a workforce with specific characteristics.

US employers have substantial flexibility regarding the design of their retirement plans. Offering a retirement plan is voluntary, and most private-sector firms that offer an employer-sponsored retirement program today include a 401(k) plan. A key element in such a plan is that the *employee* must first contribute some portion of his salary to the plan—known as the employee's 'elective deferral' or 'salary deferral amount'—before he is entitled to any matching contribution. Employees are afforded substantial tax incentives under the law for saving within 401(k) plans. Thus employee contributions from current wages are tax-deductible (up to $10,500 in 2001, the year of our data set); employer matching contributions are exempt from current taxation; and all investment earnings on the pension account are compound tax-free until withdrawal (which is typically later in life, when tax rates may be lower). By contrast, employers realize no particular tax advantage from offering a 401(k) plan: a firm can generally deduct compensation paid in the form of taxable wages or contributions to a tax-qualified retirement plan.[3]

Under the hypothesis that a 401(k) plan is used mainly as a device for obtaining tax-advantaged compensation, several factors would be anticipated to play an important role in plan design. For example, a company paying higher average compensation would be expected to have a more generous match, because salary levels will lead workers to prefer tax-deferred saving. The 401(k) plan will also be influenced by the availability of other forms of tax-advantaged compensation, such as some other defined benefit (DB) or DC retirement plan, in addition to the 401(k) plan. Larger plans are likely to be less expensive to operate, and thus benefit from economies of scale in plan administration. All of these considerations would also be shaped by the complex series of federal tax rules that govern such plans, including the rules of nondiscrimination testing about which we say more below.

An alternative view, widespread in the benefits-consulting community, is that 401(k) plans are designed to attract and retain workers according to desirable workforce traits such as age or tenure.[4] An elaboration on this view is offered by Ippolito (1997) who suggests that employers with DC plans use match rates along with deferred vesting to direct some portion of compensation to 'savers' who he concludes have lower quit rates and higher job performance ratings.[5] In such a situation, factors such as workers' compensation levels, age, tenure, and sex, as well as saving behavior within the 401(k) plan, might be important determinants of plan design and employee behaviors.

To assess these determinants of 401(k) plan design, we develop an empirical model of the employer's plan decision-making. Here employers are presumed to structure the *monetary* and *nonmonetary* features of their 401(k) plans so as to realize their plan design goals. For instance, if 401(k) plan design features were mainly driven by preferences for tax-motivated compensation among better-paid employees subject to applicable tax law constraints, we might anticipate a positive link between average compensation level and the generosity of the plan match rate. By contrast, if a firm wished to attract and retain a particularly stable workforce, plan features would be geared toward older, better-paid, and longer-tenured workers. This formulation, shown in Equation (1), thus proposes that key plan design features $(PD_j,)$ are shaped by both labor and product market factors. These include workforce characteristics (EE_j), employer-level controls (ER_j), and indicators of how constraining tax rules might be (TAX_j):

$$PD_j = \beta_0 + \beta_1 \times ER_j + \beta_2 \times EE_j + \beta_3 \times TAX_j + \varepsilon_j. \qquad (1)$$

The PD_j vector measures the presence and value of employer contribution matches as well as nonmonetary features that relate to the investment and liquidity constraints within 401(k) plans. Investment variables include how many investment funds are offered to participants; how concentrated fund investment menus are in equity funds; and whether the employer offers company stock in the plan as an investment choice. Features that reduce liquidity costs of 401(k) saving include the presence of after-tax contributions or loans. Employer-side controls include firm size, as a proxy for economies of scale, and industrial sector.

To the extent that firm-side factors drive design decisions, we would anticipate that the β_1 term would be nonzero. In addition, if design features are driven by the need to attract and retain a suitable workforce, we would expect β_2 to be nonzero. And finally, if a 401(k) plan's features are constrained by nondiscrimination or other limits, we would anticipate that the β_3 term would be nonzero.

Empirical Considerations in Nondiscrimination Testing

Analysis of 401(k) plan design is complex due to three issues: the unit of analysis, the complexity of plan design, and US tax rules governing retirement plans. Prior research has not always taken these important issues into account, yet they are of vital importance to understand plan design in the US context. To each we turn briefly.

Unit of Analysis. The 401(k) universe is highly skewed, meaning that statistical analysis will be quite sensitive to the level of aggregation used for analysis. For instance, in our sample (to be described in more detail later), the largest 3 percent of the plans account for half of all covered employees, and the largest 50 percent of plans account for 96 percent of covered employees.[6] Since we seek to explore plan design decisions at the firm level, the firm is the appropriate level of analysis. Of course, this means that this firm-level analysis will include many smaller and medium-sized firms. By contrast, employee-level analyses will be weighted toward plan features and behavior of larger firms, a point often overlooked when interpreting evidence on 401(k) plans.

Complexity of Plan Design. Few prior studies have dissected the interesting nonlinear and complex saving incentives inherent in 401(k) plan matching structures.[7] For instance, employer matches tend to be noncontinuous, bunching at particular values. Additionally, 401(k) plans contain many features that affect liquidity and investment constraints, including different investment menus and differential plan access to loans and after-tax contributions. The presence of other retirement plans will also likely to influence both saving and investment behavior within 401(k) plans, competing with 401(k) plans as a source of tax-deferred compensation, and in the case of employer- and government-guaranteed DB benefits, influencing risk-taking within the 401(k) plan. Studies which do not control on such factors will naturally find results which differ from the analysis to follow.

Tax Rules and Testing. Tax considerations play an essential role in determining 401(k) plan design and employee behavioral responses. Specifically, most forms of compensation in the USA are subject to progressive income taxes; as noted, above, pension contributions are generally tax-deferred, but only as long as they satisfy a series of tax rules, most of which restrict allowable contributions. In particular, under *Section 402(g)* of the Internal Revenue Code (IRC), employees are limited as to the amount of current wages they can contribute to a 401(k) plan—in the year of our plan data, 2001, the limit was $10,500 per year. This rule effectively censors plan saving rates; for example, someone earning $150,000 in 2001 had a maximum possible plan saving rate of 7 percent ($10,500 divided by $150,000). Meanwhile, a person earning $1 million had a maximum possible plan saving rate of about 1 percent of pay.

US retirement plans are also subject to two types of *nondiscrimination rules*. One set is called the *general nondiscrimination rules*, requiring, among other details, that the 'rights, features and benefits' of a plan be allocated equitably across eligible participants. Under this rule, no plan may offer, for example a higher match to higher-paid employees or to employees based on managerial rank. A second set of rules, particularly important for 401(k) plans, is the so-called *nondiscrimination testing (NDT)* rules, for pretax 401(k) elective deferrals. Under these rules, an employer must divide its eligible plan participants into two groups: the highly compensated employees (HCEs, earning $85,000 or more in 2001) and the non-highly compensated employees (NHCEs, or those earning below $85,000 in 2001). In the most common situation, the plan contribution rate of the HCEs may not exceed that of the NHCEs by more than 2 percent.[8]

When calculating plan saving rates under NDT rules, however, an employer may only count income subject to the *Section 401(a)* definition of compensation, which is the maximum level of pay that can be considered for retirement plan purposes; it was $170,000 per year in 2001. Thus, an employee earning $1 million and contributing $10,500 may have an *actual plan contribution rate* of just over 1 percent ($10,500 divided by $1 million). However, his plan saving rate *for federal tax purposes* is defined as 6.18 percent ($10,500 divided by $170,000). In other words, in any given 401(k) plan, as the number of highly compensated employees earning more than $170,000 and contributing $10,500 increases, saving rates for the HCE group will converge toward 6.18 percent for federal tax purposes. As a result, to comply with nondiscrimination testing rests, the employer must encourage the NHCEs to save at least 4.18 percent of earnings (2 percent less than the HCE threshold of 6.18 percent). In addition, many plans will seek to boost NHCE saving rates above this level, because not all HCEs in the plan earn more than $170,000 annually, and not all HCEs will contribute the maximum $10,500 per year.[9]

Finally, two other rules constrain highly paid employee contributions and employer matches in 401(k) plans. Under *IRS Section 415*, total employee and employer contributions to any tax-deferred retirement plan cannot exceed 25 percent of pay or $35,000. For example, a worker earning

$40,000 in 2001 could only receive total employer and employee contributions of $10,000. In addition, a *15 percent limit for profit-sharing plans* also applies, since 401(k) plans are technically organized as profit-sharing plans under US law; as a result, they must generally limit employee and employer contributions to 15 percent of the firm's total wage bill. Consequently, depending on how many eligible participants actually join the plan and the amounts contributed, plan participants could be subject to a 15 percent (or occasionally higher) limit on the sum of employer and employee contributions.

Next, we turn to an examination of data-set used in the analysis and we quantify how many employees are subject to these different tax law constraints.

Description of 401(k) Plan Features

Our analysis of the determinants of plan design draws on a unique and rich set of administrative records for 507 401(k) plans, obtained from Vanguard for the 2001 plan year.[10] Each plan record includes information on important design features including the employer's match formula, features of the plan's investment menu, the presence of other retirement plans (such as a DB or other DC plan), and indicators of participant access to plan accumulations prior to retirement. We also gained access to records for the 740,000 employees in the firms offering these plans; these data included age, sex, job tenure, earnings, plan participation, plan contribution, and asset and contribution allocation information.[11]

401(k) Plan Design Features. Key attributes of the 401(k) plans in our sample appear in Table 10-1. The mean employer is a mid-sized firm with about 1,500 employees; some 82 percent offered a match for employee 401(k) plan contributions.[12] Matching formulas range from zero (18 percent of plans) to very generous matches of more than dollar-for-dollar on at least 6 percent of pay (2 percent of plans).

Our empirical tactic divides the nonlinear 401(k) match formula into an *incentive element*, reflecting how much the employee is rewarded per dollar contributed; and a *liquidity element*, indicating how much compensation the employee must 'tie up' in the 401(k) plan in order to receive the entire employer incentive payment. Accordingly *Match_f3* indicates the value of the employer's matching contribution on the first 3 percent of pay contributed by the employee (i.e. from 0 to 3 percent); *Match_n3* captures the rate on the next 3 percent of pay (i.e. from 4 to 6 percent of pay); and *Match_n2* reflects the value of the match on an additional 2 percent of pay (i.e. over 6 percent and up to 8 percent of pay). Another variable, *Contr4 MaxMatch*, captures how much the employee must contribute to receive the maximum subsidy from the employer. For

TABLE 10-1 Employer 401(k) Plan Design: Descriptive> Statistics (Plan Level)

Panel A. Employer match rates and other plan design features'

	Variable name	Mean
Number of employees covered	Plan_size	1,460
Employer plan provides match for employee contributions	Positive_match	82%
Match rate on first 3% of compensation (0–3%) Match rate on next 3% of compensation (3–6%) Match rate on next 2% of compensation (6–8%)	Match_f3 Match_n3 Match_n2	$0.55 on $1 $0.37 on $1 $0.05 on $1
Match rates conditional on a match being offered: Match rate on first 3% of compensation (0–3%) Match rate on next 3% of compensation (3–6%) Match rate on next 2% of compensation (6–8%)		$0.67 on $1 $0.49 on $1 $0.44 on $1
Promised employer match as % of pay	MaxCostErMatch	3.00%
Employee contribution required for maximum employer plan match (the 'match cap')	Contr4MaxMatch	4.90%
Number of funds offered in plan	NFundsOffered	12.6
Fraction of funds offered that are equity funds	Fund_stock	65%
Employer stock offered in plan	ER_stock	19%
Employer plan permits after-tax contributions	After_tax	24%
Employer plan offers loan	loan	85%

Panel B. Correlations among plan design features

	Match_f3	Match_n3	Match_nn2	MaxCostE RMatch	After_tax	Nfunds	Fund_stock	ER_Stock	Loan
Match_f3	1								
Match_n3	0.63	1							
Match_n2	0.10	0.27	1						
MaxCostE RMatch	0.34	0.56	0.56	1					
After_tax	0.19	0.18	−0.05	0.08	1				
Nfunds	0.00	0.04	0.01	−0.05	0.09	1			
Fund_stock	0.06	0.13	0.03	0.09	0.06	0.32	1		
ER_Stock	0.20	0.16	−0.01	0.09	0.32	0.12	0.06	1	
Loan	0.08	0.12	−0.01	0.12	0.07	0.08	0.18	0.09	1

Source: Authors' calculations.

example, in a tiered formula that paid dollar-for-dollar up to 2 percent and 50 cents per dollar from 2 to 4 percent, the maximum required employee contribution is 4 percent. When calculating the maximum amount the employer promises in the form of matching contribution, we find that about one-third of plans promise to provide below 3 percent of pay; about one-third, exactly 3 percent; and about one-third, more than 3 percent.[13] Panel A of Table 10-1 shows that the mean match by firms offering a match is 50 cents per dollar on the first 6 percent of employee contributions, as reported in prior studies (cf. Papke 1995). But we also find that employer match patterns are extremely *nonlinear:* the average firm matches an average of 55 cents per dollar the employee contributes on his first 3 percent of salary; 37 cents per dollar on his next 3 percent of pay; and only 5 cents per dollar for his next 2 percent of pay. There is also substantial variation in the so-called 'match cap' which is the amount the employee must deposit to obtain the largest possible employer subsidy: the mean is around 5 percent of pay, while the median is 6 percent. The nonlinearity of 401(k) matching contributions is captured in Figure 10-1, which summarizes the match rate and tier for 360 single-tier formulas in our sample.

These 507 plans also offer an average of 12.6 investment choices in their plan menus; 19 percent offer employer stock as an investment choice; and two-thirds of the investment options are equity funds. It is interesting to note that the majority, but not all, of the plans (85 percent) give employees access to their retirement accounts via a *loan feature,* which affords liquidity

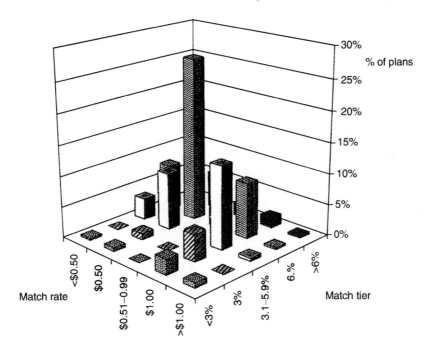

Figure 10-1. Distribution of employer match patterns in single-formula plans (360 plans).
Source: Authors' calculations.

often perceived to be particularly attractive to low-wage savers. A quarter of the plans permit *after-tax contributions*, which allow employees a way to gain preretirement access to a portion of their saving; they also offer a tax benefit, tax-deferred earnings, to those who reach pretax savings limits.[14]

Panel B of Table 10-1 shows the correlations among key plan design variables. We find that, in general, 401(k) plans are consistently generous in different design features. *Match_f3* is highly correlated *match_n3*, with the correlation coefficients at 0.63; the match cap, *Contr4MaxMatch*, is highly correlated at all levels of match (*Match_f3*, *match_n3*, and *match_n2*), with correlations at 0.34, 0.56, and 0.56 respectively. The high-correlation coefficients above indicate that generous employers not only provide higher match to every dollar that employees contribute to their 401(k) account, but also match up to a higher percentage of employees' own contribution. Panel B also tells us that the offering of employer stock is positively correlated with the first and next 3 percent of employer match. In addition, the more funds offered in a 401(k) plan, the higher the proportion of stock funds.

It is worth noting that retirement plan designs are complicated along other dimensions. Figure 10-2 indicates that the 401(k) plan designs fall into four broad categories: firms offering 401(k) plans alone (some 39 percent of plans); firms offering 401(k) plans accompanied by another DC

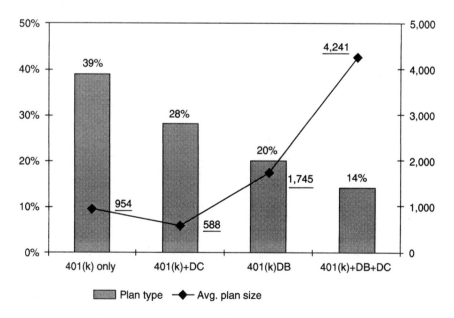

Figure 10-2. The coexistence of DC and DB plans (507 plans).
Source: Authors' calculations.

TABLE 10-2 Employee Characteristics for the Analysis
Sample

	Variable name	Plan mean
Age	Mean_age	42.7 years
Income ($000)	Mean_comp	$63.9
Job tenure	Mean_tenure	8.7 years
Sex (% female)	Female_pct	36%

Source: Authors' calculations.

plan such as a money purchase, profit-sharing, or ESOP plan (28 percent); firms providing 401(k) plans paired with a DB plan (20 percent of plans), and firms offering 401(k) accompanied by both a DB plan and other DC plans (14 percent).[15] Clearly, those who see US private pensions as being either of the DB or DC variety have far too simplistic a view. Accordingly, the analysis is to follow controls on the existence of other DB or DC plans as factors influencing 401(k) plan generosity.

A summary of plan-level employee characteristics for the more than 740,000 workers in the full sample appears in Table 10-2. The average participant in the average plan is nearly forty-three years old, earns $63,900 a year, has spent almost nine years on the job, and possesses a 401(k) account with the balance of $54,400. Comparing our data with those of the EBRI/ICI 2001 (Holden and VanDerhei 2003), these two data-sets are identical in median age and tenure. However, the median compensation and average account balance of our data-set are higher than those of EBRI/ICI at $30,130 and $43,215 respectively.

Multivariate Analysis

To evaluate how employers design 401(k) matching contributions, we turn to Table 10-3. For the set of 507 plans, we see that match generosity is clearly a function of firm size (columns 1, 2, and 6). Larger firms are more likely to provide a match in the first place and a more generous match on the first 3 percent of pay, as well as a larger overall economic value to the match (*MaxCostERMatch*). For example, a 10 percent increase in firm size evaluated at the mean will raise the value of the promised match by 9 percent. This firm size effect disappears on higher levels of pay, presumably because larger firms are more likely to offer another DB or DC plan besides the 401(k) plan. In effect, as firm size increases, employers appear to offer other retirement plans, and so they are marginally less generous with the 401(k) matching contribution.[16]

TABLE 10-3 Determinants of Employer 401(k) Plan Design: Match Features (All Employees)

	Components of employer 401(k) match					
	Positive_ Match	Match_f3	Match_n3	Match_n2	Contr4Max Match	MaxCost ERMatch
Employer characteristics						
Plan_size	0.044	4.474	−0.443	−0.027	0.104	0.187
	[0.013]**	[1.468]**	[0.919]	[0.461]	[0.069]	[0.071]**
DB	0.026	7.308	3.697	−3.933	0.016	0.32
	[0.043]	[4.100]	[2.909]	[1.714]*	[0.252]	[0.238]
DC	−0.024	−1.464	−7.288	0.168	0.26	−0.277
	[0.036]	[3.670]	[2.299]**	[1.378]	[0.226]	[0.205]
Employee characteristics						
HCE_pct	−0.003	−0.041	−0.022	−0.075	−0.023	−0.007
	[0.002]	[0.149]	[0.090]	[0.061]	[0.008]**	[0.009]
Mean_comp_ NHCE	0.007	0.729	0.315	0.075	0.022	0.05
	[0.003]**	[0.245]**	[0.124]*	[0.088]	[0.015]	[0.013]**
Mean_age	0.01	1.299	−0.496	0.524	0.044	0.083
	[0.008]	[0.694]	[0.433]	[0.313]	[0.049]	[0.046]
Mean_tenure	−0.013	−1.296	0.167	−0.171	−0.08	−0.083
	[0.007]	[0.666]	[0.434]	[0.295]	[0.040]*	[0.042]*
Female_pct	0.0004	0.126	0.065	−0.051	−0.012	0.003
	[0.001]	[0.110]	[0.070]	[0.049]	[0.006]	[0.007]
Observations	507	507	507	507	507	507
R^2	0.07	0.11	0.43	0.11	0.52	0.1

Source: Authors' calculations.

Notes: * significant at 5%; ** significant at 1%. Robust standard errors in brackets. Industry controls included. NDT_cap is controlled in all models. In the regression of higher level of match, i.e. Match_n3 and Match_n2, the lower level match rates, Match_f3 and Match_n3, are controlled.

In terms of workforce characteristics, the sponsor's 401(k) match formula proves to be positively associated with NHCE pay levels: that is, the probability of offering any match, as well as larger match rates on the first 6 percent of pay, rise with pay (columns 1–3), as does the overall economic generosity of the match (column 6). In other words, the design of the employer match pattern is clearly motivated by workforce pay levels. The effects are modest in size but statistically significant. For example, if the mean NHCE income of $42,000 increases by 10 percent, the match rate on the first 3 percent of pay rises by 6 percent (from $0.55 to $0.58), and the match rate on the next 3 percent rises by 4 percent (from $0.37 to $0.39). The variation in the match design according to different levels of NHCE income is also estimated, holding all other independent variables at their means. For example, for a workforce with a mean NHCE income of $25,000 (approximately the bottom 5 percent of firms), 80 percent of firms offer a match, and the maximum promised match amount on average to 2.3 percent of pay. For a workforce with a mean NHCE income of $55,000 (the top 5 percent of firms), all firms offer a match, and the promised match is more than one and a half times higher, at almost 4 percent of pay.

Because the general nondiscrimination rules restrict employers from favoring HCEs over NHCEs, and since the dollar contribution caps more effectively bind HCEs rather than NHCEs, we find that only NHCE income is a statistically significant factor in our regression analysis. The percentage of HCEs in a plan has no influence on plan generosity, suggesting that federal limits are binding. Equally important is what the data do not show. Plan design bears no apparent relationship to workforce characteristics *other than pay*. This finding is of interest since, if employers fashioned their match formulas to attract and retain workers with specific demographic characteristics, we might anticipate significant coefficients on such factors as employee age and tenure. However, no such relationships are evident. There is one exception: employers appear to reward shorter-tenure workforces with a higher match, but only as long as they contribute more of their own income. As we argue below, this effect is readily explained by efforts to satisfy federal nondiscrimination testing rules among short-tenured workforces. Overall, the employer match appears to be mainly motivated by the need to offer better-paid employees higher compensation in the form of 401(k) matching contributions. Yet due to the tax rules constraining contributions by the highly paid, these incentives prove to be a linear function of NCHE income only.

Next we consider the factors shaping 401(k) plan nonmonetary features, reported in Table 10-4. Here we examine three attributes of the investment menu: the number of funds (*NFundsOffered*), the percentage of the menu that represents stock funds (*Fund_Stock*), and the presence of company stock (*ER_Stock*); and also preretirement access, namely the availability of after-tax contributions and loans (*After_Tax* and *Loan*, respectively). Not surprisingly, an important determinant of the plan menu features is again plan size. Probably due to scale economies, larger employers are more likely to offer more funds in the investment menu, a larger percentage of equity funds, and company stock, and they are also more likely to permit after-tax contributions and participant loans. Firms which offer DB plans are more likely to offer employer stock in their DC plans (consistent with recent findings by Brown, Liang, and Weisbenner 2004).

TABLE 10-4 Determinants of Employer 401(k) Plan Design: Non-Monetary Plan Features (All Employees)

	Investment menu			Money access	
	NFunds offered	Fund_ stock	ER_ stock	After_ tax	Loan
Employer Characteristics					
Plan_size	0.914	1.79	0.115	0.083	0.046
	[0.172]**	[0.546]**	[0.012]**	[0.014]**	[0.011]**
DB	0.537	−3.107	0.097	0.194	0.019
	[0.699]	[1.619]	[0.040]*	[0.051]**	[0.036]
DC	−0.634	0.129	−0.004	−0.064	0.001
	[0.591]	[1.389]	[0.029]	[0.034]	[0.032]
Employee Characteristics					
Mean_comp	0.026	0.038	0.001	0.0009	0.0003
	[0.007]**	[0.012]**	[0.0003]*	[0.0004]*	[0.0003]
Mean_age	0.216	0.391	0.001	0.006	0.001
	[0.124]	[0.357]	[0.005]	[0.006]	[0.008]
Mean_tenure	−0.058	−0.398	0.01	0.002	−0.001
	[0.088]	[0.303]	[0.005]	[0.006]	[0.006]
Female_pct	0.024	0.08	−0.0003	−0.0002	0.001
	[0.014]	[0.035]*	[0.001]	[0.0008]	[0.001]
Observations	507	507	507	507	507
R^2	0.1	0.09	0.35	0.24	0.06

Source: Authors' calculations.
Notes: * significant at 5%; ** significant at 1%. Robust standard errors in brackets. Industry controls included.

Turning to workforce variables, once again relatively few employee attributes appear to be associated with plan design features. All elements of 'better' plan design are associated with employee income.[17] Better-paid employees have 401(k) plans with more funds, with a greater proportion of equity funds in their investment lineup (allowing greater diversification in what is an equity-dominated portfolio), the ability to invest in company stock (perhaps undesirable from a diversification perspective but attractive in terms of employee ownership and loyalty), and access to after-tax contributions. Most of these effects, while significant, tend to be relatively small in economic terms. For example, a 10 percent increase in mean NHCE income leads to only a 0.1 point increase in the number of funds.

From this analysis, we conclude that employer 401(k) plan design decisions are mainly driven by scale economies (firm size) and employee compensation (which for matching contributions is mean NHCE compensation due to tax limits). These results are consistent with the view of 401(k) plans as mainly a form of employee-preferred tax-deferred compensation. Better-paid NHCEs are likely to benefit from having a higher fraction of their earnings paid in the form of tax-deferred compensation, and it appears that employers design their 401(k) matching contributions plans with this consideration in mind. Arguably, without federal tax limits on contributions, both cash- and noncash incentives would both be more nearly a linear function of earnings. There seems to be little evidence that plan design is motivated by employer efforts to tailor their workforce to other demographic characteristics such as age or tenure.

Discussion and Conclusions

This paper examines the determinants of employer decisions regarding 401(k) plan design. Drawing on a unique data-set of more than 500 plans and over 740,000 employees, we find that patterns of plan design and employee behavior reflect two forces. On the one hand, better-paid workers demand 'richer' 401(k) plans from employers, but on the other hand, employers must provide minimum incentives to lower-paid workers under federal nondiscrimination testing rules. At the plan level we find that match formulas are mainly a function of NHCE income, after controlling for other key attributes. Other desirable nonfinancial elements of 401(k) plan design—such as more investment choice, 401(k) loans or after-tax contributions—are also a function of workers' earnings. In other words, 401(k) plan design appears strongly motivated by a desire to satisfy higher-paid employees' demand for tax-advantaged compensation. Controlling on pay, there is very little evidence that firms design their matching contributions to attract and retain employees with specific characteristics. This combination of findings leads us to conclude that 401(k) plans are mainly a complex form of tax-advantaged compensation, with both its provision by employers and its take-up by employees influenced by the average earnings level of a given firm.

Our findings imply that tax-motivated matching contributions in 401(k) plans may be an imperfect way of ensuring broad-based retirement security. As we note, it is better-paid workers who will demand better matching contributions from their employers in the first place, and take-up of these matching contributions will be a function of a given workforce's savings preferences. Also it appears that federal tax policy regarding nondiscrimination testing may enhance tax preferences within a firm, but tends to create inequities across firms. This is because matching incentives and participation rates tend to be more generous in companies with better-paid workers. As a result, nondiscrimination rules favor workers in companies with better-paid and longer-tenured workforces, while not helping those lacking these characteristics. Finally, because of firm-level design decisions, saving patterns in 401(k) plans tend to be 'local'. Thus, a low-wage worker employed all her life at a high-wage consulting firm would do better in retirement than if she earned the same salary but worked at a low-wage retail firm. Her high-wage colleagues in the consulting firm will demand a larger match, which will in turn induce a higher rate of plan participation by her and other lower-wage employees.

As a consequence, those seeking to enhance retirement security among low-income and low-tenured populations might consider alternatives to matching contributions in 401(k) plans. Options include automatic enrollment (cf. Madrian and Shea 2001), nonelective contributions by employers or the government, and mandatory retirement plan contributions. Reframing enrollment as a negative election encourages 401(k) saving regardless of the firm-specific match incentive, and it also induces retirement saving regardless of that specific workforce's taste for saving. Employer nonelective contributions accomplish the same goal but in a different way. By making the same retirement contribution to all eligible employees, employers in effect substitute for weak employee saving preferences with their own. The same would be true of governmental nonelective contributions made to private plans or to a reformed social security system with personal accounts. Mandatory retirement plan contributions, whether made by the employer or employee, are an option adopted by countries such as Singapore and Australia, where they create uniformity of retirement saving independent of firm-specific characteristics.

Endnotes

1. There are three times as many US workers participating in DC plans as DB plans. Since 1985, the number of DB plan participants has declined by 8 percent annually and these plans hold fewer assets than in DC plans (DB assets are estimated at $2.2 trillion; Vanguard, 2004).

2. In this chapter, we use the term '401(k)' to include both 401(k) and 403(b) salary deferral plans. The former are offered in the corporate sector, while the latter are offered by nonprofit employers, but both terms are derived from the section of the US tax code permitting contributions to these retirement plans to be tax-qualified under particular conditions (McGill et al. 2004). Our analysis excludes governmental plans (e.g. so-called Section 457 plans). More than 70 percent of US DC plans are 401(k)-type programs and 85 percent of DC plan participants have a 401(k) feature.

3. Employer retirement plan contributions are only deductible to the extent of federal tax limits. Some have argued that firms may derive a benefit from offering employer stock within a DC plan, but productivity gains from company stock tend to be negligible and may reflect employer and employee myopia about benefits and costs (Benartzi et al. 2004; Mitchell and Utkus 2003).

4. For instance, Wachovia states on its website that the 'employee benefits plan protects the most important resource of your business—your employees.

Employee benefits can be one of your most valuable recruiting tools. We can help you assemble a generous and affordable benefits plan that attracts and retains the best employees.' (*http://www.wachovia.com/small_biz/page/0,,446_610_1303_1312,00.html*)

5. In fact, Ippolito sees this compensation structure as a way to reward unobserved but valuable employee traits, such as willingness to defer gratification ('low discounters'), on the grounds that these workers may actually be more productive. He also believes that DB plans with back-loaded benefits designs permit firms to reward long tenure and experience.

6. This skewness is not unique to our sample. For instance, Mitchell and Utkus (2003) report that only 3 percent of US DC plans offer company stock, but because they are among the largest US firms, 42 percent of participants are found in these plans.

7. Engelhardt and Kumar (2003, 2004) are an important exception and provide important detail on the nature of 401(k) matching contributions.

8. In the most common case of the Actual Deferral Percentage or ADP test, if the saving rates of the NHCEs fall between 2 and 8 percent, the HCE saving rate cannot be more than 2 percent higher than the NHCE rate. There are different rules when NHCE saving rates fall below 2 percent or above 8 percent.

9. Under the NDT testing rules, should NHCE contribution rates fall short of the legally required amount, the plan is said to 'fail' nondiscrimination testing. In this case the plan can either refund HCEs' contributions, which is a laborious and time-consuming process for the employer and may require the employee to file a revised tax return, or alternatively the employer may simply limit HCE contributions to some lower rate to avoid failing the test in the first place. For example, an employer could restrict HCEs to no more than a 6 percent contribution rate to meet the nondiscrimination rules, in which case a HCE earning $100,000 would be allowed to contribute only 6 percent, rather than the statutory 10.5 percent of salary noted earlier. In practice HCEs are often capped at a flat rate (such as 6 percent) when a plan fails nondiscrimination testing, though the sponsor may also impose a dollar limit. HCEs subject to a cap in the 401(k) plan are sometimes eligible for executive compensation or nonqualified plans instead. Another option for capping HCEs is to subject those in executive plans to a smaller 401(k) limit, while allowing lower-paid HCEs not eligible for the executive plan to save at a higher rate.

10. The identity of individual firms and plan participants is masked. Union plans are excluded from our sample of 507 plans, since there the match is collectively bargained rather than determined solely by the employer.

11. The datafile does not include measures of employee educational attainment or workplace financial education programs, though all employees received plan enrollment material and a quarterly plan newsletter, and all have access to online educational materials. We also lack data on vesting schedules for employer contributions, indicating participants' ability to take employer contributions with them when they change jobs. We did investigate tenure patterns in more detail (an analysis not reported here), and the results were similar to those shown here.

12. According to the US Department of Labor, 84 percent of full-time private industry employees in the US in 2000 were in saving and thrift plans with a 'determinable' match rate (DOL 2004: 69).
13. At the employee level, since more participants are in large plans, nearly four in ten participants are provided with a match equivalent of 3 percent of pay. But this 3 percent promise can manifest itself in quite different ways in terms of required employee contribution: as a $0.50 on the dollar match on a 6 percent employee contribution, as a $1 for dollar match on a 3 percent employee contribution, or, less frequently, something in-between.
14. With after-tax contributions, employees may withdraw contributions at any time. Earnings compound tax-free and are subject to the same restrictions governing pretax contributions. Because of their liquidity, after-tax contributions compete with pretax saving, and so any regression of pretax saving against after-tax contributions should show a negative coefficient for the after-tax indicator. In a number of plan designs, employees who reach various federal tax limits on pretax contributions are able to make additional after-tax contributions, thereby gaining an additional tax benefit, the ability to defer taxes on the earnings on such contributions.
15. In the case of DC plans, a 401(k) participant may receive an employer contribution to a companion money purchase plan, profit-sharing plan, or Employee Stock Ownership Plan (ESOP). The profit-sharing or ESOP contribution may be integrated within the 401(k) plan itself, or it may be in a standalone plan.
16. All equations also control on industrial sector and, predictably, firms in sectors like manufacturing or finance and insurance had more generous designs than firms in wholesale/retail trade (results not reported here in detail but available on request).
17. We do not distinguish between NHCE and HCE employees because there are no federal constraints on nonmonetary plan design features.

References

Benartzi, Shlomo, Richard H. Thaler, Stephen P. Utkus, and Cass R. Sunstein (2004). 'Company Stock, Market Rationality and Legal Reform', University of Chicago Law and Economics, Working Paper No. 218: 1–51.

Brown, Jeffrey R., Nellie Liang, and Scott Weisbenner (2004). '401(k) Matching Contributions in Company Stock: Costs and Benefits for Firms and Workers', NBER Working Paper 10419: 1–56. *http://papers.nber.org/papers/w10419.pdf*

Engelhardt, Gary V. and Anil Kumar (2003). 'Understanding the Impact of Employer Matching on 401(k) Saving', *Research Dialogue 76*. TIAA CREF Institute. June. *www.tiaa-crefinstitute.org*.

—— (2004). 'Employer Matching and 401(k) Saving: Evidence from the Health and Retirement Study', Center for Retirement Research at Boston College WP 2004–18: 1–57. *http://www.bc.edu/centers/crr/papers/wp_2004–18.pdf*

Holden, Sarah and Jack VanDerhei (2003). '401(k) Plan Asset Allocation, Account Balances, and Loan Activity in 2001', *ICI Perspective*, 10(2): 1–16.

Ippolito, Richard A. (1997). *Pension Plans and Employee Performance*. Chicago, IL: University of Chicago Press.

Madrian, Brigitte and D. F. Shea (2001). 'The Power of Suggestion: Inertia in 401(k) Participation and Savings Behavior', *Quarterly Journal of Economics*, 116: 1149–87.

McGill, Dan, Kyle Brown, John Haley, and Sylvester Schieber (2004). *Fundamentals of Private Pensions*, 8th edn. Oxford: Oxford University Press.

Mitchell, Olivia S. and Stephen P. Utkus (2003). 'Company Stock in Defined Contribution Plans', in Olivia S. Mitchell and Kent Smetters (eds.), *The Pension Challenge: Risk Transfers and Retirement Income Security*. Oxford: Oxford University Press, pp. 33–70.

Papke, Leslie (1995). 'Participation in and Contributions to 401(k) Pension Plans: Evidence from Plan Data', *Journal of Human Resources*, 30(2): 311–25.

Poterba, James, Steve Venti, and David Wise (2004). 'The Transition to Personal Accounts and Increasing Retirement Wealth: Macro and Micro Evidence', in D. Wise (ed.), *Perspectives on the Economics of Aging*. Chicago, IL: Chicago University Press, pp. 17–71.

US Department of Labor (USDOL) (2004). *National Compensation Survey: Employee Benefits in Private Industry in the United States, 2000*. US Department of Labor, Washington, DC. *http://www.bls.gov/ncs/ebs/sp/ebbl0019.pdf*

Vanguard (2004). *How America Saves: A Report on Vanguard Defined Contribution Plans 2004*. Malvern, PA: Vanguard Center for Retirement Research. *www.vanguard-retirementresearch.com*

Chapter 11

Understanding and Allocating Investment Risks in a Hybrid Pension Plan

Peter Albrecht, Joachim Coche, Raimond Maurer, and Ralph Rogalla

First introduced in the USA by the Bank of America in 1985, hybrid types of pension plans altered the traditional form of pension plan design in the developed world.[1] The term 'hybrid' pension plan subsumes plans with elements of both defined contribution (DC) and defined benefit (DB) plans. The motivation for hybrid plans is to combine the best characteristics of DB and DC plans while circumventing their major disadvantages. Most include a DC-type individual account, but also provide minimum and/or maximum annuity benefits at retirement using a DB-type formula. Additionally, investment returns credited to the individual accounts may be subject to return guarantees and/or return caps.[2]

When setting up and running a pension plan, the costs implied by the specific plan design, as well as the asset allocation decision for the accumulated funds, are of major importance. In a pure DC plan, plan members have extensive control over their accounts' investment strategy (subject to the investment menu they are offered). This enables participants to shape their portfolio's risk/return profile to their individual risk preferences. The sponsor only promises to make a certain contribution to the account, so the investment risk is therefore completely borne by the members; consequently, the plan sponsor tends to be rather indifferent toward the individual's investment policy, as it poses no cost implications. By contrast, in a pure DB plan, the sponsor is obliged to provide adequate funds to cover the plan liabilities, so he is fully exposed to capital market risk. The asset allocation decision has direct cost implications for his funding situation. In a hybrid pension plan, both parties have an interest in influencing the plan's investment policy. This can result in a conflict of interest, which is the object of investigation of this chapter. At the same time, we scrutinize the costs inherent in different DB-type elements.

To do so, we construct several hypothetical hybrid pension plans, make assumptions about key parameters, and the optimal investment strategy for particular objective functions. These include cost minimization from the perspective of plan sponsor versus maximizing risk-adjusted pension benefits from the perspective of plan members. Although the design of the plan and the assumed parameters do not exactly match actually particular pension plans, the models draw on real-world elements. In particular, the formulation presented here draws on prior analysis of the European Central Bank retirement plan,[3] though the model plan developed here is less complex.[4]

This chapter is organized as follows. First, we discuss the main elements of the hybrid plan evaluated including the minimum pensions guarantee, maximum pension limits, and the return guarantee/caps. Next, we focus on technical aspects of the model and the decision-making process assumed. Finally, we analyze the optimal investment strategy, both from the perspective of the plan sponsor as well as plan members.

Designing a Hybrid Pension Plan

The pension arrangement analyzed in this study is taken to be a mandatory plan whose members do not contribute to any other public or private pension scheme. It is a noncontributory funded pension plan, consisting of two types of accounts. First, every plan member owns an individual account endowed by the plan sponsor with an assumed payment of 17 percent of the members' annual salary,[5] representing the employer's regular plan contributions. In addition to this, the plan sponsor owns a separate account, called the *contingency reserve*, which plays the role of a settlement account for transfers to or from the individual accounts. The funds in both the individual accounts as well as the contingency reserve represent total plan assets. All plan funds must be invested in the same asset allocation, and the return on this portfolio is credited *pro rata* to the individual accounts and the contingency reserve.

In addition to the plan sponsor's pledge to finance the individual accounts with regular contributions, the plan design includes a combination of additional guarantees and/or limits. These are related to the level of benefits at retirement and/or to the asset return credited to the individual accounts. Incorporating this element influences plan obligations, and it may require additional payments from the sponsor (in addition to regular contributions). These supplementary contributions may be triggered in two cases. First, when guaranteeing a minimum return on the plan assets, the plan sponsor must cover shortfalls below the target return by replenishing the individual accounts through supplementary contributions. Second, supplementary contributions may be needed if there are guaranteed minimum pension benefits. Specifically, we posit that if the market value of the total plan assets falls below 90 percent of the actuarial present value of the plan liabilities (i.e. the solvency ratio falls below 0.9), the plan sponsor must immediately endow the contingency reserve with enough funds to reestablish a solvency ratio of one.

In this plan, participants cannot withdraw funds during the accumulation phase. Members leaving the plan before retirement (e.g. due to workforce turnover) may either leave their funds in the plan, or receive the balance of their individual account as a lump sum (limited to the actuarial value of the maximum pension where applicable). At the retirement age of 65, the available funds are converted into a life annuity. This conversion may be subject to the guaranteed minimum pension benefits and to maximum pension limits, depending on the exact design of the benefit structure, to be discussed subsequently.

Benefit Structure. In what follows, six distinct hybrid pension plan benefit designs are scrutinized. Every plan is characterized by a unique combination of the elements mentioned earlier. The reason to compare these designs is to investigate their differential effects on plan costs and pension benefit levels, and implications for optimal plan asset allocation.

In Case I, which we term the 'benchmark' design, the pension plan consists of an individual account for every plan member endowed by the plan sponsor with regular contributions of 17 percent of the current salary. These funds are invested in the capital markets. Beneficiaries are protected from return shortfalls by an annual capital guarantee, i.e. a guaranteed yearly minimum return of 0 percent.[6] In case the funds earn less than 0 percent in any given year, the sponsor must make additional contributions. If the funds accumulated over a plan member's career are insufficient to pay for an adequate pension, this plan also will guarantee a minimum level of pension benefits, corresponding to 2 percent of the career-average salary per year of service. In addition, this plan limits the maximum level of benefits to 2 percent of the beneficiaries' final salary (times years of service).[7] In the event of a member either leaving the plan or retiring, any funds in the individual account that exceed the actuarial value of the maximum benefits are transferred to the contingency reserve.

The subsequent Cases II–V are constructed by eliminating certain plan elements, compared to the benchmark case. Case II excludes the capital guarantee, and in Case III, the maximum benefits are also removed. Case IV eliminates the minimum benefit from the benchmark case, while Case V only includes the annual capital guarantee. Case VI includes the annual capital guarantee and additionally a return cap of 10 percent per year, but provides no further benefit elements relating to salary and years of service. If the asset return on the funds in the individual accounts in any year exceeds the 10 percent level, the excess return will be credited to the contingency reserve. Case VII does not include any guarantees or caps and, therefore, can be interpreted as a pure defined contribution plan. Table 11-1 summarizes the various plan designs.

The minimum rate of return guarantee increases the complexity of the pension plan substantially. More specifically, the minimum rate of return guarantee *may* introduce an asymmetric link between assets and liabilities. Suppose the value of a given investment account corresponds to a pension

TABLE 11.1 Summary of Hybrid Pension Plan Designs

	Case I	Case II	Case III	Case IV	Case V	Case VI	Case VII
Individual account	√	√	√	√	√	√	√
Minimum benefits	√	√	√	—	—	—	—
Maximum benefits	√	√	—	√	—	—	—
Capital guarantee	√	—	—	√	√	√	—
Return cap	—	—	—	—	—	√	—

Source: Authors' compilations.

Notes: Minimum benefits are defined as 2 percent of career-average salary per year of service; maximum benefits are defined as 2 percent of final salary per year of service; capital guarantee refers to a guaranteed minimal return of 0 percent per year for the individual accounts; the return cap limits the annual return credited to the individual accounts to 10 percent.

payment in-between the minimum and the maximum pension limit. In this situation, a high asset return in any given year permanently increases the sponsors' liabilities for the current and future years. Negative returns in subsequent years do not decrease the liability as the minimum rate of return guarantee requires the sponsor to replenish the investment account. Thus the high asset return in the first year had a permanent effect on the liabilities.[8] However, in a situation where the investment account corresponds to a pension payment either below the minimum pension guarantee or above the maximum pension limit, asset returns do not have an immediate effect on the sponsor's liabilities.

Asset Liability Modeling and the Pension Decision-Making Process. Next we evaluate the asset–liability model and decision-making process needed to determine the fund's asset allocation behavior. To do so, we describe the key assumptions about how assets and liabilities are projected forward, and then specify decision rules used either by the plan sponsor or by the beneficiaries to identify the optimal asset allocation. Regardless of whether the asset allocation decision is made by the sponsor or by the beneficiaries, a two-step heuristic method is applied which is often found in practical decision-making formats. In the first step, the set of mean-variance efficient asset allocations is determined using a standard Markowitz-type portfolio optimization. In the second step, all portfolios from the efficient frontier are assessed against a projection of asset and liabilities over a horizon of thirty years.

To project the return and risk effects of a certain asset allocation over time, it is necessary to specify the stochastic processes governing asset class returns, interest rates for maturities of three months (representing money market investments) and ten years, as well as inflation rates. The difference between the nominal ten-year interest rate and the inflation rate (i.e. the real ten-year interest rate) is used to discount future pension liabilities. The stochastic dynamics of the (uncertain) market values of the assets are modeled as geometric Brownian motion, which implies that the log return of every asset is independent and identically normally distributed. Long- and short-term interest rates as well as the inflation rate are modeled using the multidimensional Ornstein/Uhlenbeck process, to cover the empirically observable mean reversion characteristics in these time series.[9]

The investment universe comprises the broad asset classes, money market instruments, euro area bonds, worldwide diversified equities, and emerging market equities. A regime-switching model is used to derive expected returns for the fixed-income asset classes (i.e. money market instruments and Eurobonds). This technique allows consistent generation of yield curve projections contingent on expectations about economic activity (Bernadell et al. 2005). In the long-term projection of the macroeconomic environment, we rely on the economist intelligence unit (EIU) as an external provider of forecasts for the Euro area, the US, and Japan.[10] Expected returns on equity investments are approximated by add-ons to the long-term yields on government bonds. In the analysis, the equity risk premium is fixed at 2.5 percent annually for worldwide diversified equity. Reflecting higher risk of emerging market investments we assume an equity risk premium of 4 percent for this asset class. All asset classes are subject to short selling constraints and, in addition, the investment in emerging market equity is restricted to a maximum of 5 percent of overall investments.

The projection of liabilities is based on a discontinuance valuation method usually applied by plan actuaries; this relies on the assumption that service of each participant ceases on the respective valuation date. It assumes that at a given valuation date the individual investment accounts are translated into a (usually deferred) life annuity with inflation-adjusted payments, whereby the minimum and maximum pension limits laid out earlier are applied. The real discount rates used for this exercise are the real ten-year interest rates determined by the asset model. Discontinuance valuation is performed for each year over the thirty-year analysis horizon (Bacinello 2000). The valuation of liabilities requires projecting population dynamics comprising the evolution of the number and composition of staff, salaries, number of retirees, and dependents. For this purpose a hypothetical population comprising initially of 1,000 staff members is constructed. The population is evolved forward using an inhomogeneous, discrete-time Markov chain. Transition probabilities are derived using assumptions for the company's recruitment, promotion and turnover patterns, evolution of salaries as a function of consumer price inflation, and mortality rates.

TABLE 11-2 Parameter Assumptions for Asset Returns, Interest Rates, and Inflation Dynamics

	Mean	Volatility	Correlations		
			Eurobonds	Global equities	EM equities
Eurobonds	5.1	3.7	1	—	—
Global equities	7.6	17.9	0.21	1	—
EM equities	9.1	27.5	0.1	0.73	1

	θ	κ	σ	Correlations of innovations		
				3-m interest rate	10-y interest rate	Inflation rate
3-m interest rate	0.043	0.114	0.012	1	—	—
10-y interest rate	0.05	0.075	0.01	0.8461	1	—
Inflation rate	0.02	0.286	0.011	0.7757	0.8103	1
Eurobonds	—	—	—	0.0683	0.1396	0.0740
Global equities	—	—	—	−0.0100	0.0000	0.0100
EM equities	—	—	—	−0.0100	0.0000	0.0100

Source: Authors' calculations.

Notes: Return expectations are derived using yield curve projections as laid down in Bernadell et al. (2005) as well as the assumption of equity risk premia of 2.5 and 4% for global equities and emerging markets (EM) equities. Furthermore, the return dynamics are assumed to follow a geometric Brownian motion. The three-month and ten-year interest rates as well as the inflation rate are modeled using the process specified by $dX_t = \kappa(\theta - X_t)dt + \sigma dW_t$ where X_t is the value of the Ornstein/Uhlenbeck process in t, kappa (κ) is the speed of mean-reversion, theta (θ) is the long-run mean, and sigma (σ) is the volatility of changes of the process. dW_t is the increment of a standard Wiener process. The above estimates are made on the basis of monthly data from January 1986 throughout December 2002 for the JP Morgan European Bond index (Eurobonds), MSCI World ex EMU index (Global Equities), and MSCI Emerging Markets Free index (EM Equities), as well as German inflation rates, three-month Euribor and REX ten-year yields.

Comparing the value of liabilities with the projected value of assets at the respective valuation date allows for the evolution of the plan's solvency ratio to be determined and supplementary contributions to be made by the sponsor and average benefits. Given the complexity of the plan design, solutions are determined using Monte Carlo simulation over 1,000 simulation runs. In the process, we make a number of specific assumptions about selection criteria used to determine the plan's optimal asset allocation. To this end, two different regimes are introduced. Under the first regime, arguably the standard for hybrid pension plans, the plan sponsor is solely responsible for the investment strategy. Correspondingly, the second regime assumes that decisions are made by the beneficiaries. In both

cases, investment decisions apply simultaneously to all individual investment accounts and the contingency reserve.

For the sponsor, we assume the objective is to minimize the costs of
running the plan. More specifically the sponsor is modeled as minimizing
the worst-case value of discounted supplementary contributions, where the
worst-case value is defined as the 5 percent quantile of the distribution of
the sum of discounted supplementary contributions over the 30-year
investment horizon. Thus, decision criteria other than costs (such as plan
solvency) are not considered explicitly. Plan funding is accounted for by
the solvency rule, as specified later, according to which the funding ratio
cannot fall short of 90 percent in any single year. More formally, let SC_t be
the total amount of supplementary contributions to be made by the plan
sponsor in period t and r the appropriate discount rate, then the objective
function is given by:

$$\min VaR_{5\%}\left[\sum_{t=1}^{30}\frac{SC_t}{(1+r)^t}\right] \tag{1}$$

Investment decisions for the plan are made collaboratively for all investment accounts. These decisions may be made in the context of an
investment committee composed of staff representatives. Such a body is
assumed to maximize the expected value of the constant-relative-risk-aver-
sion (CRRA) utility function $u(PBF)$ with risk-aversion parameter $\gamma > 0$.

$$\max E[u(PBF)] = \max E\left[\left(\frac{PBF^{1-\gamma}}{1-\gamma}\right)\right] \tag{2}$$

Utility is defined over the pension benefit factor PBF which refers to
pension payments per year service expressed as the percentage of final
salary at time of retirement. Factor PBF comprises all simulation runs and
all plan members retiring over the thirty-year investment horizon.

The Plan Sponsor's Investment Decision

We next take the perspective of the plan sponsor, to evaluate the interrela-
tion between asset allocation in the individual pension accounts and the
resulting plan costs measured in terms of supplementary contributions by
the plan sponsor. Figure 11-1 depicts the worst-case supplementary contributions for Cases I–IV for different portfolio allocations, and Figure 11-2
for Cases V and VI. Worst-case costs are measured as the 5 percent value at
risk of the supplementary contributions, i.e. the present value of contributions by the plan sponsor exceeding the regular payments of 17 percent of
the salaries. Portfolio allocations are represented by the mean-variance
efficient portfolio returns. Details of the cost-optimal asset allocations,
including the asset weights for cash, Eurobonds, global, and emerging

market equities appear in Panel 1 of Table 11-3. Panel 2 contains the distributional characteristics of the discounted supplementary contributions for the cost-optimal asset allocations. Finally, Panel 3 reports the pension benefits for these allocations in terms of certainty equivalents.[11] These certainty equivalents are calculated according to the utility function stated earlier and for four different parameters of relative risk aversion.

TABLE 11-3 Optimal Investment Decisions: The Plan Sponsor's Perspective

	Case I	Case II	Case III	Case IV	Case V	Case VI
Panel 1: Cost-optimal asset allocation (%)						
Mean return	5.57	5.70	5.76	5.63	4.55	5.95
Volatility	4.68	5.23	5.53	4.94	2.17	6.53
Cash	0.00	0.00	0.00	0.00	71.28	0.00
Eurobonds	84.27	79.16	76.61	81.72	28.04	68.95
Global equities	10.73	15.84	18.39	13.28	0.68	26.05
Emerging markets equities	5.00	5.00	5.00	5.00	0.00	5.00
Panel 2: Distributional characteristics of DSC with optimal asset allocation (%)						
Mean DSC	19.64	18.44	22.14	9.24	13.02	7.00
Std. DSC	13.03	12.89	12.60	9.62	8.01	9.17
5%-VaR DSC	42.49	41.50	43.95	27.01	28.04	25.87
25%-Q DSC	10.27	9.04	12.71	0.00	6.95	0.00
50%-Q DSC	17.56	16.12	19.87	6.70	12.15	2.77
75%-Q DSC	26.92	25.65	29.41	15.17	17.96	11.39
Panel 3: Distributional characteristics of PB with optimal asset allocation (%)						
Mean PB	1.875	1.872	2.257	1.793	1.531	1.939
Std. PB	0.045	0.050	0.415	0.102	0.205	0.307
Certainty equivalent ($\gamma = 1$)	1.874	1.872	2.223	1.790	1.517	1.915
Certainty equivalent ($\gamma = 5$)	1.872	1.869	2.121	1.776	1.470	1.827
Certainty equivalent ($\gamma = 10$)	1.869	1.866	2.040	1.750	1.421	1.726

Source: Authors' calculations.
Notes: Asset weights in percent; DSC (i.e. discounted supplementary contributions): contributions required on top of fixed regular contributions to fully fund the pension plan (in percent of expected discounted regular contributions); PB (i.e. pension benefits): attainable income replacement factor (in percent of final salary per year of service); Gamma (γ): parameter of risk aversion in a constant relative risk aversion (CRRA-) utility function of the type: $u(W) = W^{1-\gamma}/(1 - \gamma)$; Objective function: Minimize the 5 percent VaR of DSC; Q: quantile; Case I: DC + minimum benefits + maximum benefits + capital guarantee; Case II: DC + minimum benefits + maximum benefits; Case III: DC + minimum benefits; Case IV: DC + maximum benefits + capital guarantee; Case V: DC + capital guarantee; Case VI: DC + capital guarantee + 10% cap on asset return.

Focusing first on the benchmark, Figure 11-1 shows that the worst-case plan costs for Case I follow a U-shaped curve. With increasing expected portfolio returns, the costs first decrease and then rise, resulting in minimum supplementary contributions for an asset allocation with an expected return of 5.57 percent. This portfolio consists of about 84 percent bonds and 16 percent equities. The minimum supplementary contributions amount to 43 percent of the expected regular contributions. Hence, for every discounted Euro the sponsor regularly paid into the plan, additional payments of 43 discounted cents are required to cover the costs of the plan. The U-shape of the cost curve can be directly related to the guarantees included in Case I. Investing in portfolios mainly consisting of cash or bonds will result in assets not being able to generate enough return to cover the costs of the guaranteed minimum benefits. These costs have to be borne by the plan sponsor. As the expected return on the portfolio increases, it becomes more and more likely that the funds will suffice to at least pay the minimum pension without further contributions by the plan sponsor. The rise in expected portfolio return is in turn accompanied by an increase in return volatility, which induces costs resulting from falling short of the guaranteed minimum annual asset return of 0 percent. From a certain level of volatility onwards, these newly induced costs overcompensate the cost savings related to the minimum pension benefits and the overall costs increase again.

Changing the structural design of the plan has some interesting effects. Eliminating the annual return guarantee for the individual accounts in Case II cuts the amount of supplementary contributions, especially in the case of a more risky asset allocation. However, the asset allocation which minimizes costs is only slightly different compared to Case I (i.e. about 5 percent less bonds and more equities). The worst-case costs only fall from 43 to 42 percent of regular contributions. This results from the fact that for a low-risk asset allocation the costs from the annual return guarantee are relatively low.[12]

In Case III, not only the capital guarantee but also the maximum pension regulation is eliminated; now the plan is basically DC but the beneficiaries are protected by a DB minimum pension benefit in the event of adverse capital market developments. Therefore, the amount of supplementary contributions increases compared to Case II, as there are no longer funds in excess of those needed to provide maximum pension benefits which could be credited to the plan sponsor. Looking at the cost minimizing asset allocation, the equity exposure is slightly further increased to about 13 percent with overall worst-case supplementary contributions of 44 percent.

Case IV shows a quite different curve. The general U-shape is maintained showing a minimum of supplementary contributions for a portfolio return of 5.6 percent, which corresponds to an asset allocation of 82 percent bonds and 18 percent equities. While the asset allocation is comparable to Cases I–III, the level of supplementary contributions with 27 percent of regular contributions is substantially lower than in the previous cases. Additionally, the left branch of the cost curve (low-risk portfolios) is nearly flat while the right branch (more risky portfolios) shows a strong increase. Economically, this can be explained as follows. As discussed for Case I, the predominant source of costs, especially when investing in low-risk allocations, is the minimum benefit guarantee. This guarantee is not included in Case IV, leading to substantially lower costs compared to Case I. Increasing the expected return and the volatility of the portfolio now has two opposing effects. The higher the (expected) portfolio return, the more often the plan sponsor will profit from cashing in funds from the individual retirement accounts that exceed the amount necessary to cover the maximum pension benefits. Contrarily, the higher the return volatility, the more often supplementary contributions will be triggered due to the annual capital guarantee. Since the former effect dominates the latter for less risky portfolios, the overall costs first decrease with increasing

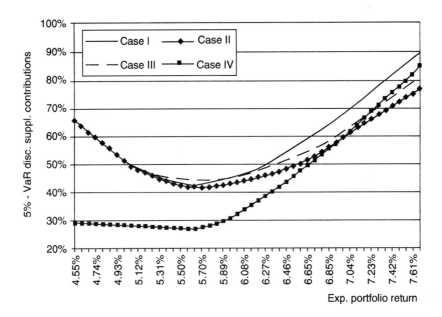

Figure 11-1. Worst-case plan costs vs. asset allocation.
Source: Authors' calculations.
Notes: Discounted supplementary contributions (DSC) in percent of expected discounted regular contributions; Case I: DC + minimum benefits + maximum benefits + capital guarantee; Case II: DC + minimum benefits + maximum benefits; Case III: DC + minimum benefits; Case IV: DC + maximum benefits + capital guarantee.

expected portfolio return. For more risky allocations the latter effect dominates the former, which leads to rapidly growing contributions. As the cost impact of the minimum benefit guarantee is diminishing for increasing portfolio returns, Cases I and IV hardly differ for highly risky portfolios.

We now turn to the cases with no explicit defined minimum or maximum benefit, depicted in Figure 11-2. Case V shows a plan with unlimited upside potential but with a shortfall protection resulting from the annual return guarantee. It is clear that such a plan design results in increasing supplementary contributions, the higher the equity exposure. Hence, minimizing the costs in terms of supplementary contributions leads to the minimum volatility portfolio, consisting of 71 percent cash, 28 percent bonds, and only 1 percent equities. The resulting costs amount to 28 percent of regular contributions.

As in Case V, Case VI offers an annual capital guarantee and therefore protection against return shortfalls. However, the upside potential is limited due to the 10 percent return cap. This structural change has a significant impact on the shape of the cost curve. While the amount of supplementary contributions in Cases V and VI is approximately equal for low-risk asset allocations, the costs in Case VI begins to decrease again

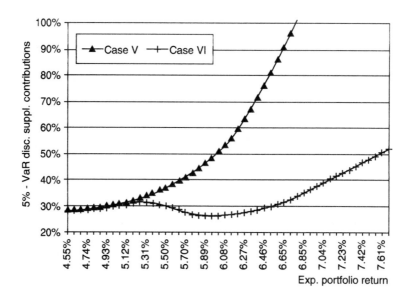

Figure 11-2. Worst-case plan costs vs. asset allocation.
Source: Authors' calculations.
Notes: Discounted supplementary contributions (DSC) in percent of expected discounted regular contributions; Case V: DC + capital guarantee; Case VI: DC + capital guarantee + 10% cap on asset return.

for increasing portfolio return and volatility. For these allocations, the increasing costs resulting from the capital guarantee are overcompensated by the profits the plan sponsor can generate through cashing in any returns that exceed the 10 percent cap. With even more increasing volatility, the costs of the capital guarantee increase disproportionately, leading to over-all growing supplementary contributions. With minimum worst-case costs of 26 percent resulting from investing in about 69 percent bonds and 21 percent equities, this case proves to be the cheapest of all plan designs discussed. This holds for the minimum cost asset allocation and especially for all portfolios with high expected returns and volatilities.

Implications for Plan Beneficiaries. The implications of investing in the cost-minimizing portfolios for expected pension benefits can now be derived (see Figure 11-3). Panel 3 of Table 11-3 summarizes expected pension benefit factors and their standard deviation, expressing the pension benefits as a percent of final salary per year of service. In order to relate the whole probability distribution of the pension benefit factors to the risk aversion of a representative beneficiary, the pension factor certainty equivalents are calculated for a range of risk-aversion parameters using the standard CRRA utility function. This allows a direct evaluation of the cost-optimal asset allocation for the various plan designs, Cases I–VI, from the perspective of plan members with different levels of risk aversion. Figure 11-3 depicts the certainty equivalents for all parameters of risk aversion from one to ten in half steps. Additionally, numerical results for selected levels of risk aversion ($\gamma = 1$, 5, and 10) are presented in Panel 3 of Table 11-3.

The figure shows that Case III results in the highest pension benefit factors for all levels of risk aversion under scrutiny, with the mean benefit factor being 2.257 percent (see also Table 11-3, Panel 3). At the same time, Case V always produces the lowest factors, on average 1.531 percent. This is an interesting result, as both cases show structural similarities. Cases III and V both offer downside protection to the beneficiaries, Case III by means of guaranteed minimum pension benefits, Case V with the annual capital guarantee for the individual accounts. Neither case limits the upside potential.

An explanation for this can be found when looking at the different cost-minimal asset allocations. Optimizing the amount of supplementary contributions in Case V, the plan sponsor will only invest in cash and bonds, resulting in the lowest risk exposure with respect to the capital guarantee. With highly conservative risk and return profile of the assets simultaneously low pension benefits are expected. Such an asset allocation, however, is not appropriate in Case III, since its return expectations are insufficient to cover the costs resulting from the guaranteed minimum benefits, i.e. 2 percent of the career-average salary per year of service.

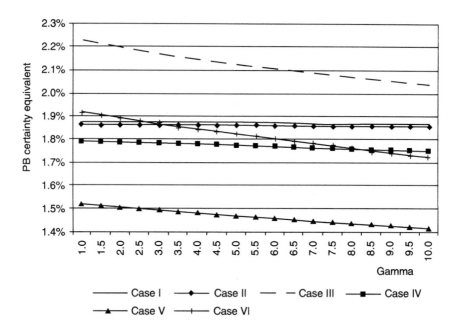

Figure 11-3. Certainty equivalents of pension benefit factors for different plan designs with sponsor's optimal asset allocation.

Source: Authors' calculations.

Notes: PB certainty equivalent: certain pension benefit (PB) factor, i.e. retirement income in percent of final salary per year of service, that has the same utility to the beneficiary as the random pension benefit factor provided by the pension plan. Gamma: parameter of risk aversion in a constant relative risk aversion (CRRA-) utility function of the type: $u(W) = W^{1-\gamma}/(1 - \gamma)$; Case I: DC + minimum benefits + maximum benefits + capital guarantee; Case II: DC + minimum benefits + maximum benefits; Case III: DC + minimum benefits; Case IV: DC + maximum benefits + capital guarantee; Case V: DC + capital guarantee; Case VI: DC + capital guarantee + 10% cap on asset return.

Rather, it is necessary to implement a portfolio strategy that offers higher mean returns, coming at the cost of higher volatility. This, in turn, leads to substantially higher supplementary contributions, since the plan sponsor fully bears the downside volatility while only the beneficiaries profit from the upside volatility.

Implementing a maximum benefit cap (2 percent of final salary per year of service) results in considerably reduced volatilities of the pension benefit factors, i.e. 0.045 percent for Case I, 0.05 percent for Case II, and 0.102 percent for Case IV (see Table 11-3, Panel 3). Consequently, the certainty equivalents of the pension benefit factors are nearly constant for the various risk-aversion coefficients reported in Figure 11-3. Among these cases, Case I offers the highest pension benefits but is also the most costly design. Case II only offers slightly lower benefits combined with slightly lower costs.

In general, it can be concluded that hybrid plans that offer the highest expected pension benefits tend to cause the highest amount of supplementary contributions. Yet there are two exceptions: Case V offers by far the lowest pension benefits, but even given optimal asset allocation patterns, additional costs are not small. By contrast, Case VI has the lowest supplementary contribution, and will lead to expected pensions benefits that exceed all but one other case. The rather high volatility of the pension benefit factor, however, causes the certainty equivalents to drop below those of most other cases for higher levels of risk aversion.

Beneficiaries' Investment Decisions

In this section we assume that the asset allocation decisions are made by the plan participants, rather than the plan sponsor; here, the plan members' objective function is to maximize the expected utility of pension benefits by choosing an appropriate asset allocation. This analysis is undertaken for Cases I–VI and also for Case VII, a pure defined contribution plan. Our interest here is to look at the resulting pension benefits for plan members with different levels of risk aversion, as well as the composition of the optimal asset allocation. For simplicity, we assume that the asset allocation decision made by the beneficiaries and their cost impact have no repercussive effects on plan member salaries; neither will rising supplementary contributions lead to lower salaries/salary increases nor will reductions of plan costs be passed on to the workers.

As earlier, we represent the plan's portfolio allocations by the mean-variance efficient portfolio returns; details of the benefit-optimal investment weights (i.e. the mean and volatility of asset returns, mean and certainty equivalents of pension benefit factors for plan members as well the resulting costs in terms of supplementary contributions for the plan sponsor) appear in Table 11-4. The first Panel contains the results for a representative plan member with a low coefficient of risk aversion ($\gamma = 1$), while the other panels show findings for a medium ($\gamma = 5$) and a high ($\gamma = 10$) coefficient. Table 11-5 provides details regarding the investment weights.

The results show that, independent of risk aversion, plan beneficiaries would opt to invest in the asset allocation that offers the highest or almost the highest expected return and the highest or almost the highest volatility in Cases I–V. Table 11-5 indicates that the optimal asset allocation consists of 100 percent stocks. This is because beneficiaries are protected against downside volatility of the international equity markets by guaranteed minimum pension benefits and the annual capital guarantee. The value of this downside protection *ceteris paribus* increases with the volatility. By analogy to option pricing theory, the minimum pension benefit and the capital

TABLE 11-4 Optimal Investment Decision: The Plan Participants' Perspective

	Case I	Case II	Case III	Case IV	Case V	Case VI	Case VII
Panel 1: Low level of risk aversion ($\gamma = 1$) (%)							
Mean return	7.68	7.68	7.68	7.68	7.68	7.68	7.68
Volatility	17.27	17.27	17.27	17.27	17.27	17.27	17.27
Mean DSC	30.91	24.60	29.80	26.58	126.85	14.29	0.00
5%-VaR DSC	87.93	75.71	79.28	84.52	246.62	51.33	0.00
Mean PB	1.974	1.915	3.937	1.949	6.890	1.948	3.793
Certainty equivalent	1.974	1.914	3.355	1.948	6.014	1.918	3.093
Panel 2: Medium level of risk aversion ($\gamma = 5$)(%)							
Mean return	7.68	7.61	7.68	7.68	7.68	5.89	6.33
Volatility	17.27	16.83	17.27	17.27	17.27	6.18	8.74
Mean DSC	30.91	24.14	29.80	26.58	126.85	7.35	0.00
5%-VaR DSC	87.93	74.14	79.28	84.52	246.62	26.06	0.00
Mean PB	1.974	1.915	3.937	1.949	6.890	1.937	2.543
Certainty equivalent	1.973	1.909	2.449	1.947	4.011	1.827	2.007
Panel 3: High level of risk aversion ($\gamma = 10$) (%)							
Mean return	7.68	7.61	7.61	7.68	7.68	5.76	5.76
Volatility	17.27	16.83	16.83	17.27	17.27	5.53	5.53
Mean DSC	30.91	24.14	29.22	26.58	126.85	7.98	0.00
5%-VaR DSC	87.93	74.14	77.68	84.52	246.62	26.31	0.00
Mean PB	1.974	1.915	3.847	1.949	6.890	1.930	2.155
Certainty equivalent	1.973	1.902	2.160	1.944	2.990	1.729	1.760

Source: Authors' calculations.

Notes: DSC (i.e. discounted supplementary contributions): contributions required on top of fixed regular contributions to fully fund the pension plan (in percent of expected discounted regular contributions); PB (i.e. pension benefits): attainable income replacement factor (in percent of final salary per year of service); Gamma (γ): parameter of risk aversion in a constant relative risk aversion (CRRA-) utility function of the type: $u(W) = W^{1-\gamma}/(1 - \gamma)$; Objective function: maximize the expected utility of pension benefits using a CRRA-utility function defined over the pension benefits in percent of final salary per year of service; Case I: DC + minimum benefits + maximum benefits + capital guarantee; Case II: DC + minimum benefits + maximum benefits; Case III: DC + minimum benefits; Case IV: DC + maximum benefits + capital guarantee; Case V: DC + capital guarantee; Case VI: DC + capital guarantee + 10% cap on asset return; Case VII: DC.

guarantee can be interpreted as a call option, for which the value is also positively related to the volatility of the underlying.

Looking at the level of supplementary contributions associated with these asset allocations, it would appear that costs for the plan sponsor would be prohibitively high. This is particularly true for Case V, in which the members' individual accounts are protected against negative fluctuations in the capital markets while at the same time offering full participation in positive returns. Here, the certainty equivalents of the pension

TABLE 11-5 Optimal Asset Allocations: Participant Perspectives

	Case I	Case II	Case III	Case IV	Case V	Case VI	Case VII
Panel 1: Low level of risk aversion ($\gamma = 1$) (%)							
Cash	0.00	0.00	0.00	0.00	0.00	0.00	0.00
Eurobonds	0.00	0.00	0.00	0.00	0.00	0.00	0.00
Global equities	95.00	95.00	95.00	95.00	95.00	95.00	95.00
EM equities	5.00	5.00	5.00	5.00	5.00	5.00	5.00
Panel 2: Medium level of risk aversion ($\gamma = 5$) (%)							
Cash	0.00	0.00	0.00	0.00	0.00	0.00	0.00
Eurobonds	0.00	2.55	0.00	0.00	0.00	71.50	53.63
Global equities	95.00	92.45	95.00	95.00	95.00	23.50	41.37
EM equities	5.00	5.00	5.00	5.00	5.00	5.00	5.00
Panel 3: High level of risk aversion ($\gamma = 10$) (%)							
Cash	0.00	0.00	0.00	0.00	0.00	0.00	0.00
Eurobonds	0.00	2.55	2.55	0.00	0.00	76.61	76.61
Global equities	95.00	92.45	92.45	95.00	95.00	18.39	18.39
EM equities	5.00	5.00	5.00	5.00	5.00	5.00	5.00

Source: Authors' calculations.

Notes: Objective function: maximize the expected utility of pension benefits using a CRRA-utility function defined over the pension benefits in percent of final salary per year of service; Case I: DC + minimum benefits + maximum benefits + capital guarantee; Case II: DC + minimum benefits + maximum benefits; Case III: DC + minimum benefits; Case IV: DC + maximum benefits + capital guarantee; Case V: DC + capital guarantee; Case VI: DC + capital guarantee + 10% cap on asset return; Case VII: DC.

benefit factors vary between 6.014 percent for a low-risk aversion ($\gamma = 1$) and 2.99 percent for a higher risk aversion ($\gamma = 10$). These high pension benefits are associated with worst-case (mean) supplementary contributions of 247 percent (127 percent).

Cases I, II, and IV limit the upside potential available to the beneficiaries by incorporating the maximum pension benefit restriction. This results in lower benefits and lower costs compared to Case V, yet plan members still have the incentive to choose portfolios with very high volatility. Even though the costs are substantially reduced, they are still intolerably high. For example in Case IV, i.e. Case V with incorporated maximum benefit limit, the worst-case (expected) supplementary contributions amount to 85 percent (27 percent), being about three times as high as in case the plan sponsor chooses the asset allocation.

Case VI produces a different picture: now, the annual capital guarantee and a 10 percent cap on the maximum annual asset return is credited to the beneficiaries' individual accounts. Beneficiaries with a low level of risk aversion ($\gamma = 1$) will still invest in the maximum expected return/maximum volatility portfolio, but more risk-averse plan members will choose an asset allocation with substantially reduced exposure to capital market risk. For a medium (high) level of risk aversion ($\gamma = 5$ vs. 10), the allocation to bonds will increase from none (at $\gamma = 1$), to 72 (79) percent (see Table 11-5). We compare this benefit optimal asset allocation from the members' perspective (with moderate-to-high risk aversion) to the cost optimal asset allocation from the sponsor's perspective in Panel 1 of Table 11-3. It is interesting that from both perspectives, the optimal investment strategy is nearly identical—to have high exposure to bonds and low exposure to equities. This results in quite similar cost implication in terms of supplementary contributions. If the plan sponsor were to set the asset allocation, the 5 percent Value-at-Risk of supplementary contributions would be 26 percent (Panel 2 of Table 11-3); if the representative member with a medium- or high-risk aversion selected the optimal asset allocation for him, this would result in supplementary contributions for the plan sponsor of 26 percent. Hence, if the benefit structure of the pension plan is designed according to Case VI, this will lead to 'harmony' of the members' and sponsor's interests, at least with respect to the asset allocation decision for a given plan design.

Case VI might seem to be most suitable for a hybrid pension plan, as it combines acceptable cost consequences for the sponsor and attractive pension benefit factors for the plan members. Nevertheless, a superior plan design exists. Case VII is a pure defined contribution plan with no capital guarantee and no return cap. By construction, this plan causes no additional costs in term of supplementary contributions for the sponsor. Additionally, as shown in Table 11-4, a pure DC plan provides higher mean pension benefits as well as certainty equivalents for all levels of risk aversion. This result is due to the specification of the floor/cap structure, i.e. a minimum rate of return of 0 percent per year and a return maximum of 10 percent per year. Setting the cap to an annual return of 12.5 percent and leaving the floor constant at 0 percent leads to the following results: For members with a low level of risk aversion ($\gamma = 1$), the certainty equivalent for the benefit factor of the hybrid plan is still lower than in the case of a pure DC plan (2 percent compared to 3 percent). For members with medium to high levels of risk aversion ($\gamma = 5$ or 10), the hybrid plan is more attractive than the pure defined contribution plan.[13] Yet when increasing the cap to 12.5 percent, the plan members will again choose the maximum volatility portfolio (i.e. 100 percent equities), independent of their level of risk aversion. Unfortunately this will cause unacceptable costs in terms of supplementary contributions for the plan sponsor.

Conclusions

This chapter evaluates key properties of hypothetical hybrid pension plans in terms of their cost consequences, by adapting a pure defined contribution scheme to include minimum and maximum limits for pension benefits, as well as minimum guarantees and return caps on individual investment accounts. We also explore optimal investment strategies from the perspectives of both plan sponsor and beneficiaries. We find that introducing DB elements substantially increases the overall costs of running the pension plan and has a major impact on the resulting optimal portfolios.

The investment strategy chosen and the additional plan costs show strong interrelationship. If only minimum rate of return guarantees are included in the plan design, additional costs increase exponentially as a function of higher expected asset return and volatility. Consequently, plan sponsors choose the minimum risk portfolio consisting of around 70 percent cash, around 30 percent bonds, and virtually no equities. Enhancing this plan with a cap on returns credited to the individual accounts leads to a U-shaped cost curve for a broad range of possible asset allocations. Here, the optimal portfolio consists of about 69 percent bonds and 31 percent equities, i.e. about 50 percent more equities than for any other plan design optimized from the sponsor's perspective. At the same time, with this design the additional costs are reduced to 26 percent from 28 percent in the case without the return cap.

For plan designs that guarantee minimum pension benefits, the implied additional costs (expected and worst-case values) are also U-shaped as a function of expected investment returns. Therefore, assuming the objective to minimize the worst-case value of additional costs, the sponsor will opt for asset allocations which deviate from the minimum risk allocation as well. These portfolios comprise between 77 and 84 percent bonds and between 16 and 23 percent equities. The additional costs for these plans lie in the range of 42 and 44 percent of regular contributions, i.e. about 50 percent above the costs of a plan only guaranteeing a minimum rate of return.

Taking beneficiaries' perspective, we also evaluate the utility implications of alternative DB elements and sponsor pension fund asset allocation decisions. To this end, certainty equivalents of pension benefits are calculated for a range of risk aversion parameters. Generally higher additional costs imply higher expected pension benefits, but the introduction of caps on credited asset returns allows cost reductions with only slightly lower certainty equivalents of random pension benefits. We also evaluate optimal investment choices from the beneficiaries' perspective, and we find that almost independent of risk aversion, plan members tend to select maximum return, maximum risk asset allocations where the plan either guarantees minimum pension benefits or minimum return guarantees. However, if the minimum rate of return guarantees are combined with a cap on the maximum return credited to individual accounts, risk-averse members opt for less risky asset allocations. In this case, the optimal asset allocation includes about 72 percent in bonds and 28 percent in equities.

Our results are directly relevant to the moral hazard problem faced by agencies' insurance pension plan defaults, including the PBGC in the USA, and the newly established Pension Protection Fund in the UK (see, e.g. Coronado and Liang 2006; McCarthy and Neuberger 2006; Warshawsky et al. 2006). Like the plan sponsor in this chapter, those organizations issue a put option on the value of the assets invested in the insured pension plans. They therefore should be interested in rather conservative pension fund asset allocations mainly concentrated in bonds. If, as for the beneficiaries in this chapter, the price of such an option (i.e. the insurance premium) is set independently of its value, and if the insured party can influence the value, there is a chance that the insured party will seek to boost the probability of exercising the option—by investing in high-risk assets or by underfunding the pension plan. A possible solution to this moral hazard problem is to implement funding requirements that take into account both current level of funding as well as investment risk, as for example is done for the German Individual Investment Accounts ('Riester' accounts; cf. Maurer and Schlag 2004).

The analysis presented in this study can be useful when discussing possible designs of hybrid pension plans. Some plan designs appear to be Pareto-inefficient (e.g. minimum and maximum pension benefits in combination with minimum rate of return guarantee) as they are dominated by others which imply lower additional costs and higher expected utility for plan members. Furthermore, if plan sponsors and beneficiaries are jointly responsible for investment decision, caps on investment returns may reduce conflicts of interest as asset allocations will diverge less between the parties.

Endnotes

1. Pension promises in the USA have traditionally been either of the pure DB or pure DC type (Schieber 2003). In a DB scheme, the plan sponsor promises to the plan beneficiaries a final level of pension benefits. This level is usually defined according to a benefit formula, as a function of salary trajectory and years of service. Benefits are usually paid as a life annuity rather than as a lump sum. As Bodie et al. (1988) note, the foremost advantage of a DB plan is that it offers stable income replacement rates to retired beneficiaries. The major drawbacks of DB schemes include the lack of benefit portability when leaving the company and the complex valuation of plan liabilities. Moreover, the plan sponsor is exposed to substantial investment and longevity risk, which could result in significant contribution expenses. In a DC scheme, by contrast, the plan sponsor commits to paying funds into the beneficiaries' individual accounts according to a specified formula, e.g. a fixed percentage of annual salary. The most prominent feature of a DC scheme is its inherent flexibility: by construction, it is fully funded in individual accounts. The value of the pension benefits is simply determined as the market value of the backing assets. Therefore, the pension

benefits are easily portable in case of job change. Additionally, the beneficiaries have control over their funds' investment strategy and at retirement can usually take the money as a life annuity, a phased withdrawal plan, a lump sum payment, or some combination of these. While the employer is only obliged to make regular contributions, the employee bears the risk of uncertain replacement rates, especially caused by fluctuations in the capital markets (Bodie and Merton 1992).

2. An in-depth discussion of the implications of introducing hybrid pension plans in the USA can—among others—be found in Clark and Schieber (2004), Coronado and Copeland (2004), Johnson and Steuerle (2004), and Mitchell and Mulvey (2004).

3. The European Central Bank (ECB) operates a hybrid pension scheme; plan assets, which exist solely for the purpose of providing benefits for members of the plan and their dependents, are included in the other assets of the ECB. Benefits payable, resulting from the ECB's contributions, have minimum guarantees underpinning the DC benefits.

4. For example, we do not handle dependent benefits and we assume a simplified population model.

5. A contribution rate of 17 percent can be considered as reasonable assumption given the typical structure of European pension plans. For example, in Germany, contributions to the state-run pay-as-you-go pension system currently amount to 19.5 percent of salaries. As provisions for dependents' pensions are neglected in this study, reducing the contribution rate by 2.5 percent compared to the German state pension system seems a reasonable assumption.

6. Alternatively to a focus on absolute return, a minimum fixed rate of return guarantee could be applied to a relative rate of return. For example, Chile's private pension funds were long required to earn an annual real rate of return that depended on the average annual real rate of return earned by all of Chile's private pension funds (Pennacchi 1999). Or the guarantee may be applied to the account balance at the time of retirement, instead of the assumed annual basis.

7. As is typical for public employees, the wage path until retirement is nondecreasing and so the guaranteed minimum pension benefits will always be lower than the maximum pension benefit limit.

8. This link between assets and liabilities is in contrast to the analogy developed by Bodie and Davis (2000), who compare a pension plan to an equipment trust such as those set up by an airline to finance the purchase of airplanes. Here the equipment serves as specific collateral for the associated debt obligation. The borrowing firm's liability is not affected by the value of the collateral. So, for instance, if the market value of the equipment were to double, this would greatly increase the security of the promised payments, but it would not increase their size. As opposed to this scenario, in the scheme developed in this chapter, the value of the assets may well affect the liabilities as a high return in a given year may increase the value of the liabilities as outlined above.

9. A drawback of the Ornstein/Uhlenbeck process is the theoretically positive probability of negative nominal interest rates, but this is eliminated in the simulation procedure by cutting off the negative nominal interest rates.

10. The EIU forecasts are constructed with the aid of an econometric world model, maintained by the UK-based Oxford Economic Forecasting.
11. The certainty equivalent of a lottery is defined as the fixed payment that provides the same utility as the random lottery.
12. Analyzing the costs of Individual Account guarantees, Lachance and Mitchell (2004) argue that guarantee costs tend to be insensitive to the asset allocation in cases where the exercise of the guarantees is either extremely likely or extremely unlikely.
13. The certainty equivalents are 2.100 percent compared to 2.007 percent for $\gamma = 5$, and 1.913 percent compared to 1.760 percent for $\gamma = 10$.

References

Bacinello, Anna R. (2000). 'Valuation of Contingent-Claims Characterizing Particular Pension Schemes', *Insurance: Mathematics and Economics*, 27: 177–88.

Bernadell, Carlos, Joachim Coche, and Ken Nyholm (2005). 'Yield Curve Prediction for the Strategic Investor', Working Paper, European Central Bank, forthcoming.

Bodie, Zvi and E. Philip Davis (2000). *The Foundations of Pension Finance*. Cheltenham, UK: Edward Elgar, p. xvi.

—— and Robert C. Merton (1992). 'Pension Benefit Guarantees in the United States: A Functional Analysis', in Raymond Schmitt (ed.), *The Future of Pensions in the United States*. Philadelphia, PA: University of Pennsylvania Press, pp. 194–234.

—— Alan J. Marcus, and Robert C. Merton (1988). 'Defined Benefit versus Defined Contribution Pension Plans: What Are the Real Tradeoffs?' in Zvi Bodie, John B. Shoven, and David A. Wise (eds.), *Pensions in the U.S. Economy*. Chicago, IL: University of Chicago Press, pp. 139–62.

Clark, Robert and Sylvester J. Schieber (2004). 'Adopting Cash Balance Pension Plans: Implications and Issues', *The Journal of Pension Economics and Finance*, 3(3): 271–95.

Coronado, Julia L. and Nellie Liang (2006). 'The Influence of PBGC Insurance on Pension Fund Finances', this volume.

—— and Philip C. Copeland (2004). 'Cash Balance Pension Plan Conversions and the New Economy', *The Journal of Pension Economics and Finance*, 3(3): 297–314.

Johnson, Richard W. and Eugene Steuerle (2004). 'Promoting Work at Older Ages: The Role of Hybrid Pension Plans in an Aging Population', *The Journal of Pension Economics and Finance*, 3(3): 315–37.

Lachance, Marie-Eve and Olivia S. Mitchell (2004). 'Understanding Individual Account Guarantees', in Olivia S. Mitchell and Kent Smetters (eds.), *The Pension Challenge: Risk Transfers and Retirement Income Security*. Oxford: Oxford University Press, pp. 159–86.

Maurer, Raimond and Christian Schlag (2004). 'Money-Back Guarantees in Individual Account Pensions: Evidence from the German Pension Reform', in Olivia S. Mitchell and Kent Smetters (eds.), *The Pension Challenge: Risk Transfers and Retirement Income Security*. Oxford University Press, pp. 187–213.

McCarthy, David and Anthony Neuberger (2006). 'The UK Approach to Insuring Defined Benefit Pension Plans', this volume.

Mitchell, Olivia S. and Janemarie Mulvey (2004). 'Potential Implications of Mandating Choice in Corporate Defined Benefit Plans', *The Journal of Pension Economics and Finance*, 3(3): 339–54.

Pennacchi, George G. (1999). 'The Value of Guarantees on Pension Fund Returns', *The Journal of Risk and Insurance*, 66(2): 219–37.

Pesando, James E. (1996). 'The Government's Role in Insuring Pensions', in Zvi Bodie, Olivia S. Mitchell, and John A. Turner (eds.), *Securing Employer Based Pensions: An International Perspective*. Philadelphia, PA: University of Pennsylvania Press, pp. 286–305.

Sylvester J. Schieber (2003). A Symposium on Cash Balance Pensions: Background and Introduction', Pension Research Council Working Paper, Wharton School, *http://rider.wharton.upenn. edu/~prc/wpcashbalance.html*

Warshawsky, Mark J., Neal McCall, and John D. Worth (2006). 'Regulating Single Employer Defined Benefit Plans: A Modern Approach', this volume.

Chapter 12

Market Innovations to Better Allocate Generational Risk

Salvador Valdés-Prieto

In Western nations and Japan, social security payroll taxes are mainly used to pay benefits to middle-class workers. These systems operate like a mandatory old-age annuity-saving scheme paying a rate of return below market rates for similarly long-term and illiquid saving. In many these nations, two issues are of primary concern. First, these social security systems face prospective or actual insolvency, meaning they will be unable to fulfill benefit promises unless benefits are cut or taxes are raised. Second, and much less well known, these systems offer large opportunities for improving risk-sharing and reducing political risk. In this chapter we explore these opportunities and argue that substantial gains are available, without incurring transition costs and without increasing the public debt. These gains could be available to facilitate resolution of systemic long-term insolvency in social security schemes.

Political Risk and Social Security Adjustments

Pay-as-you-go (PAYGO) social security systems are often forced to adapt when subject to demographic, economic, and other shocks. In practice, these changes tend to occur via emergency changes in legislation, with the sponsoring government seeking to restore order while maintaining system-wide control. In such cases, politicians are often forced to consider the demands of critical interest groups and constituencies who influence the political process. Accordingly, politicians confronted with present-focused interest groups are apt to delay dealing with economic and demographic shocks as long as possible, rather than concerning themselves enough with future generations' well-being (Holzmann et al. 2005).

In the past, emergency legislation has been used to alter many system parameters including retirement ages and eligibility rules, benefit formulas, the period over which past earnings are averaged, the indexation of past earnings, the indexing rate for benefits in payment, coverage and levels of payroll taxes, and more. Such parametric changes seem highly unpredictable from the viewpoint of individual workers and pensioners, transforming the mandatory old-age system into a lottery where parties may experience either huge gains or huge losses, depending on whether they are lucky or take cuts. Such political risk also impinges on national fiscal health, because social security programs tend to loom large relative to government budgets. For this reason, social security insolvency can boost the risk premium required by holders of public debt, which in turn damages taxpayers and beneficiaries of federal transfers in unpredictable ways.

Of course, policy discretion can sometimes be a valuable tool, if used to deal with uncertainty that cannot be pooled at low cost. For example, subsidies for disadvantaged groups which may appear in the future may be developed *ex post*, at the discretion of future legislators. Nevertheless, discretion in social security systems to date often appears to have been more harmful than beneficial, to date. A possible response would be to improve the way that government discretion works. For example, in Sweden, automatic stabilizers were built into benefit formulas for their notional accounts, as a means of preserving the traditional PAYGO financing approach for the old-age system. Yet political risk remains, since such schemes do not attain full financial stability in the face of economic and demographic shocks. Moreover, if government-controlled funds are invested in corporate securities, they can be subject to 'socially targeted' political investment rules which might curtail participant returns. Having the government control the Trust Fund investments may expose a social security system to political and social suasion at the expense of the economy's performance (Cogan and Mitchell 2003).

Evidence on Political Risk. When social security systems run short of financing, interest groups may oppose even minor changes today—even if these changes would improve the system's long-term sustainability (Müller 2003). Reluctance to take on reforms is often sustained by efforts to suppress information about the financial status of social security programs. For example, in the USA, policymakers have habitually truncated the social security liability computation at an arbitrary seventy-five-year horizon, which severely understates the full scope of the problems faces (Gokhale and Smetters 2003; Kotlikoff and Burns 2004). In Europe some governments have actually boosted pension generosity during the 1990s (Boldrin et al. 1999), due to lack of awareness of the financing consequences of doing so.[1]

There is also ample evidence that social security benefits are often changed quite arbitrarily, when the political need arises. For instance, the US Congress cut benefits in 1977, reducing promises by 19 percent for workers age 62 in 1980, and by 30 percent for those age 54 and younger in 1980. It also subjected more benefits to taxes, thus dropping replacement rates by about 7 percent, and raised the retirement age which will cut replacement rates by 14 percent when fully phased in. Other nations have seen even sharper cuts, as in the case of retirees in Russia and other former Soviet Union countries during the 1990s. The Mexican social security system had promised benefits that replaced 40–80 percent of preretirement earnings plus health benefits in the 1970s, but when the 1982 debt crisis struck, the government defaulted on these promises with inflation over 50 percent per annum decimating real payments.[2] A similar history of fiscal unsustainability explains the benefit cuts behind the 1980 Chilean pension reform, the 1994 Argentinean reform, the 1993 Peruvian reform, and many others. The lottery aspect of political risk is evident in the case of Hungary: after a large shock to real wages and four legislated changes to the indexation of different components of the pension formula 1991–7, the benefits of retirees 1986–90 averaged 20–25 percent higher than those for persons who retired later (Augusztinovics et al. 2002). Holst (2005) calculates that political risk creates a welfare loss equivalent to 2–4 percent of the pension amount in the USA and Germany (Holst 2005).

A Better Representation of Social Security Finances. A symptom of this present focus is the reluctance to publish an annual balance sheet such as that in Table 12-1, illustrating the long-term insolvency problems facing a national social security system. If benefit and tax parameters are such that expected cash flows require the sponsor to provide additional future support to keep the system going, as in the right-hand panel of Table 12-1, the social security program is said to be insolvent.[3] Conversely, if the program's assets (the PAYGO asset is defined below) are large enough to cover all anticipated liabilities, the social security program would be said to be solvent. The 'Implicit Fiscal Liability' (IFL) represents the gap—namely the present discounted value of the expected support to be provided by the federal government over the infinite horizon (following Geanokoplos et al. 1999).

The economics literature has shown that PAYGO social security system debt is similar to public debt (Auerbach and Kotlikoff 1987). That is, economically rational participants who contributed in the past perceive

TABLE 12-1 Balance Sheets for Partially Funded Retirement Systems

Solvent Plan		Insolvent Plan	
Assets	*Liabilities*	*Assets*	*Liabilities*
Pension Fund	Payments promised to current members, retired and active	Pension Fund	Payments promised to current members, retired and active
PAYGO Asset		PAYGO Asset	
		Implicit Fiscal Liability	

Source: Valdés-Prieto (2005a).

benefit promises as akin to public debt, both in their household portfolios and in the national public finance balance sheet. Indeed, in a world with no uncertainty, implicit social security debt and ordinary public debt are perfect substitutes; the subsidy received by the initial generation of retirees in a PAYGO plan equals the present value of the net lifetime taxes (see later) that must be levied on future generations (Geanokoplos et al. 1999; Sinn 2000).

While the accrued liability does not depend on whether social security uses pure PAYGO finance, partial funding or full funding, there are differences across countries in the way the benefits are paid for. A partially funded social security system, such as that in the USA, backs part of its accrued liability with a Trust Fund, with the remainder of the liability financed by the promise of two types of hidden or implicit future tax revenue. Let us define the *net lifetime tax* levied by social security on a particular generation, as the difference between the present discounted value of the payroll taxes that this generation expects to pay, and the expected discounted value of benefits that this same generation expects to collect. When this net lifetime tax is positive, the social security program collects a positive cash flow from this generation. It is useful to think of the present value of future net lifetime taxes as an asset, which here we shall call a PAYGO asset (see Table 12-1). A solvent PAYGO-financed system levies a positive net lifetime tax on the average generation, because the payroll tax is *larger* than the expected present discounted value of benefits accrued, when the economy is dynamically efficient. If the system is insolvent, there are *two* implicit taxes: one is the net lifetime tax whose revenue is the PAYGO asset, and the other is the potential new tax needed to finance the Implicit Fiscal Liability (IFL, see Table 12-1), if benefits promises are honored.

Long-term system solvency then requires that the present value of future promised benefits is no larger than the PAYGO asset, without requiring additional revenue support. In the US case, the social security system faces insolvency since the PAYGO asset is approximately $11 trillion less than the present value of future benefits promised (Cogan and Mitchell 2003). In terms of Table 12-1, the IFL is $11 trillion is promised benefits are honored. However, under current law, the system may not collect additional revenue beyond the PAYGO asset. What this means is that when the Trust Fund runs out, the system cannot legally continue paying promised benefits. In terms of Table 12-1, if promised benefits are not honored the IFL disappears.

Moving to a Market-Based Social Security System

Compared to politically vulnerable social security systems, we propose that a market-based approach would offer many advantages. The idea would be to establish individual accounts with a rule-based approach to risk allocation, a concept familiar from financial contracts. As an example, mutual funds regularly stipulate that fund shares will be priced daily at the 'net asset value', a concept that refers to the net value of all securities held by the fund at yesterday's closing price, divided by the number of outstanding shares. Under this rule, capital market risks are shared by participants in proportion to the number of shares each holds. This approach is also what DC pensions do. A different rule-based approach applies to the lifetime real annuity contract sold by life insurance companies. Here the annuitant is generally exempted from bearing investment and inflation risk (assuming the pension benefit is indexed to the CPI); these risks, instead, are absorbed by the insurer's capital and the issuers of the inflation-indexed bonds in which the life insurance company's investments are held.

Of course other risk-sharing rules are possible, but these two have the advantage of having legal support. Rules of this sort also offer transparency which can improve the policy process itself and reduce political risk. Such rules also allow workers to diversify and trade the underlying risks in the financial markets, and to choose among diverse balanced portfolios. And finally, financial regulators would be less subject to conflicts of interest created by being subordinate to the same political coalition that experiences reelection concerns. Nevertheless, a rule-based approach must rely on the accounts to have capital assets backing the promises, which many PAYGO social security systems lack. That is, if financial markets are to take on a risk-sharing role in the case of social security, we must confront the question of where the money comes from to fund the system.

Securitization of Future PAYGO Taxes. Our proposal would devise a new financing mechanism that does not increase the public debt. It does not require decade-long consumption sacrifices because it does not redistribute across generations. This approach involves five steps (Valdés-Prieto 2002, 2005*a*):

(1) Determine what additional social security tax would be required over and above the current payroll tax, to honor current benefit promises for an infinite horizon. Also determine how much benefit promises would have to be cut below the current promises (say by reducing the degree of wage indexation of past earnings to calculate initial benefits), to finance a solvent system with the current payroll tax. Choose some combination between these extremes, appealing to the gains of the next steps in the reform.

(2) In the reformed system, determine the size of average net lifetime taxes as a share of earnings. Convert this rate, currently an *implicit tax on earnings*, into an *explicit* residual payroll tax, and endow the Social Security Trust Fund with property rights over the revenue from this residual payroll tax. The remaining portion of the current payroll tax

would be transformed into contributions to personal saving accounts;

(3) Securitize the revenue of the residual payroll tax, creating new 'Covered Wage Bill' (CWB) securities. Set their prices in competitive financial markets;

(4) Change the social security benefit formula to link benefits to the overall financial return achieved by the Trust Fund. The continuation benefits to the initial elderly are almost identical to the current ones. Benefits for initial workers are similar to the current ones because they would initially get portfolios heavily invested in CWB securities. Still, initial workers would benefit from the cut in the political risk they currently bear; and

(5) Allow each participant to select from a limited set of balanced portfolios and to choose his own asset manager to administer his personal account assets.

In other words, this process involves relabeling the difference between social security projected future benefits versus future taxes as an explicit residual tax, specified as a percentage of covered payroll. The Trust Fund would then be endowed with property rights to the future revenue collected by the residual tax. No new explicit public debt is issued, and no new debt-servicing costs appear. The CWB securities would reflect the value of the residual tax revenue, defined as the dividend on the new CWB securities. This cash flow would be owed by future participants (contributors) rather than the federal government. Finally, there would be no government guarantee on the CWB dividend payout: if the covered wage bill varied for any reason (e.g. due to demographic, productivity, or other shocks), only the owners of the CWB securities would be affected. Holders of CWB securities would take a loss if dividend growth fell below expectations, and they would appropriate any gains when dividend growth was above expectations. The fact that CWB securities would behave like equity protects fiscal stability, i.e. protects beneficiaries of federal transfers and taxpayers.[4] After relabelling PAYGO as individual accounts, the addition of property rights makes the system fully transparent, cutting political risk and allowing access to financial markets.

In order to implement this strategy, current social security benefit formulas based on workers' years of service and Average Indexed Monthly Earnings (AIME) would be replaced by a rule-based system of personal accounts. Initially, active workers would be issued shares in the Social Security Trust Fund, and its net asset value would be the value of the Trust Fund including the CWB securities, divided by the number of shares outstanding. Contributions by active workers would purchase additional shares, while retirees would sell shares back to finance a pension or to purchase an annuity. Here risks would be shared only among participants in proportion to the number of shares each held, just as in DC pension plans. Retirees would be given variable annuities backed by CWB securities, so the risks transferred to pensioners would be much smaller than feasible in current financial markets.

Later, individual choice would be feasible; for instance, market-based social security could offer retirees a choice between variable annuities indexed to a portfolio that holds CPI-indexed CWB securities (for maximum stability), or a balanced portfolio offered to active participants. Annuities might pass along to members the risk that the life table itself could change, along the lines of the CREF annuity formula pioneered by TIAA–CREF in the USA. Alternatively a retiree could be offered a fixed annuity from a life-insurance company.

The innovation under this approach is that the social security system offers no guarantees to participants as a group. Of course, workers and retirees may purchase guarantees from issuers of fixed-income securities in the capital market, and participants could be allowed to sell their claims on market-based social security to outside investors, provided that the funds raised would purchase annuities from life insurers meeting solvency conditions. Naturally supervision of life insurers would continue to be necessary, since otherwise insurers might select risky asset portfolios and then hope for a bailout via an implicit government guarantee (Gollier 2005).

One condition that all these arrangements must meet is asset–liability matching. In other words, the value of CWB securities of any given type held in the Trust Fund must equal the value of program liabilities. This ensures that the sum of payouts linked to the returns of each type of CWB security is equal to the combined dividends earned by all the CWB securities of that same type in any state of nature.

Transition Costs. Let us explain why this transition proposal does not increase the public debt and does not require decade-long consumption sacrifices, despite achieving a new situation which appears to be full funding. The label 'funding' has been assigned three different meanings, creating some confusion. The first type of funding, also called 'narrow' or 'financial', is the degree to which benefit promises are backed by assets protected with property rights such as securities and real estate. The degree of narrow funding of an employer pension plan is independent from the paths of national saving and of the public debt (Bernheim and Shoven 1988).

The second type of funding is the degree to which changes in benefit promises translate into changes in national savings, and therefore into changes in consumption, possibly sacrifices, redistributing across generations. This is 'ultimate' or 'broad' funding, which depends on changes in the stock of voluntary savings (tax-favored and normal financial saving, housing equity), changes in the national debt, nationalizations and privatizations, and changes in government programs which create intergenerational transfers such as health subsidies for the old and educational subsidies (Lee 1994). Third, consider 'fiscal' funding. This is the degree to which changes in benefit liabilities bring about changes in the net fiscal debt, or affect the riskiness of the payment profile of the net public debt. For this purpose, the 'net public debt' is the standard public debt, minus publicly owned assets, plus the implicit fiscal debt to insolvent health and old-age benefit programs.[5]

The gains from market-based social security come from narrow funding. The consumption sacrifices are caused by increases in broad funding and the fiscally costly 'transition costs' are caused by restructuring of fiscal funding. The transition path analyzed in this paper achieves narrow funding without touching either broad or fiscal funding.

Responding to Aggregate Shocks. The next issue is to specify how the proposed system would adjust if uninsurable shocks strike, which could involve discretionary *ex post* adjustments; adopting prespecified rules *ex ante*, or some blend of the two. In provident funds and DB corporate plans, the fiduciaries are generally given some discretion to adjust parameters *ex post*, so as to preserve solvency, and sometimes this works well but the last decade of DB failures in the USA underscores the risk in this approach.

Alternatively, preset rules can be derived to preserve cash-flow equilibrium, though a problem with such cash-flow rules is that they tend not to respond to predictable events but rather delay action until cash-flow problems materialize. As an example, the Swedish Notional Account program maintains PAYGO financing, while crediting benefit promises to each participant's 'notional' account with a hypothetical interest rate. If the economy maintained a steady growth path, the internal rate of return on social security taxes would equal the growth rate of payroll tax revenue; in reality, however, shocks produce substantial cash flow deficits or surplus that can last for decades and whose accumulated value may attain 8 percent of GDP (Valdés-Prieto 2000). In addition, the Swedish benefit formula deviates from the theoretical ideal by crediting individual accounts with an interest rate that equals the growth rate of average covered wages rather than the growth of payroll tax revenue. In general, a notional account approach is backward rather than forward looking, as it does not attempt to match assets and liabilities on a continuing basis; the latter would require a reliable method to construct projections such as those provided by prices in a competitive financial market. Instead, the Swedish system relies on projections made by a single government bureau which then adjusts benefits in an ad hoc manner. This makes the system subject to political risk all over again.

Some forward-looking rules are in use in financial markets, as in the case of annuities where longevity and investment risks are absorbed by life insurance companies, and by the issuers of bonds in which assets are invested. The DC rule used by mutual funds also meets this objective, as uninsurable aggregate financial shocks are allocated among plan members in proportion to the market value of their claims on the plan.

In the present context, let us consider the case where a panic struck financial markets and knocked down the value of the CWB securities. If all CWB securities were perpetuities, a solvent social security program would not have to sell any of its holdings because all benefits could be paid in full using the dividend payout of CWB securities—which equals the revenue of the residual payroll tax plus the revenue from new contributions. Of course retirees would sell some of their holdings to younger participants every month, and since these trade at prices set in financial markets, a panic there affects the terms of trade. If this change is permanent, a response by participants is not a problem but rather is economically justified.[6] Similarly, a pure PAYGO system would have to adopt new legislation if news arrived to modify expected payroll tax revenues or benefits. By contrast, a rule-based approach as proposed here offers immediate and objective adjustments that guarantee continued solvency. For example, if longevity were to rise faster than anticipated, holders of variable annuities and the life insurance companies that issued the fixed annuities would take a loss.

If new information were to show that the aggregate future payout of the CWB securities held by younger participants would fall, benefits would have to be cut to restore solvency. Of course provident workers facing this loss would respond both by deferring retirement and raising their saving rates. Therefore, a market-based social security program that allowed flexibility in the contribution rate in response to forward-looking changes could actually reduce risk exposure.

Financial Market Implications

Next we turn to the possible financial market implications of moving to a market-based social security system, and we also discuss ways to organize the new market for asset management services provided to participants.

Access to a More Efficient Portfolio. Initially, the social security program would trade CWB securities sufficient to establish pricing, which would be a small volume relative to the complete stock of CWB securities. This alone would create new financial markets. Subsequently, social security may gradually trade much larger blocks of CWB securities with outside investors.

The literature suggests that real-world investors are often beset by information deficiencies and behavioral quirks making them less skilled than professional asset managers (Mitchell and Utkus 2004). In addition, small investors pay more for trading than do large institutional investors. For both reasons, having the government participate in financial markets via the CWBs is likely to have important effects. Currently, the portfolio owned by the social security system is undiversified, and it is unlikely to be optimal for all or most workers; accordingly, as Valdés-Prieto (2002 and 2005a) suggests, allowing people to exchange some CWBs for equities could achieve significant diversification gains. Of course, the value of this diversification depends also on the holdings of human capital, housing, and company-based pensions.

Creation of New Markets. It is also likely that the payment profile of CWB securities across states of nature is not spanned by the payment profiles of current financial assets, so if the social security program were to sell small amounts of CWB securities, it would immediately create new financial markets.[7] Completing the financial markets could generate substantial new value (Shiller 1993), though there is a theoretical possibility that if markets remain incomplete after the new security is introduced, this could make people worse off (Hart 1975).[8] In practice, we believe that CWB securities would be attractive investments for domestic corporate and occupational pension plans seeking to curtail exposure to inflation risk, because the covered wage bill is protected from inflation (at least in the medium term). Trade of CWB securities between countries would also permit participants to access new international risk diversification, that is to permit trade in aggregate human capital.[9]

Organizing the Asset Management Market. If workers are to be required to save in personal accounts, it would be important to make the market efficient and competitive, and respond to changes in optimal portfolio weights over time. Since most participants are insufficiently financially literate to design balanced portfolios and adjust them over time, some oppose letting individual workers select their own investment options in their personal accounts (Kotlikoff and Burns 2004). An obvious solution would be to pass the responsibility for balancing and updating portfolios to the experts, while ensuring that the experts compete among themselves. For example, asset managers could be required to offer just a handful of *balanced* portfolios and then each participant could be asked to choose a *single* balanced portfolio; this has been implemented in Chile, for instance. Participants would be well protected from the downside risk of investing in equities, because these portfolios would hold significant shares in CWB securities and corporate and government bonds.[10]

Competition between the asset managers would allow participants to switch between competing registered asset managers; further, asset management firms could set their own commission levels, with competition preventing commissions from being raised to exorbitant levels. One way to achieve intense price rivalry and keep cross-selling low would be to rely on large employers, employer associations, and unions to find low-cost asset managers as in the Netherlands and Denmark. Another approach would offer participants a 'bidding service', where participants can identify the asset management company that would charge them the least, identified via bidding contests (Valdés-Prieto 2005*b*). Such a service would create a distribution channel that avoids contacting each participant, while at the same time reducing participants' information costs.

Redistributive Concerns

Next we turn to an assessment of how this plan for market-based social security affects redistribution within and between generations.[11] Some have worried that moving away from the current system would undo social security redistribution within cohorts, as they argue that the current old-age benefit formula replaces a larger share of previous earnings for lower than higher earners. But the reality is different: in fact, very little redistribution is achieved by the US social security system. For instance, Gustman and Steinmeier (2000) show that less than 3 percent of current social security payroll tax revenue is redistributed across income deciles. This is because most of the redistribution in the benefit formula is offset within households, since relatively lower-paid wives receive bigger benefits that offset the smaller benefits going to their well-paid husbands. Consequently, adopting individual accounts would not alter the system's degree of redistribution. In fact with a progressive income tax, more redistribution can be achieved by an individual accounts system.[12]

Another issue is whether intergenerational risk-sharing would be improved by market-based social security. On the one hand, the availability of CWB securities in financial markets would allow young participants and other investors to sell guarantees to participants in their 70s and beyond, enhancing intergenerational risk-sharing. Moreover, if the investors included institutions representing even younger persons (e.g. wealthy dynasties altruistic toward the welfare of grandchildren, or wealthy foundations devoted to child welfare), risk-sharing could span 100 years. On the other hand, governments can be thought of as even longer-lived so that PAYGO finance offers the potential for even longer risk-sharing. Yet as we have seen, permitting this implies allowing legislators to make discretionary and unpredictable decisions. We would argue that if market-based social security is coupled with CWB securities, the span of generations covered by financial market trades can replicate that achieved by conventional PAYGO social security, while offering less political risk, a wider set of portfolios, and more individual choice.

A separate issue concerns the possibility that poorer generations might need to be helped by richer generations. This has been accomplished by

Congress under discretionary social security rules by changing the level of prefunding for promised liabilities. That is, poorer generations (e.g. during the Depression) spent more than they paid into the Trust Fund, while richer generations have been forced to build it up. Yet an alternative would be to change the value of the net public debt as well as the present discounted value of promised Medicare benefits. If a government wanted to improve the welfare of future generations, it could always do so by running a budget surplus and using it to purchase CWB securities in the market. The revenue from these bonds could then be used to pay a subsidy to covered labor earnings, or the securities could simply be cancelled and the residual payroll tax cut proportionately. Therefore, the adoption of market-based social security does not constrain intergenerational redistribution in any way.

Credibility of the Mandate to Pay the Residual Payroll Tax

Will future governments be willing to mandate workers to pay the residual payroll tax, if many holders of CWB securities are domestic investors or even foreign investors? There is the notion that the highest credibility that the residual payroll tax will be levied is achieved by allocating the benefits of that revenue to the most powerful interest group. If retirees are assumed to be the most powerful interest group, then to maximize credibility, they and not investors should receive all the revenue from the residual payroll tax (Bovenberg 2005).[13]

However, the historical evidence shows that frequently the promises to retirees have been broken, so their political strength must have been limited. Although retirees have created national political parties in some countries, in many episodes they have borne the brunt of the cost of fiscal crises. Moreover, governments can be pressed into action by entities different from interest groups. Investors in financial markets can put significant constraints on fiscal behavior too, without any need to coordinate among themselves, simply by moving their money out when a government fails to meet its promises. Many governments have opened up the capital account of the Balance of Payments to take advantage of the gains from full participation in the world economy, and this has increased the ability of international investors to move their funds when risk increases.

The contrast between retirees and investors blurs under market-based social security. Older and retired participants are highly likely to keep claims to a big share of the CWB securities, simply because these will be the safest investments available. Therefore, retirees and older workers will contribute their political clout to ensure respect for their property rights over the residual payroll tax paid by the younger workers. This political clout would combine with the market pressure applied by investors, to keep the government willing to mandate active workers to pay the residual payroll tax.

Now consider the polar opposite objection: because the revenue of CWB securities relies on the willingness of the government to mandate workers to pay the residual payroll tax, CWB securities would be 'owed' by the government. This is a mistake, because the existence of *most* privately owned cash flows relies on the continuing use of force by the government. Corporations keep their machinery because the government is willing to use force to stop thieves, and landlords collect rents because governments are willing to expel intruders. If it appears bizarre to count all these cash flows as 'owed' by the government, then counting CWB securities as fiscal liabilities is equally inappropriate.

Conclusions

We have shown that implementing market-based social security reforms can enhance well-being, by allowing risk diversification and trading in guarantees on the underlying economic and demographic risks. A key benefit of this approach is that participants may gain access to new financial markets rather than having the government impose risk and return portfolios unlikely to be optimal for all participants. Another advantage of a market-based approach to social security is that the system can be better adapted to suit individual needs. For example, if risk tolerance falls with age, participants can move to safer pension portfolios, a practice not permitted when a centrally run PAYGO social security system imposes uniform risk levels on everyone. We also show that between- and within-cohort redistribution can exist under market-based social security.

Covered wage bill securities are a key element of this plan. It is important to underscore the fact that these would be the responsibility of future workers who pay the residual payroll tax to social security so that this residual tax acknowledges the 'legacy debt' implicit in the starting point of a PAYGO system. The role of government would be limited to ensuring the obligation that workers pay the residual payroll tax. Shocks to economic growth or fertility are borne by owners of the CWB securities, because taxpayers do not guarantee the revenue of the residual payroll tax. Similarly, CWB owners appropriate the ensuing gains in the event of better-than-expected economic performance.

In this sense, the new securities are akin to equity and are not part of the public debt. Yet these CWB securities are much safer than equities over the business cycle, because the residual payroll tax backing them is proportional to the covered wage bill which tends to be more stable than profits at horizons shorter than ten years. In addition, nominal wages tend to keep up with inflation in the medium term, as compared to nominal corporate or treasury bonds. Moreover, CWB securities are perpetual (having no expiry date), so renewal risk and vulnerability to investor panics are minimal. Portfolios containing a substantial share of CWB securities also reduce replacement rate risk (cf. Burtless 2000).

As a final benefit, these CWB securities would permit financial markets to hedge and diversify the risk in aggregate human capital (reflected in the present discounted value of earnings). Indeed CWB securities would permit all GDP to be traded, as espoused by Shiller (1993). The young as a group, who hold substantial human capital, would benefit by choosing a portfolio short on human capital and long in corporate securities, while the old as a group would benefit by choosing a portfolio heavy in human capital (Merton 1983). If market-based social security reduces the equilibrium equity risk premium through this route, higher levels of innovative risk-taking would be supported, and growth rates could increase. In addition, new CWB securities can permit investors to hedge separately shocks to real average earnings, and covered employment (influenced by demographic risks and labor force participation trends). This separation is possible because the revenue of the residual payroll tax can always be decomposed in this way. These gains would be available to facilitate step (1) in the proposal, where parameters are adjusted to resolve the initial insolvency situation.

Endnotes

1. This has been noted by Browning (1975), Tabellini (1991), and Casamatta et al. (2000).
2. Legislation to index the minimum pension to the consumer price index in Mexico was passed only in 1989, *after* the large inflation of the 1980s wiped out the value of most social security benefits.
3. Insolvency is compatible with a cash-flow surplus for a few decades, as with the US social security system; see OASDI (2005).
4. Payouts on CWB securities could be uniform, meaning that a simple pro rata share of the total dividend payout would be received in the future, or they could take other shapes. Valdés-Prieto (2005a) conjectures that one CWB security type would include wage-indexed bonds, while others could be indexed to demography and participation in the covered labor force or to CPI-indexed bonds.
5. For example, if the introduction of individual-account-based social security *de novo* (in a country with no previous social security) and the ensuing accumulation of pension funds, induces the political system to issue new public debt in equal amounts, then the degree of fiscal funding falls as much as when PAYGO financed social security is introduced (Holzmann 2005: 83). If future generations service this 'legacy debt' with an extra payroll tax, then the parallel with balanced PAYGO finance becomes exact.
6. Valdés-Prieto (2005a) argues that properly chosen option contracts such as collars between the portfolios held by active participants and retirees could help insulate prices for twelve months ahead without interfering in the market's valuation of the CWB bonds.

7. Financial innovation is efficient when short sales of the new security are effectively limited by costs, which seems to be the case (Allen and Gale 1994).

8. An important example provided by Dow (1998) considers a single consumption good with asymmetric information. In this example, risk-averse traders use the new market to hedge their positions in a preexisting security, but this reduces liquidity in the old market, and this last effect dominates.

9. For instance, European and Japanese corporate pensions would benefit from buying US CWBs; emerging nation Central Banks might also desire to hold a portion of their international reserves in CWB securities issued by American workers versus nominal bonds. The correlation between shocks to the covered wage bill across countries is likely to be below unity after taking into account real exchange rate risk.

10. A sophisticated participant who preferred more variety, even at higher cost, could allocate voluntary saving and debt to undo the balanced portfolio.

11. An important redistribution question refers to poverty-based assistance for the elderly. This issue is unrelated to market-based social security, because such support is generally provided by a separate tax-financed scheme, as with the US Supplemental Security Income program.

12. Another important issue is integration of disability insurance and survivorship insurance, which would remain mandatory under market-based social security. A capital payment would be made into the individual accounts of beneficiaries equal to the difference between the market price of a set of immediate annuities for the beneficiaries, whose initial amounts are specified by law, and the account balance as of the date of the claim. This means that the accounts would help participants when they need it most. In addition, the indemnity would be larger for those who become disabled relatively young, compared to that for those falling disabled closer to retirement. The premium for this insurance can also be determined by bidding contests. Contrary to Diamond and Orszag (2004), market-based social security can treat the disabled, widows, and orphans as generously as the society deems necessary, and the premium will adjust accordingly.

13. This objection was first raised by Andrea Prat in an *Economic Policy* panel discussion in October 2004 and then refined by Bovenberg (2005). This is my first opportunity to respond.

References

Auerbach, Alan J. and Laurence J. Kotlikoff (1987). *Dynamic Fiscal Policy*. Cambridge: Cambridge University Press, pp. 150–1.

Augusztinovics, Maria, Robert Gál, Agnes Matits, Levente Máté, András Simonovits, and János Stahl (2002). 'The Hungarian Pension System Before and After the 1998 Reform', in Elaine Fultz (ed.), *Pension Reform in Central and Eastern Europe* vol. 1. Budapest: International Labour Office, pp. 25–93.

Bernheim, B. Douglas and John B. Shoven (1988). 'Pension Funding and Saving', in Zvie Bodie, John B. Shoven, and David A. Wise (eds.), *Pensions in the U.S. Economy*. NBER: University of Chicago Press, pp. 85–114.

Boldrin, Michele, Juan J. Dolado, Juan F. Jimeno, and Franco Peracchi (1999). 'The Future of Pensions in Europe', *Economic Policy*, 29: 289–320.

Browning, Edgar K. (1975). 'Why the Social Insurance Budget Is Too Large in a Democracy', *Economic Inquiry*, 13(3): 373–88. (See *http://ideas.repec.org/a/oup/ecinqu/v13y1975i3p373–88.html*)

Bovenberg, Lans (2005). 'Discussion of Pay-as-you-go Securities', *Economic Policy*, 20(42): 251–5.

Burtless, Gary (2000). 'Social Security Privatization and Financial Market Risk', Center on Social and Economic Dynamics Working Paper 10. Washington, DC: Brookings Institution.

Casamatta, Georges, Helmuth Cremer, and Pierre Pestieau (2000). 'The Political Economy of Social Security', *Scandinavian Journal of Economics*, 102(3): 503–22.

Cogan, John F. and Olivia S. Mitchell (2003). 'Perspectives from the President's Commission on Social Security Reform', *Journal of Economic Perspectives*, 17(2): 149–72.

Commission to Strengthen Social Security (2001). CSSS *Final Report http://www.csss.gov/ reports/Final_report.pdf/*

Diamond, Peter A. and Peter R. Orszag (2004). *Saving Social Security: A Balanced Approach.* Washington, DC: Brookings Institution Press.

Geanokoplos, John, Olivia S. Mitchell, and Stephen Zeldes (1999). 'Social Security Money's Worth', in Olivia Mitchell, Robert Myers, and Howard Young (eds.), *Prospects for Social Security Reform.* Philadelphia, PA: University of Pennsylvania Press, pp. 79–151.

Gokhale, Jagadeesh and Kent Smetters (2003). *Fiscal and Generational Imbalances: New Budget Measures for New Budget Priorities.* Washington, DC: American Enterprise Institute Press.

Gollier, Christian (2005). 'Discussion of Pay-as-you-go Securities', *Economic Policy*, 20(42): 255–7.

Gustman, Alan and Thomas Steinmeier (2000). 'How Effective is Redistribution Under the Social Security Benefit Formula?' NBER Working Paper No. 7597, March.

Hart, Oliver D. (1975). 'On the Optimality of Equilibrium When the Market Structure is Incomplete', *Journal of Economic Theory*, 11: 418–43.

Holst, Roland (2005). 'Policy Risk: Some Evidence, its Relevance and Welfare Costs in Retirement Programs', Department of Economics Working Paper, University of Chicago.

Robert Holzmann, Richard Hinz, and World Bank Staff (2005). *Old Age Income Support in the 21st Century: an International Perspective on Pension Systems and Reform.* Washington, DC: World Bank.

Kotlikoff, Laurence J. and Scott Burns (2004). *The Coming Generational Storm: What You Need to Know about America's Economic Future.* Cambridge, MA: MIT Press.

Lee, Ronald (1994). 'Population Age Structure, Intergenerational Transfers and Wealth: A New Approach with Application to the U.S.', *Journal of Human Resources*, 29(4): 1027–63.

Merton, Robert C. (1983). 'On the Role of Social Security as a Means for Efficient Risk-Bearing in an Economy Where Human Capital Is Not Tradeable', in Zvi Bodie and John B. Shoven (eds.), *Financial Aspects of the U.S. Pension System.* Chicago, IL: University of Chicago Press, pp. 259–89.

Mitchell, Olivia S. and Stephen P. Utkus (eds.) (2004). *Pension Design and Structure: New Lessons from Behavioral Finance.* Oxford: Oxford University Press.

Müller, Katharina (2003). *Privatizing Old Age Security: Latin America and Eastern Europe Compared.* Northampton, MA: Edward Elgar.

Old-Age and Survivors Insurance and Disability Insurance Trustees (OASDI) (2005). *Annual Report of the Board of Trustees of the Federal Old-Age and Survivors Insurance and Disability Insurance Trust Funds,* March. Washington, DC: USGPO.

Shiller, Robert J. (1993). *Macro Markets: Creating Institutions for Managing Society's Largest Economic Risks.* Oxford: Oxford University Press.

Sinn, Hans-Werner (2000). 'Why a Funded Pension Is Useful and Why It Is Not', *International Tax and Public Finance,* 7(4–5): 389–410.

Tabellini, Guido (1991). 'The Politics of Intergenerational Redistribution', *Journal of Political Economy,* 99(2): 335–57.

Valdés-Prieto, Salvador (2000). 'The Financial Stability of Notional Account Pensions', *Scandinavian Journal of Economics,* 102(3): 395–417.

—— (2002). *Políticas y Mercados de Pensiones: Un texto Universitario para América Latina.* Santiago, Chile: Ediciones Universidad Católica.

—— (2005a). 'Pay-as-you-go Securities', *Economic Policy,* 20(42): 215–51.

—— (2005b). 'Para Aumentar la Competencia Entre las AFP', *Estudios Públicos,* 98 (Otoño): 87–142, Santiago, Chile.

Index